# Woman and Leadership in Higher Education

A Volume in
Women and Leadership: Research, Theory, and Practice

*Series Editors:*
Faith Ngunjiri, *Concordia College*
Susan R. Madsen, *Utah Valley University*
Karen A. Longman, *Azusa Pacific University*

# Women and Leadership:
# Research, Theory, and Practice

Faith Ngunjiri, Susan R. Madsen, and Karen A. Longman, *Series Editors*

*Women and Leadership in Higher Education* (2014)
edited by Karen A. Longman and Susan R. Madsen

# Women and Leadership in Higher Education

### Edited by

### Karen A. Longman
*Azusa Pacific University*

### and

### Susan R. Madsen
*Utah Valley University*

**Information Age Publishing, Inc.**
Charlotte, North Carolina • www.infoagepub.com

**Library of Congress Cataloging-in-Publication Data**

CIP data for this book can be found on the Library of Congress website:
http://www.loc.gov/index.html

**Paperback:** 978-1-62396-819-9
**Hardcover:** 978-1-62396-820-5
**E-Book:** 978-1-62396-821-2

# CONTENTS

v

# FOREWORD

**Warren G. Bennis**

Reading through the thoughtful and provocative chapters in this manuscript reminded me of a quote by Marcel Proust, "The real discovery consists not in finding new lands but in seeing with new eyes." This book gives a fresh perspective to the important issue of women's leadership in society.

The opening chapters present a clear articulation of the trends and demographic realities in terms of women and leadership across various sectors of the United States, focusing on higher education in particular. Given that the college graduates today at all levels (associate's through doctoral degrees) are predominately female, the significant underrepresentation of women in senior-level leadership across higher education is troubling.

The middle section of this book summarizes the approaches and curricular content used by three well-respected women's leadership development programs—the American Council on Education, the Higher Education Resource Services, and the University of San Diego's Women's Leadership Academy. In reading these chapters I found myself thinking that, for too long, we have assumed that the male-normed models of leadership development would work to inspire and prepare high-potential women to move into institutional leadership roles. Simply put, our attempts to put new "wine" into "old wineskins" has not worked. The strategies and curricular approaches identified in this section can shape future leadership development programming at the state, regional, or institutional level.

Drawing upon a rich array of research literature, several chapters argue for the importance of bringing women's perspectives to the leadership

*Women and Leadership in Higher Education,* pp. vii–viii
Copyright © 2014 by Information Age Publishing

table. Yet doing so has not been easy, given the male-normed cultures of most institutions. Overt and subtle forms of adversity lead to discouragement or opting out, often related to differing systems of values and rewards between men and women. Understanding the dynamics of privilege, internalizing a respect for the value of different perspectives, and being open to fresh thinking can move our campuses beyond the constraints that have held back highly competent women for too long. The final section contains five short and illuminating chapters containing "leadership lessons" from former and current college and university presidents.

As a leadership scholar who has had a front row seat to the evolution of the leadership field for more than 50 years, I want to say "thank you" to the International Leadership Association for supporting this new "Women and Leadership" book series. The focus on higher education in launching the series is both timely and critical. Those involved in higher education, and particularly those who lead institutions of higher education, shape the future in ways that directly influence the vitality and well-being of the United States and our world. Best wishes as the International Leadership Association book series begins to influence both theorists and practitioners to advance a broader and better understanding of the contributors to effective leadership.

*Warren Bennis, University Professor and Distinguished Professor of Business Administration at USC. Author of over 30 books on leadership and change. His latest is:* Still Surprised: A Memoir of a Life in Leadership.

# INTRODUCTION

## Karen A. Longman and Susan R. Madsen

Some leaders are born female. Despite this fact, many women who could develop into highly talented leaders find their potential dampened by an array of internal and external factors, and those constraints are evident even in the field of higher education. This book focuses particular attention on the status of women in college and university leadership in the United States, describes the experiences and contributions of women in those leadership roles, and offers strategies and best practices for opening more doors for women to serve in positions of influence across all sectors of higher education. The importance of this work is evident in the fact that, within the United States, women now comprise the majority of students at all levels—associate degrees through doctorates, as well as first professional degrees (National Center for Education Statistics, 2012), yet only 26% of university presidents, 10% of full professors, and less than 30% of the college and university board members are women (Colorado Women's College, 2013).

Reasons for the significant underrepresentation of women in senior-level leadership roles across all sectors are complex and multifaceted, as summarized in a book chapter by Ely and Rhode (2010) titled "Women and Leadership: Defining the Challenges." Specifically related to the experiences of women in higher education, many of the factors emerge from "the male norms that define the academy [which] can be daunting" (Van Ummersen, 2009, p. ix). The implications of working in male-normed cultures shape the aspirations and experiences of women who have much to offer as current and future leaders in higher education, yet fledgling talent is too rarely identified and developed. The same holds true across most sectors in the United States today. Expressing concern

*Women and Leadership in Higher Education*, pp. ix–xvii
Copyright © 2014 by Information Age Publishing
All rights of reproduction in any form reserved.

for the limited presence of senior-level women in corporate leadership roles, Ibarra, Ely, and Kolb (2013) in a September 2013 cover story of *Harvard Business Review* discuss blockages faced by women that are related to "the often fragile process of coming to see oneself, and to be seen by others as a leader" (p. 62).

Factors that hinder women's advancement into leadership often relate to a disconnect between the values of many women and the reward structures and goals that shape the culture of most organizations (Helgesen & Johnson, 2010). Thus women may be reticent to "Lean In" (Sandberg, 2013) to their own professional advancement. In exploring the question of whether women lack ambition, Fels (2004) reported research findings indicating that women's identity is often oriented around giving rather than drawing attention to themselves; this dynamic can negatively impact women's motivation to pursue leadership. Stated succinctly, cultural norms have traditionally contributed to young girls aspiring to be cheerleaders while boys aspire to be quarterbacks … a highly visible role that requires risk-taking yet offers the platform for individualistic accolades. The implications of these deeply ingrained and societally recognized roles are profound.

Many of the chapters in this volume articulate various ways that higher education "loses" as a result of the lack of women's voices at the highest levels of leadership—administrative, faculty, and board leadership. Our students, both male and female, lack important role models; our decision-making processes are often biased as the result of the lack of diverse perspectives around the senior leadership table. Interestingly, a 2013 publication by Jossey-Bass carries the title *The Athena Doctrine: How Women (and the Men Who Think Like Them) Will Rule the Future* (Gerzema & D'Antonio, 2013). Reporting on the findings of a massive international survey of 64,000 respondents about preferred leadership styles, the book emphasizes that "Nearly two thirds of the people around the world—including the majority of men—feel that the world would be a better place if men thought more like women" (p. 7). Higher education has much to gain by identifying, preparing, and advancing more high-potential women into leadership roles.

This book, divided into four parts and containing the chapters briefly described below, presents both the hard facts of the current demographic realities and fresh thinking about how progress can and must be made. The world is changing; higher education collectively, as well as institutions of all types, must change. Bringing more women into leadership is critical to the goal of moving our society and world forward in healthier ways.

## PART I: THE STATE OF WOMEN AND LEADERSHIP
## IN HIGHER EDUCATION

Given the importance of providing foundational information about "The State of Women and Leadership in Higher Education," this opening section contains three provocative chapters that establish the current demographics, trends, and areas of concern. The first chapter, "Benchmarking Women's Leadership in Academia and Beyond," was written by Drs. Lynn M. Gangone and Tiffani Lennon from the Women's College within the University of Denver. These coauthors highlight the fact that over the four decades since the passage of Title IX, the number of women in leadership positions has remained relatively small. Evidence of the paucity of women in leadership has been much documented; for example, *The White House Project: Benchmarking Women's Leadership* (2009) report, a multisector examination of women's presence in the "C-Suite," concluded that, on average, women held only 18% of the chief executive positions across 10 sectors in the United States. Recently Colorado Women's College of the University of Denver released *Benchmarking Women's Leadership in the United States 2013*; this report expanded the original *Benchmarking* study beyond the C-Suite to include senior leaders, such as vice presidents, in 14 sectors. The study concluded that females represent 19% of senior leaders, while males represent 81%. The study also explored industry-specific performance indicators, salary comparisons, and debunked several myths surrounding women and work. This opening chapter presents and discusses the data and recommendations from the 2013 report.

The second chapter, written by Barbara Kellerman (Harvard Kennedy School) and Deborah L. Rhode (Stanford Law School), is titled "Women at the Top: The Pipeline Reconsidered." This chapter explores the status of women in higher education and strategies to improve that status. Contrary to the widespread view that barriers are coming down, that women are moving up, and that the pipeline will take care of any resulting inequalities, this chapter offers a more sobering assessment. Drs. Kellerman and Rhode argue that women, particularly women of color, are dramatically underrepresented at leadership levels, and that the playing field is far from level. True equality will require challenging the gender stereotypes, in-group favoritism, and unequal domestic roles that continue to keep women from realizing their full potential.

The third chapter, "Leadership Out Front and Behind the Scenes: Young Women's Ambitions for Leadership Today," was written by Dr. Nannerl O. Keohane, former president of Wellesley College and Duke University. This chapter explores the attitudes toward leadership of contemporary female undergraduates, drawing from the results of a 2011 study she chaired at Princeton University on the occasion of the 40th anniversary of Princeton becoming a coeducational institution. The female students at Princeton reported that they prefer "high impact" rather than "high profile" jobs; they want to make a difference in a cause they care about or work "behind the scenes" to get the job done. Notably, Princeton's female students were less involved in the top leadership of traditional campus organizations than their male peers, but many of them were committed to top-level posts in cause-oriented organizations. These findings suggest that young women should be encouraged to think more positively about top posts in traditional organizations. Beyond this, however, the findings also suggest that a more capacious conception of leadership might encourage more female students to pursue significant leadership roles in a variety of contexts.

## PART II: STRATEGIES FOR WOMEN'S LEADERSHIP DEVELOPMENT

The status quo of underrepresentation of women in top-level leadership roles across higher education, as described in the opening chapters, is problematic for many reasons. In response to the current realities, Part II of this volume provides descriptions of three prominent women's leadership development programs and/or initiatives that offer fresh thinking on how progress can be made. The first, written by Leah Witcher Jackson Teague (associate dean of the Baylor Law School) and Kim Bobby (director of the Inclusive Excellence Group at the American Council on Education), is titled "American Council on Education's IDEALS for Women Leaders: Identify, Develop, Encourage, Advance, Link, and Support." These coauthors argue that leading higher education institutions is difficult but critically important in shaping society's future, and that diversity improves innovation and performance yet is sorely lacking at the highest levels of leadership. This chapter discusses the 40-year commitment of the American Council on Education to advancing women into leadership through an extensive system of state, regional, and national leadership development programs. Also discussed is the Moving the Needle initiative, a collaborative effort to raise national awareness of the importance of gender parity and to establish a blueprint for achieving gender parity through deliberate action by higher education decision and policy makers.

Judith S. White, executive director of the Higher Education Resource Services (HERS), authored the fifth chapter, titled "HERS at 50: Curriculum and Connections for Empowering the Next Generation of Women Leaders in Higher Education." Dr. White shares the conviction that the development of a new generation of women for senior posts in higher education is critically important to meet the need for a diverse cadre of leaders that is capable of responding to the challenges of a rapidly changing environment. The work of HERS has assisted in meeting this need since 1976, providing leadership development training for more than 5,000 women from over 1,200 campuses in the United States and other nations. HERS complements the best practices learned from decades of experience with its signature residential program, HERS Institutes, with fresh research-based insights about curricular and pedagogical approaches that will best prepare women to lead effectively in future years.

The third chapter in this section, titled "Developing Women's Leadership: An Innovative and Unique Approach to Raising Leadership Capacity," was written by Dr. Lorri Sulpizio, coordinator of the Women's Leadership Academy (WLA) in the School of Leadership and Education Sciences at the University of San Diego. This chapter describes how the WLA has created uniquely designed programs to develop women's leadership capacity. The WLA programs make a clear distinction between leadership and authority, acknowledge the existing organizational gender bias, encourage a balance of a feminine and masculine expression, and utilize a pedagogical method based on group dynamics. The theoretical foundation for the WLA programs is presented in this chapter, with examples that illustrate how a safe environment is provided for women to explore leadership identity and to learn about advanced concepts of authority and leadership, while sharpening the skills that are most difficult for women leaders.

## PART III: WOMEN'S EXPERIENCES AND CONTRIBUTIONS IN HIGHER EDUCATION LEADERSHIP

This section of the book focuses on women's experiences in higher education leadership and the contributions of women who hold positional leadership roles. Chapter 7, "Women's Contributions to Leadership and the Road Ahead," was written by Dr. Adrianna Kezar from the University of Southern California. She argues that one of the major contributions of women leaders is a fundamental rethinking of what leadership is as a phenomenon and how it can be enacted. In contrast to past hierarchical and command-and-control perspectives, images of leadership based on studies of women must now reflect mutual power and influence processes, attention to relationships and tasks, and democratic and participatory forms of decision making. Leadership is now more focused on ethics and values than was the case in past eras. Furthermore, a variety of studies have identified that the characteristics associated with women's leadership are related with more effective leadership. While acknowledging the contributions that women bring to leadership, it is important to note that higher education is increasingly a market-driven, corporate environment that does not favor the important leadership approaches typical of women. This chapter concludes with the suggestion that to be successful in this neoliberal environment, women may need to implement a hybrid form of leadership that integrates the effective style of leadership that women have brought in the past, but blend it with strategies that have also been associated with the agentic style of men's leadership in order to navigate strategically on today's campuses.

Amy Diehl, from Shippensburg University of Pennsylvania, authored Chapter 8, titled "Approaches of Women Leaders in Higher Education: Navigating Adversity, Barriers, and Obstacles," based on her dissertation research. This qualitative study involved face-to-face interviews with 26 women in senior leadership roles in higher education; the chapter addresses the findings related to her research question: "How do women leaders in higher education make meaning of adversity?" The goal of the research was to explore whether participants have experienced adversity, what such experiences meant to their lives both personally and professionally, and how they responded to such events. Adversity negatively impacted the self-esteem and perceived sense of power for many participants. To navigate adversity, the women used strategies to empower themselves and reach out to others. This chapter provides details and insights around three themes related to how participants made it through adversity: reframing, resilience, and self-efficacy.

"Women Leaders, Authenticity, and Higher Education: Convictions and Contradictions" is the title for Chapter 9 of this book. Similarly drawing from a recent dissertation study, Rita Gardiner, from the University of Western Ontario, presents the findings of her research. This chapter considers the interconnections among women's leadership experiences in higher education, authenticity, and an ethic of care. In addition to drawing upon relevant literature, key findings from a phenomenological inquiry conducted with 10 senior women leaders in higher education are presented and discussed. Three main themes emerged from an analysis of the interview data in this study. The first theme related to care and relationships. The effects of gender socialization constituted the second theme. The third theme concerned the conflicts that arose in the minds of the participants when organizational expectations were perceived to be incongruent with their personal convictions. The chapter concludes by suggesting that focusing on women's leadership experiences in the context of higher education, alongside an ethic of care, may open up new directions for research into authentic leadership.

The final chapter in this section, "Madame President: Gender's Impact in the Presidential Suite," emerged from the dissertation research of the author, Mary L. Bucklin from Northern Kentucky University. She noted that even with the gradual increase of women in presidential roles, these leaders experience the job differently than do their male counterparts for reasons related to their gender; more specifically, related to role incongruity. Dr. Bucklin conducted interviews with eight women presidents of doctoral-granting universities (i.e., women at the top of their field). Her findings indicated that these women continued to be judged against the stereotypical model of how women should look, speak, and behave. In general, the presidents were aware of gender's influence, but took intentional steps to lessen its impact on their ability to fulfill their presidential responsibilities.

## PART IV: LESSONS FROM THE TRENCHES: PERSPECTIVES FROM FEMALE PRESIDENTS

This final section of the book, titled "Lessons from the Trenches," offers essays from five former or current college or university presidents. Rita Bornstein, former president of Rollins College, shares her insights in a chapter titled "Leadership Legitimacy, Managed Authenticity, and Emotional Stability: Keys to a Successful Presidency." After 14 years in the presidency, Dr. Bornstein reflects on three themes that she views to be key to a successful presidency: (1) the quest for legitimacy, (2) managed authenticity, and (3) emotional intelligence. Clearly, presidents must establish their legitimacy based largely on the competent handling of their responsibilities and demonstrating appreciation for the institutional culture. Yet equally important is the ability to fulfill the responsibilities of the presidency with skills related to management style and personality.

In Chapter 12, Ann Hart, current president of the University of Arizona, summarizes some of the lessons she has learned in her chapter titled "Docs, Jocks, and Other Wildlife: The Challenges and Potential for Women Leaders in the 21st Century Public Research University." Dr. Hart notes that the proportion of women presidents at colleges and universities throughout the United States has increased significantly over the past several decades, yet the number of women leaders at research universities remains low compared to other sectors. She argues that for women who fill these roles, four components of the public research university—major research achievements, land-grant roles, big-time sports, and academic medicine—often combine to present unique challenges (and opportunities) that compound traditional gender dynamics and therefore merit attention. This chapter describes the interaction of these components of the modern public research university and how women leaders can prepare to manage them effectively.

Sherry Penney, as a former president of the University of Massachusetts Boston, summarizes her lessons learned in the chapter titled "Twenty-First Century Presidents Must Work With Multiple Stakeholders and Be Agents of Change." Dr. Penney describes the many skills and experiences that one needs to be effective in the presidency and provides suggestions about how to develop those skills. Encouragement and advice are offered for those who plan to take the presidential route are offered. In addition, her chapter outlines ways in which presidents must work with the many constituencies that are part of the larger university community. The concluding section offers a discussion of the changes that need to take place in postsecondary education and how presidents can and must be successful change agents.

Chapter 14, "*No Te Dejes*: Giving Voice to Issues that Choose You," was written by Juliet García, president of the University of Texas at Brownsville. Dr. García's personal story of growing up between the cultures of Mexico and the United States illustrates the power of higher education to transform lives. In just one generation, the university education that had been urged by her parents resulted in families that now include lawyers, physicians, engineers, and teachers. From the perspective of her service as the first female Mexican American-appointed president of a college or university in the United States, Dr. García communicates her passion for others to have the same educational opportunities. This chapter, which challenges institutional leaders to be people of conviction and courage, recounts the author's experience of opposing the division of her campus by an 18-foot wall as mandated by the Secure Fence Act. The act required the U.S. government to build a 700-mile barrier along the Texas-Mexico border by the end of 2008.

The final chapter in this section and in the book is one titled "Grounded" by Karen Holbrook, who previously served as president of The Ohio State University. Drawing from her experiences over more than 40 years in higher education, Dr. Holbrook describes searching for a thread that had been present throughout her career—a career that spanned six research universities, one liberal arts college, and various positions with increasing levels of responsibility. Throughout the transitions, the concept of "grounding" provided a source of strength and represented an attribute that provided identity. For Dr. Holbrook, part of that grounding has been reflected in a commitment to maintain an inquisitive mind, and embracing what is fun and exciting about the academic life. This chapter concludes with a challenge for academics to recognize and live into their grounding—whether it is professional, personal, or spiritual—thereby finding both personal peace of mind and fulfillment as a leader of many.

## CONCLUSION

"Some leaders are born female" were the opening words of this introduction. Scholars and practitioners across U.S. higher education would agree that the complexities facing postsecondary education are greater today than ever before; indeed, the challenges facing our world are greater than ever before. Wise and courageous leaders are needed in the senior ranks of faculty, staff, and administrators and across all institutional types. In Sheryl Sandberg's *Lean In* (2013), legendary investor Warren Buffett is cited as having remarked that "one of the reasons for his great success was that he was competing with only half of the population" (p. 7). Sandberg continues, "The Warren Buffetts of my generation are still largely enjoying this advantage. When more people get in the race, more records will be broken. And the achievements will extend beyond those individuals to benefit us all" (p. 7). The hope of the authors who have contributed to this volume is that many records will be broken because more women are encouraged and equipped to enter senior-level leadership roles. If that goal is not achieved expeditiously, higher education will continue to lose, our students will lose, and eventually the entire world will lose as high-potential women are overlooked and their talents left untapped.

## REFERENCES

Colorado Women's College. (2013). *Benchmarking women's leadership in the United States 2013*. Denver, CO: Colorado Women's College.

Ely, R., & Rhode. D. (2010). Women and leadership: Defining the challenges. In N. Nohria & R. Khurana (Eds.), *Handbook of leadership theory and practice* (pp. 377–410). Boston, MA: Harvard Business Press.

Fels, A. (2004, April). Do women lack ambition? *Harvard Business Review*, 50–60.

Gerzema, J., & D'Antonio, M. (2013). *The Athena doctrine: How women (and the men who think like them) will rule the future*. San Francisco, CA: Jossey-Bass.

Helgesen, S., & Johnson, J. (2010). *The female vision: Women's real power at work*. San Francisco, CA: Berrett-Koehler.

Ibarra, H., Ely, R., & Kolb, D. (2013). Women rising: The unseen barriers. *Harvard Business Review, 91*(9), 61–66.

National Center for Education Statistics. (2012). *Digest of educational statistics 2011*. U.S. Retrieved from http://nces.ed.gov/pubs2012/2012001.pdf

Sandberg, S. (2013). *Lean in: Women, work, and the will to lead*. New York, NY: Alfred A. Knoph.

Van Ummersen, C. (2009). Foreword. In D. R. Dean, S. J. Bracken, & J. K. Allen (Eds.), *Women in academic leadership* (pp. ix–xii). Sterling, VA: Stylus.

The White House Project. (2009). *The White House Project: Benchmarking women's leadership*. New York, NY: The White House Project.

# PART I

## THE STATE OF WOMEN AND LEADERSHIP IN HIGHER EDUCATION

CHAPTER 1

# BENCHMARKING WOMEN'S LEADERSHIP IN ACADEMIA AND BEYOND

**Lynn M. Gangone and Tiffani Lennon**

We write this chapter based on our professional and personal perspectives and from different places inside the academy. One author is a sitting dean, a seasoned university administrator, and a nationally noted speaker and writer dedicated to the advancement of women in higher education. The other is a current faculty member and academic chair, a legal scholar by training, and a qualitative and descriptive researcher, as well as the author of *Benchmarking Women's Leadership in the United States 2013* (Colorado Women's College, 2013). We are colleagues at Colorado Women's College, an institution in its 125th year, which is the only women's college in the country to exist as a single-gender academic unit following a 1982 merger with a coeducational institution, the University of Denver. Together, we bridge practitioner and scholar, administrator and faculty member, baby-boomer and Gen Xer, and we share a common cause—to use quantitative and qualitative data to illuminate the ways in which women are advancing into leadership positions—or not. In this first chapter of *Women and Leadership in Higher Education*, we will examine where women sit in positional leadership roles and provide qualitative and quantitative data from *Benchmarking Women's Leadership in the United States 2013* to lay the foundation for understanding where women are—or are

*Women and Leadership in Higher Education,* pp. 3–22
Copyright © 2014 by Information Age Publishing
All rights of reproduction in any form reserved.

not—in positional leadership roles and influence in the academy and beyond.

## WHERE ARE THE WOMEN LEADERS?

Title IX, part of the Educational Amendments of 1972, was created with the stated purpose of eliminating sex discrimination in education. Title IX held the promise of creating educational equity that would ultimately advance women's influence and participation throughout society. One goal of Title IX was to level the playing field among women and men through educational equity, with the hope that in developing a pipeline of women ready to assume leadership positions across all sectors of U.S. society, the face of leadership in future years would be more equitable as well. However, despite significant educational attainment for women at the undergraduate and graduate levels over four decades since the passage of Title IX, the goal of increased presence, achievement, and influence of women across all sectors still leaves much to be desired.

In the introduction to her book, *In the Company of Educated Women*, author Solomon (1985) wrote, "While the impact of women's education has had revolutionary implications for the whole society, educated women have still not achieved equal status with men either within or outside the sphere of education" (p. xvii). Twenty-three years later, Glazer-Raymo (2008) similarly commented that:

> among my concerns … has been the often-repeated but erroneous observation that women's majority status as undergraduate and graduate students means that gender equality has been achieved, and that as a result, women no longer require the protection afforded them through affirmative action and antibias legislation. (p. 1)

Both Solomon and Glazer-Raymo, among other authors (Chamberlain, 1991; Myers, 2008; Tarr-Whelan, 2009; Wilson, 2007), have rightly noted that the sheer presence of women in the academy, and the creation of the "pipeline" of educated women, have not necessarily had a direct correlation in moving women up and into parity with men, inside or outside the academy.

Evidence of the paucity of women in senior leadership roles has been much documented and discussed throughout the 21st century. On April 19, 2012, the *Wall Street Journal* had a full series of reports under the headline of "Women in the Workplace," asking the question "Where are the women leaders?" This series explored the factors, potential, and the possibilities inherent in advancing women (Lublin & Eggers, 2012). Discussions and commentary related to these reports noted that women make a powerful impact on the economy, and posed the question whether companies could harness the opportunities offered by this vital segment of the workforce. A number of studies have pointed to the ways women exhibit leadership and capacity, or lack thereof. Factors often cited for women not pursuing leadership roles include choosing to invest in family responsibilities, choice of professional fields and lifestyle, and the hesitation of women to adequately negotiate pay and other forms of compensation (Appelbaum, Audet, & Miller, 2003; Burke & Collins 2001; Eagly & Johnson, 1990; Sandberg, 2013). Sandberg, chief operating officer of Facebook, wrote *Lean in: Women, Work, and the Will to Lead* and emphasized an important perspective within the national dialogue about women's progress in senior leadership roles. *Lean In* offered some explanation as to why women have not reached parity with their male counterparts and focused on women's reluctance to take professional and personal risks. Reactions to Sandberg included those who questioned the systems in which women are expected to function. For example, will leaning in be a fully viable option unless companies rethink the time clock (Greenstone Miller, 2013)? Do women truly make better leaders (Andersen, 2012), or is great leadership gender neutral? Do salary inequities exist because women have not negotiated well enough and need to just ask for higher salaries (Babcock & Laschever, 2007)? Do women simply need more difficult work assignments to prove their worth or are there gender-based pay inequities that linger due to continued sex-role stereotyping and bias (Darity, 1998)? Will the "four Ps"—Pay at first job, Parenthood, Part-time or nontraditional trajectories, or Penalized by plumbing—always dictate women's capacity for career advancement (Fondas, 2010)?

Regardless of reasons, studies continue to document the lack of women in positional leadership roles. Measuring the presence of women in senior leadership roles has often been sector specific; for example, Catalyst, a nonprofit organization in New York dedicated to advancing women and business, has conducted business-specific studies of women since its inception in 1962 (Catalyst, 2013). The White House Project (TWHP), founded in 1988 by Marie C. Wilson, sought to advance women's leadership in all communities and sectors, up to and into the U.S. presidency. TWHP published the 2009 report titled, *The White House Project: Benchmarking Women's Leadership*, in seeking to advance its objective of furthering women's leadership. This report marked the first time that a multisector, quantitative examination of women's presence in the "C-Suite" (e.g., chief executive officer, chief financial officer, chief operating officer) was conducted. Using secondary data sources, the report concluded that women, on average, held only 18% of the positional leaders across 10 sectors, belying the results of a 2008 poll conducted by GfK Roper for The White House Project, which concluded "that one big battle has been won—large majorities of Americans (overall, about 90% and never lower than 70%) are comfortable with women as top leaders in all sectors, from academia and business to media and the military" (p. 5).

Recognizing the need to conduct an updated and expanded study, and with the goal of partnering with a like-minded academic institution, The White House Project president, Marie C. Wilson, requested that Colorado Women's College become the intellectual proprietors of the next phase of this research. In accepting this responsibility, the college dean, Lynn M. Gangone, ultimately secured external funds from two primary sources—the Emily Spencer Endowment for Women's Leadership assisted to disseminate the 2013 study after the unexpected closing of TWHP in 2012 (Franke-Rhuta, 2013) and Teachers Insurance and Annuity Association - College Retirement Equities Fund supported expanded marketing of the study to the higher education community. The 2013 study broadened the scope from the originally studied 10 sectors to 14 sectors, including medicine, entrepreneurship, technology, and K–12 education. In the 2009 report, women averaged 18% of the positional leaders across 10 sectors, and in 2013 women averaged 19% of the positional leaders across 14 sectors (Colorado Women's College, 2013). Researchers also found that pay inequities continue to exist, even among the most senior-level women, in comparison to their male counterparts (Colorado Women's College, 2013).

## BENCHMARKING WOMEN'S LEADERSHIP IN THE UNITED STATES 2013

The findings and the resulting ramifications contained in *Benchmarking Women's Leadership in the United States 2013* (Colorado Women's College, 2013) illuminate existing data and offer new data that had been missing as part of the public discourse on women's leadership and this country's future as a global competitor. This descriptive study marks the first time researchers calculated an overall percentage of female leaders across 14 sectors. Researchers examined approximately 500 for-profit companies, not-for-profit businesses, organizations, universities, and associations as well as thousands of senior and executive leadership positions throughout the United States (Colorado Women's College, 2013). In doing so, researchers relied on and culled public information available on original source data sites, annual reports, and numerous databases to analyze descriptive data on positional leaders and top performers in each sector. The percentage of female leaders overall was examined and compared to the percentage of female leaders in the top echelons of each sector; researchers determined the top institutions and organizations by size, profitability, budget, and influence, and then narrowed the scope to the top 10 in each industry (Colorado Women's College, 2013). This comparison between the percentage of female leaders overall, to top echelon female leaders, provided a larger perspective of where women sat in leadership positions on the whole and among the industry's elite.

The project's lead researcher and author, Tiffani Lennon, convened a research team of University of Denver and Colorado Women's College alumnae and students to conduct this descriptive study, examining hundreds of organizations and institutions and thousands of senior leadership positions. Whenever possible, the researchers noted the leaders' racial demography. Based on various Bureau of Labor Statistic studies, the study concluded that approximately 57% of middle-level managers across the sectors studied represented the pipeline of women for potential sector leadership (Colorado Women's College, 2013). The researchers then compared the pipeline of potential women leaders to the actual percentage of women leaders and found tremendous disparity, with women representing approximately 19% of positional senior and executive leaders, and, conversely, men representing 81% of positional senior and executive leaders.

The dearth of women in positional leadership roles, as well as the continued presence of pay inequities, prompted the researchers to look at performance indicators to determine whether women actually performed comparably to their male counterparts (Colorado Women's College, 2013). Researchers embarked on this maiden task, since little, if any, research precedence exists, by employing industry-specific standards and benchmarks to determine the top performers in each sector. To illustrate from the sector of academia, those faculty who receive research dollars (e.g., awardees of the National Science Foundation, National Institutes of Health, and the Social Science Research Council prizes, grants, and awards) are considered industry-specific top performers. Researchers also used industry-specific standards such as the Carnegie Classifications to determine the top-ranked universities, and researchers then identified the positional leaders inside those top-ranked institutions. Researchers found that female academicians earned the majority of research awards, and that female administrators were more likely to hold the presidency or chancellorship within the top-ranked, top-10 institutions than among all doctoral-granting institutions as a whole (Colorado Women's College, 2013). Additionally, in the business sector, researchers compared the percentage of female leadership in Fortune 500 to the Fortune 10 companies. *Fortune* magazine ranks each company numerically according to fiscal year revenues; therefore, Fortune 10 companies earn significantly more than Fortune 11-500 companies. A higher percentage of women lead Fortune 10 companies than Fortune 500 companies as a whole.

The research team compared the industry's gender (and whenever possible race) demography to the top echelon in each industry. Invariably, female leaders were more likely to appear among the "most distinguished" performance lists than were their male counterparts across nearly all sectors except in the technology sector, where women did not earn more patents than men, although the percentage of patents earned by women is beginning to rise dramatically. While researchers do not seek to position the industry-specific criteria as the only or superior approach to measure performance, the criteria used, albeit limited, serves as a first attempt to understand how women perform compared to men. Additionally, the rationale for examining the top performers was to eliminate the arguments based on individual achievement; for example, women were "choosing" less demanding jobs due to child care needs, were not negotiating as well as men, or were not ambitious enough to achieve senior leadership status (Babcock & Laschever, 2009; Fondas, 2010; Lublin & Eggers, 2012; Sandberg, 2013). In looking at top performers, the idea was that these women had moved beyond any set of individually imposed limitations and were full participants in their respective sectors; this allowed researchers to look more definitively within the systems and thereby avoid conclusive assumptions about why women may earn less than their male counterparts.

Data trends across all 14 sectors revealed that women are often among the highest performers, and yet disproportionately underrepresented in leadership roles. In fact, those organizations and institutions in which women hold positional leadership frequently perform better than peer institutions without female leaders (Colorado Women's College, 2013). For example, institutions with a higher percentage of female leaders boast higher revenue for businesses and receive more national research funding. Benchmarking women's leadership in academia, as well as benchmarking women's leadership presence across sectors, provides evidence that filling the pipeline with educated women has not achieved gender parity in leadership, and that ensuring a greater presence of female leaders would serve all institutions and organizations.

The national study consists of percentages of leadership positions in the sector as a whole and among each of the 10 most elite and influential industry organizations and institutions, salary comparisons, and some indicators of performance as defined by the sector and/or industry. When researchers closely examined an industry's top 10 institutions and organizations, they included all senior and executive positions, and boards of trustees and directors. To illustrate, among the Fortune 10 companies, there exist hundreds of senior executives. A summary of the findings contained in the study include:

- Women's achievements at the most senior levels of each sector indicate that they may be outperforming men, but are not earning salaries or obtaining titles that reflect their high performance, particularly in academe.
- When comparing the nation's top businesses and organizations to each sector as a whole, women are better represented among the industry's top performers.
- Women are the majority in the leadership pipeline, yet are vastly underrepresented in leadership positions.
- When a significant representation of women leaders is present, studies show that revenue is greater, sales are increased, impact and reach are more expansive, and industry distinctions are more prolific.
- Taking all evidence into consideration, a major contributor to the lack of women in positional leadership roles is due to continued inherent biases against women as leaders.
- Without strategies to address promotion and advancement of women, U.S. corporations and organizations will continue to fall behind their competition.
- As stakeholders become aware of the potential for overall greater returns with women in leadership roles, they will likely act and apply pressure to change business practices accordingly.
- Throughout the 14 sectors, women in general were underpaid and underrepresented in leadership, regardless of their performance.

An important recommendation that emerged throughout all sectors, which became the focal point of *Recognizing Women's Leadership: Employing Best Practices and Strategies for Excellence* (2014), is that a performance-based, inclusive climate is essential for women and men of color to rise to leadership positions and for an institution to be successful.

## ACADEMIA: BENCHMARKING WOMEN'S LEADERSHIP IN HIGHER EDUCATION

The field identified of higher education is a specific sector examined in *Benchmarking Women's Leadership in the United States 2013* (Colorado Women's College, 2013). This "Academia" section examines all facets of higher education—students, faculty, administration, and boards of trustees. Overall, researchers found continued increases in the numbers of women attending college and attaining degrees at most levels and slight improvements among certain leadership positions, yet not much significant improvement in the overall presence of women leaders or in their compensation. More specifically, the 2013 report noted that while women represented 57% of all college students, women were only 10% of full professors, and 26% of university presidents. Women accounted for less than 30% of the college and university board members. Using baseline data from 1972, female faculty had not made any progress in closing the salary gap with their male counterparts. In 1972, women earned 83% of what male faculty made, and in the 2009, that percentage had declined to 82%. On average, females accounted for 31% of chief academic officers (CAOs), presidents or chancellors, and members of boards of trustees among all colleges and universities in 2011. When full professors, as determined by the American Association of University Professors (AAUP), are included in the senior leadership average, the overall percentage declines to 26%. As Glazer-Raymo (2008) noted, majority presence does not dictate majority leadership in the academy or, indeed, elsewhere. A brief review of the status of women in higher education follows.

## Students

The presence of women students continues to increase throughout higher education. Female students comprised 57% of all undergraduate enrollments and received 59% of all degrees conferred in 2009–2010 (National Center for Education Statistics [NCES], 2012). More specifically, in 2009–2010, women received 62% of associate degrees, 57% of bachelor's degrees, 60% of master's degrees, and 52% of doctoral and first professional degrees (NCES, 2012). The rate of women's participation in colleges and universities is rising, aided by the presence of women of color, who are obtaining degrees and increasing the number of women students and graduates overall. In 2010, women of color comprised approximately 20% of total fall enrollments, 22.2% of all undergraduate enrollments, and 17.6% of all postbaccalaureate enrollments (NCES, 2011). A quick look at professional degree attainment for women reflects that female law students have declined from 50.4% in 1992–1993, to 49% in 2003, and 47% in 2010 (American Bar Association, 2012), while in 2011 female medical students comprised 47% of first-year classes (Catalyst, 2012).

With the aggregate growth of women students across all levels of higher education, educational leaders have grown concerned about a seeming lack of incoming male students. Some media reports have latched onto this discussion by expressing concerns for all young males, as evidenced by various op-ed articles, PBS specials, and other press coverage (A Voice for Male Students, 2013; Hoff Sommers, 2013; Lamm, 2013;

Rocky Mountain PBS, 2011). When data are disaggregated, the alarm over the decreased presence of men must be examined very carefully. White women are receiving degrees at higher rates than ever, and women of color and older women are also earning degrees at higher rates, creating a large aggregate number of women students in higher education (Mead, 2006). White males are receiving degrees at higher rates than ever (Mead, 2006), although that fact is often absent from cries for affirmative action for men (Lamm, 2013) in higher education. Yet, young men of color are lagging behind their White counterparts in entering and completing higher education (Mead, 2006), thus impacting the overall number of men in higher education.

## Faculty

Women continue to be a strong presence among college and university faculty; however, the ranks of women faculty continue to be disproportionately in the mid- to lower levels. Women are more likely than men to have entry-level faculty positions such as lecturers and/or instructors. Women now comprise 50% of instructors and lecturers, which has remained virtually unchanged since 2006, with only a slight average increase of 2.7% (AAUP, 2011). At all degree-granting institutions today, women account for 43% of the full-time faculty, an increase from 32% in 1991. While this increase represents substantial progress, women are still underrepresented among the more prestigious faculty ranks. As was found in all sectors, the percentage of women steadily declines in moving up the ranks. Moreover, the nontenure track jobs typically held by women often exclude them from attaining senior-level roles in academia, because universities tend to draw from tenured faculty to fill top administrative positions. Additionally, universities typically support the research agendas and professional development of their tenured faculty.

As previously stated, the percentage of women appears to have reached near parity with men in faculty positions. Yet, a closer examination indicates that the representation of women at colleges and universities differs significantly by institution type and faculty rank. Women are well represented among community colleges and baccalaureate institutions. Yet, female faculty representation declines significantly among doctoral institutions, particularly in tenure and tenure-track positions. Women make up 38% of faculty at doctoral institutions, 45% of faculty at master's and baccalaureate institutions, and 53% of faculty at associate degree-granting institutions (AAUP, 2011). Overall, there are more male faculty members than female in all categories, except among associate's degree-granting institutions. In this category—often the least paid and least recognized—women outnumber men 52.7% to 47.3% (AAUP, 2011).

According to an NCES study conducted in 2010–2011, when all institution types are averaged, the percentages of women and men differ in terms of faculty rank. Women constitute 28% of full professors—the top faculty rank—(up from 15% in 1991), 41% of associate professors (up from 28% in 1991), 48% of assistant professors (up from 40% in 1991), 55% of instructors (up from 47% in 1991), and 53% of lecturers (up from 43% in 1991) (NCES, 2011). It is important to note that the data derived from NCES in academic years 2010–2011 were notably different than the percentages reported by AAUP during the same academic years. NCES reported much higher full professorships (28%) among women than did AAUP (10%) within all institution types. NCES reported approximately 45% of associate and assistant professorships among women versus AAUP's 25% (AAUP, 2011; NCES, 2011). NCES reports on all faculty at all institutions, including for-profits, while AAUP reports on full-time faculty at not-for-profit institutions only, which likely accounts for the differences in data reporting.

The data uniformly reflect a gender disparity predominantly among the full professor rank within all institutional types. Yet, when researchers disaggregate the data by institutional type, the disparity is more marked. Among the most valued and rewarded tenure-track positions within doctoral institutions specifically, women comprise just 21.1% of assistant and associate professors, and 8% of full professors (AAUP, 2011). Men average 28.4% of assistant and associate professors and 27.4% of full professors at these same institutions. The gender disparity reflected in the areas of faculty hires and promotions demonstrates that the gap will remain for at least the next 30 years unless a significant and profound shift occurs. Moreover, institutions typically promote senior leaders from within tenure-track ranks, leaving women at a serious disadvantage for advancement.

Among all medical school faculties, in 2009–2010 women comprised 36%, which includes lecturers and instructors (Catalyst, 2012). Among female assistant professors in medical schools, 59% had achieved the rank of associate or full professor, compared to 83% of men (Selhat, 2011). Just 5% of women had achieved full professor status compared to 23% of men. Additionally, the *Journal of the American Association of Medical Colleges* reported that females represent 13% of deans nationally, a decrease from 15% in 2006 (Scott White, 2012). Law school faculties have gained modest increases in the percentage of females since 1994, comprising approximately 40% in 2012 (American Bar Association, 2012). Interestingly, females comprise 60% of associate and assistant deanships, an overrepresentation, considering that most assistant and associate deans are selected from the faculties. Yet, females represent 26% of law school deans nationally, a significant underrepresentation (American Bar Association, 2012). In other words, males comprise 74% of deans, 40% of associate and assistant deans, and 60% of the faculties. Thus, men are overrepresented on faculties and in deanships, again, the most prestigious roles.

## Chief Academic Officers, Presidents, and Boards of Trustees

Across higher education in the United States, women comprise 40% of chief academic officers (CAOs). Within subsets by institutional type, women comprise 50% of community college CAOs; 38% at baccalaureate institutions; 37% at masters'-granting institutions, and 32% at doctoral institutions (American Council on Education, 2011). Universities tend to select CAOs from the associate and full professor ranks. Noting this, women are slightly underrepresented among baccalaureate and masters' institutions and overrepresented in CAO positions at doctoral institutions. Women are more likely than men to attain a college or university presidency from CAO positions; among all college and university presidents, 52% of female presidents and 42% of males were previously provosts or CAOs (Cook, 2012). Conversely, men are more likely to be considered for presidencies with a wider variety of educational and professional backgrounds than women, thus narrowing opportunities for women who possess less than traditional academic or professional backgrounds.

The percent of female college and university presidents increased from 23% in 2006 to 26% in 2011, and 22% of presidents at the doctoral degree-granting institutions (Cook, 2012). Yet, among the top-10 elite institutions, women comprise 36% of sitting presidents, a notable difference ("Best Colleges," 2012). The data indicate that women are much more likely to hold presidencies at community colleges (33%) than at doctoral-granting institutions (22%) (Cook, 2012). In 2013, women were leading half of the eight Ivy League institutions (Zweifler, 2012). In examining female presidents of color as a demographic category, the percent has increased from 4.4% in 2006 to 17% in 2011 (Cook, 2012), a significant increase over that five-year period.

Since 1997, the percentage of female board of trustee members across all institutional types has slightly decreased from 30% to 28% in 2010 (Association of Governing Boards, 2010). The gap is particularly evident on public boards. While the presence of women on private boards reflects a modest 1.8% increase since 2004, men still outnumber women by two to one (Association of Governing Boards, 2010). Conversely, people of color are better represented on the boards of public institutions (23%) than on private postsecondary boards (12%), and there have been increases on both. Men of color, in particular, significantly increase the overall percentage of people of color on boards. In a 2009 article in *Forbes.com* (Brown, 2009), Molly Broad, president of the American Council on Education, noted that board demographics can significantly influence presidential hiring decisions. Brown observed: "Since a president is selected by an institution's board of trustees—women, especially minority women, are virtually absent from most [searches]—tips on navigating the interview process and news about job openings tend to stay among the insiders: men."

## Compensation and Performance

Women faculty members earn less than their male counterparts at nearly all institution types, with the exception of two-year (associate-granting) private institutions, where they earn roughly equal amounts (AAUP, 2011). At four-year institutions the gap is the largest, with women earning 20% less than their male counterparts, reflecting a pay gap comparable to the 1980s (NCES, 2011). Further, only two females were included on the list of the 10 highest salaried college and university presidents. One female president self-identified as a woman of color (Newman & O'Leary, 2011) and holds her presidency at a private university; the other serves at a public university.

In attempting to understand how women perform in higher education, researchers employed industry distinctions to determine how women compare to men. Researchers analyzed awardees of the major science, health, social sciences, and education institutions including the National Science Foundation, Institute of Education Science, National Institutes of Health, and the Social Science Research Council. Despite the underrepresentation of women in tenure-track positions at doctoral institutions (29.1%), women researchers received approximately 56% of national research distinctions (derived from National Institutes of Health, Institute of Education Science, National Science Foundation, Social Science Research Council grantee reports). Stated differently, tenure-track faculties comprise nearly 60% of men, and these men earn 44% of national research awards (Colorado Women's College, 2013).

Women leaders were more likely to be found among the elite institutions than in the academy as a whole. To illustrate, while women comprise 13% of medical school deans nationally, when we examined the top 10 medical colleges in the United States women comprise 21% of deans. Among the top-10 institutions in the United States ranked by *U.S. News & World Report*, 36% of the presidents were women, compared to the industry average of 26% and the associate-degree granting institutions at 33% (Cook, 2012). Among the top-funded National Science Foundation and the National Institutes of Health institutions, 32% of presidents were female (Colorado Women's College, 2013).

## CONCLUSION

Having examined where the women leaders are, we have provided the data and conclusions from *Benchmarking Women's Leadership in the United States 2013* (Colorado Women's College, 2013) and other sources to look at the status of women's positional leadership across various sectors, with a particular focus on higher education—its students, faculty, administrators, and trustees. We have shared a set of common themes that emerged from the *Benchmarking* report and illustrated the ways in which women, across sectors, may be outperforming men in some respects. Employing data specific to higher education, we illustrated the current state of women's participation and leadership in academia. Additionally, we noted circumstances in which women in higher education outperform men, specifically examining tenured faculty and research awards, as well as noted gender-based rank and pay discrepancies that remain in the academy. Finally, we offer three evidence-based recommendations that have emerged from the descriptive study conducted in *Benchmarking Women's Leadership in the United States* (Colorado Women's College, 2013), and the qualitative study conducted in *Recognizing Women's Leadership: Employing Best Practices and Strategies for Excellence* (Lennon, 2014).

The first recommendation is that mentors and sponsorship matter, and in particular, active sponsorship of women, rather than just mentorship. Women and men must actively sponsor women as they navigate the labyrinth of higher education advancement. Sponsorship is "active support by someone appropriately placed in the organization who has significant influence on decision-making processes or structures and who is advocating for, protecting, and fighting for the career advancement of an individual" (Catalyst, 2011, p. 4). Sponsors put themselves in the position of being active advocates for those being mentored (Catalyst, 2011; Klotz, 2012; Lennon, 2014; Schulte, 2013).

A 2012 *Business Week* article, entitled "Ivy Leaders Thank One Man for Inspiring Women Presidents" (Hymowitz, 2012), acknowledged Harold T. Shapiro, former president of Princeton, for his mentorship and sponsorship of emerging female leaders. Shapiro actively sponsored several women for college and university presidencies: Shirley Tilghman (current president of Princeton University), Amy Gutmann (president of the University of Pennsylvania), Ruth Simmons (former president of Brown University), as well as Nancy Cantor (chancellor and president of Syracuse University), and S. Georgia Nugent (former president of Kenyon College). Men and women in positions of power and influence make a difference for women who are still underrepresented throughout higher education, whether at the presidential level or as part of the hiring and promotion processes on faculties. As a woman sponsor stated in the Catalyst (2011) report "A lot of decisions are made when you're not in the room, so you need somebody who can advocate for you. I can't think of a person who rose without a sponsor or significant sponsors" (p. 1).

The second recommendation is that performance matters and is instrumental to women's positional advancement. Performance can be the great equalizer if institutions promote and hire leaders based on performance. While this may seem obvious, researchers discovered that many institutions, both inside and outside the academy, rarely employed performance metrics uniformly and/or among the institution's senior leaders (Barsh & Yee, 2011; Kenexa, 2012; Lennon, 2014; Pinto, 2009). Kenexa, an IBM company, in a company-produced white paper entitled "Women Leaders' Career Advancement: A Three-Level Framework" (2011) noted that:

> While objective assessment methods, such as assessment centers, have been shown to predict supervisors' performance ratings of employees ... the more senior an appointment is the less likely that objective assessment methods will be used. Senior roles are frequently filled by decision-makers who rely on informal endorsements of a candidate by others in their own network. Therefore an individual's social capital, or by whom the individual is known at a senior level, becomes more important than the human capital the individual has acquired (Broadbridge, 2010). Women's exclusion from powerful networks disadvantages them when appointments are made through personal networks rather than through formal selection processes. (p. 7)

Organizations and companies dedicated to gender equity in leadership can move away from relying on social capital—and who one knows—to a more objective, performance-based assessment of potential leadership candidates. In *Benchmarking Women's Leadership in the United States 2013*, Lennon and her colleagues (Colorado Women's College, 2013) found in their review of federal agencies that typically, when an agency was headed by a woman, or a man or woman of color, women and people of color excelled. However, there were two notable exceptions. The first notable exception was the U.S. Department of Treasury, which—until 2014—was always led by a White man; in that agency women excelled and were represented in higher proportions in senior leadership. The second notable exception was the Social Security Agency where, on the other hand, with a history of women and people of color at the helm, there was less presence of women in senior leadership. In reviewing the qualitative data filed by both agencies employees, it was clear that Treasury relied on performance-based measures, while Social Security employees noted that the informal network determined which employees were advanced. It was this finding, among others, that prompted Tiffani Lennon to write *Recognizing Women's Leadership: Best Practices and Strategies for Excellence* (2014), which further examines institutions and organizations where women excel as leaders in performance-based environments.

The final recommendation is that the climate of the institution matters. Often the descriptors that comprise the institution's leadership speak volumes of the existing climate. To illustrate, if the institution has never had a female president or a chief academic or budget officer, it is more likely that inherent, covert gender (and racial) biases exist within the institution. Additionally, if the institution has a consistent pattern of hiring female leaders from outside the institution rather than promoting from within the ranks, a lack of inclusive climate may be present for there exists a lack of willingness to trust existing leaders in the pipeline. Evidence demonstrates that such institutions are also far less likely to employ performance-based metrics and emphasize a performance-based climate, particularly in hiring and/or promoting senior leaders (Lennon, 2014). Performance and inclusivity, intrinsically linked, create a climate that rewards the best and brightest and, as a result, women and men of color will rise in leadership ranks (Lennon, 2014).

While nearly all institutions have a multicultural, diversity, or inclusive excellence office, few recognize and reward the contributions of the non-hegemony. Professional development opportunities seeking to improve climate only serve an institution when a performance-based, inclusive climate exists and when the existing climate and performance metrics align with the development programs (Lennon, 2014). Moreover, for professional development to impact climate, all members of the college and university community must participate, including senior administrators and boards of trustees.

In the corporate world, much of the dialog centers on improving profits and retaining employees through gender and racial diversity (Nishii, 2012). Higher education must also create an inclusive climate for its students and employees—faculty, staff, and administration. The discourse on academic climate that often focuses on student retention, and/or creating an optimal learning environment (Manning & Munoz, 2011) is essential to the student experience, and yet a sustainable inclusive environment must also include other members of the campus community as well (Elliott et al., 2013). Tackling institutional climate change is challenging albeit possible if the will of existing positional leaders is present to realize an inclusive and performance-based climate.

We close by sharing an experience we had as colleagues with women from around the globe. In reflecting on the recommendations and sobering statistics of women's leadership in the United States, we are reminded of the prudent words echoed by international delegates convoyed by the U.S. State Department. These delegates included women leaders from Africa, Eastern Europe, and the Middle East, recently hosted by World Denver, a Denver-based nonprofit organization, and Colorado Women's College for exchange and discourse with local leaders. As we welcomed our sisters from other countries, we were struck by their remarkable presence and profound experiences. All of us were women with seemingly different journeys and paths, and yet a common thread brought us together—our experiences as females transcended sociopolitical and sociolegal distinctions. In particular, we recalled the surprise and accompanying care Iraqi and African academicians expressed after spending three weeks in the United States visiting major cities and institutions, as well as meeting with national leaders. The delegates had been expecting to learn how American women reached noteworthy levels in society, business, academe, and instead found themselves offering advice for those of us from the United States. One Iraqi leader exclaimed, "You (U.S. women) think you have rights, but you do not. What is speech when you do not influence policy and (do not) have mandatory paid maternity leave" (Anonymous Iraqi Delegate, 2011). An African academician offered, "You must prepare for the onslaught of criticism when you become a leader so that you do not become discouraged when it happens" (Anonymous African Delegate, 2012). Many of these women are from countries that boast higher percentages of women in leadership than the U.S., despite threats of bodily harm and even death.

The outsiders' perspective conveyed that the absence of female leaders is apparent, and yet U.S. women appear fragmented as a group and/or resigned to their plight. Some of the Colorado Women's College students present felt emotionally and intellectually challenged by how these "disadvantaged" women viewed American women and our capacity to advance into leadership and influence, and we suspect many readers will experience a similar visceral reaction. This juxtaposition informs one aspect of where women sit in leadership, albeit an important one. Non-U.S. perspectives are helpful in considering how we in the United States characterize and address the dearth of women leaders in positional roles. Our colleagues from other countries often pointed to systemic opportunities present when constitutions require a certain percentage of women in elected office or public policies required a certain number of women boards of directors. These systemic interventions by governments are anathema in the United States and, instead, the individual woman is often left to absorb the "blame" for her lack of advancement. However, what we have found through *Benchmarking Women's Leadership in the United States 2013* is that U.S. women are performing despite significant systemic obstacles, and by some measures outperforming their male colleagues, and that their advancement into senior leadership roles is, by any estimation, a complicated journey. The question that remains is the following: What will it take to move women from the significant pipeline of leadership candidates into equitable representation among the senior leaders across sectors in the United States?

Our goal in this chapter has been to use the data and observations from *Benchmarking Women's Leadership in the United States 2013* to shed light on the dark complexity of women's lack of advancement into senior leadership roles in general, and in higher education particularly. The following chapters offer a variety of strategies for women's leadership development, a discussion of the contributions that women bring to leadership, and the perspectives of five women presidents who offer professional and personal lessons from their own journeys that can inform the work of future women in leadership.

## REFERENCES

American Association of University Professors. (2011). It's not over yet: The annual report on the economic status of the profession 2010-2011. Retrieved from http://www.aaup.org/reports-publications/2010-11salarysurvey

American Bar Association. (2012). First year and total JD enrollment by gender 1947-2011. Retrieved from http://www.americanbar.org/content/dam/aba/administrative/legal_education_and_admissions_to_the_bar/statistics/jd_enrollment_1yr_total_gender.authcheckdam.pd

American Council on Education. (2009, March). *The 2009 CAO census: A national profile of chief academic officers.* Washington, DC: Author.

Andersen, E. (2012, March 26). The results are in: Women are better leaders. *Forbes.* Retrieved from www.forbes.com/sites/erikaandersen/2012/03/26/the-results-are-in-women-are-better-leaders/

Appelbaum, S., Audet, L., & Miller, J. (2003). Gender and leadership? Leadership and gender? A journey through the landscape of theories. *Leadership & Organization Development Journal, 24*(1), 43–51.

Association of Governing Boards. (2011). 2011 policies, practices, and composition of institutionally related foundation board: Executive summary. Retrieved from http://agb.org/sites/agb.org/files/u3/AGB_Foun-dation_Board_Exec_Summary.pdf

A Voice for Male Students. (2013). *Educational equity for men and boys.* Retrieved from http://www.avoiceformalestudents.com/know-the-issues/issues/educational-attainment-and-well-being-of-men-and-boys/

Babcock, L., & Laschever, S. (2007). *Women don't ask.* New York, NY: Bantam Books.

Barsh, J., & Yee, L. (2011). Unlocking the full potential of women in the U.S. economy. Retrieved from http://www.mckinsey.com/client_service/organization/latest_thinking/unlocking_the_full_potential

Best colleges and universities rankings 2012. (2012). *U.S. News & World Report.* Retrieved from http://colleges.usnews.rankingsandreviews.com/best-colleges/rankings/national-universities

Brown, H. (2009, October 6). Women college presidents' tough test. *Forbes.* Retrieved from http://www.forbes.com/2009/10/06/female-college-presidents-forbes-woman-power-women-tenure.html

Burke, S., & Collins, K. (2001). Gender differences in leadership styles and management skills. *Women in Management Review, 16*(5), 244–257.

Catalyst. (2011, August 17). *Sponsoring women to success.* Retrieved from http://www.catalyst.org/knowledge/sponsoring-women-success

Catalyst. (2012). *U.S. labor force, population, and education.* Retrieved from http://www.catalyst.org/publication/202/us-labor-force-population-and-education

Catalyst. (2013). *Our history.* Retrieved from http://www.catalyst.org/who-we-are/our-history

Chamberlain, M. (Ed). (1988). *Women in academe: Progress and prospects.* New York, NY: Russell Sage Foundation.

Colorado Women's College. (2013). *Benchmarking women's leadership in the United States 2013.* Denver, CO: Author.

Cook, S. (2012, May). Women presidents: Now 26.4% but still underrepresented. *Women in Higher Education, 21*(5), 1–3. Retrieved from http://www.wihe.com/printBlog.jsp?id=36400

Darity, W., & Mason, P. (1998). Evidence on discrimination in employment: Codes of color, codes of gender. *Journal of Economic Perspectives, 12*(2), 63–90.

Eagly, A., & Johnson, B. (1990). Gender and leadership styles: A meta-analysis. *University of Connecticut Center for Health, Intervention, and Prevention, 108*(2), 233–256.

Elliott, C., Stransky, O., Negron, R., Bowlby, M., Lickiss, J., Dutt, D., & Barbosa, P. (2013). Institutional barriers to diversity change work in higher education. *Sage Open, 3(2)*, 1–9.

Fondas, N. (2010, April 20). Peaceful revolution: Equal at birth but not at work [Web blog]. Retrieved from http://www.huffingtonpost.com/nanette-fondas/ipeaceful-revolutioni-equ_b_544244.html

Franke-Ruta, G. (2013, January 28). The White House Project shutters its doors [Web blog]. Retrieved from http://www.theatlantic.com/politics/archive/2013/01/the-white-house-project-shutters-its-doors/272576/

Glazer-Raymo, J. (2008). *Unfinished agendas: New and continuing challenges in higher education.* Baltimore, MD: Johns Hopkins University Press.

Greenstone Miller, J. (2013, March 8). Designing a workplace for ambitious women [Video file]. Retrieved from http://live.wsj.com/video/designing-a-workplace-for-ambitious-women/D27188F5-5328-481A-8537-A88F248E69D7.html

Hoff Sommers, C. (2013). *The war against boys: How misguided feminism is harming our young men* (2nd ed). New York, NY: Simon & Schuster.

Hymowitz, C. (2012, October 12). Ivy leaders thank one man for inspiring women presidents. *Business Week*. Retrieved from http://www.businessweek.com/news/2012-10-12/ivy-leaders-thank-one-man-for-inspiring-women-presidents

Kenexa. (2011). *Women leaders' career advancement: A three-level framework*. Retrieved from http://www.kenexa.com/Portals/0/Downloads/Women%20Leaders%20Career%20Advancement.pdf

Klotz, F. (2012, February 24). Why women need sponsors, not mentors. *Forbes Magazine*. Retrieved from http://www.forbes.com/sites/friedaklotz/2012/02/24/why-women-need-sponsors-not-mentors/

Lamm, D. (2013, July 14). Affirmative action for college men. *The Denver Post*. Retrieved from http://www.denverpost.com/ci_23644027/lamm-affirmative-action-college-men

Lennon, T. (2014). *Recognizing women's leadership: Employing best practices and strategies for excellence*. Santa Barbara, CA: Praeger.

Lublin, J. S., & Eggers, K. (2012, April 30). More women are primed to land CEO roles. *The Wall Street Journal*. Retrieved from http://online.wsj.com/news/articles/SB10001424052702303990604577368344256435440

Manning, K., & Munoz, F. (2011). Re-visioning the future of multi-cultural student services. In D. Stewart (Ed.), *Building bridges, re-visioning community: Multicultural student services on campus* (pp. 282–300). Washington, DC: American College Personnel Association Media.

Mead, S. (2006). The truth about girls and boys. *The Education Sector*. Retrieved from http://www.educationsector.org/publications/truth-about-boys-and-girls

Myers, D. (2008). *Why women should rule the world*. New York, NY: HarperCollins.

National Center for Education Statistics. (2011). *The condition of education 2011*. Retrieved from http://nces.ed.gov/pubs2011/2011033.pdf

National Center for Education Statistics. (2012). *Digest of educational statistics 2011. U.S.* Retrieved from http://nces.ed.gov/pubs2012/2012001.pdf

Newman, J., & O'Leary, B. (2011). Highest-paid public-college presidents, 2011 fiscal year. *The Chronicle of Higher Education*. Retrieved from http://chronicle.com/article/Executive-Compensation/129979

Nishii, L. (2013). The benefits of climate for gender-diverse groups. *Academy of Management Journal, 56*(6), 1754–1774.

Pinto, C. (2009, Spring). Eliminating barriers to women's advancement: Focusing on the performance evaluation process. *Perspectives, 17*(4). Retrieved from http://www.americanbar.org/content/dam/aba/publishing/perspectives_magazine/women_perspectives_Spring09_evaluations.authcheckdam.pdf

Rocky Mountain PBS. (2011, January 28). *Colorado state of mind, Colorado quarterly* [Video file]. Retrieved from http://video.rmpbs.org/video/1771981476/

Sandberg, S. (2013). *Lean in: Women, work, and the will to lead*. New York, NY: Alfred A. Knoph.

Selhat, L. (2011, Winter). The goal is transformation. Retrieved from http://www.uphs.upenn.edu/news/publications/PENNMedicine/files/PennMedicine-2011-01-winter-12-transforming-academic-culture.pdf

Schulte, B. (2013, November 4). Major national companies try 'sponsorship' to break to glass ceiling. *Washington Post*. Retrieved from http://www.washingtonpost.com/local/major-national-companies-try-sponsorship-as-new-hammer-to-break-glass-ceiling/2013/11/13/6f7663c0-3ba8-11e3-b7ba-503fb5822c3e_story.html

Scott White, F. (2012, August). Gender-related differences in the pathway to and characteristics of U.S. medical school deanships. *Journal of the Association of American Medical Colleges, 87*(8), 1015–1023.

Social Science Research Council. (2012). *SSRC fellows around the globe*. Retrieved from http://www.ssrc.org/fellowships/map

Solomon, B. (1985). *In the company of educated women*. New Haven, CT: Yale University Press.

Tarr-Whelan, L. (2009). *Women lead the way: Your guide to stepping up to leadership and changing the world*. San Francisco, CA: Berett-Koehler.

The White House Project. (2009). *The White House Project: Benchmarking women's leadership*. New York, NY: The White House Project.

Wilson, M. C. (2007). *Closing the leadership gap: Add women, change everything*. New York, NY: Penguin Books.

Zweifler, S. (2012, May 8). Gutmann's contract to be extended through 2019. *The Daily Pennsylvanian*. Retrieved from http://www.thedp.com/article/2012/05/gutmanns_contract_extended_through_2019

CHAPTER 2

# WOMEN AT THE TOP

## The Pipeline Reconsidered

### Barbara Kellerman and Deborah L. Rhode

From the perspective of gender, the conventional wisdom about higher education is a happy story. Women are moving up, barriers are coming down, and full equality is just around the corner. This chapter questions that view, and offers a more sobering assessment of the status of women in leadership in higher education, as well as strategies that might improve that status.

Let's be clear at the outset. What we say about the pipeline in higher education applies equally to the professions more generally. The theory is, of course, that in the fullness of time the larger number of women at the lower levels of the professions will yield larger numbers of women at the higher levels. This theory presumes, first, that women and men are more or less the same in qualifications, since it takes as a given that once women are in the system, they will ascend to the top at a rate similar to that of men. This theory presumes, second, an absence of gender bias; no gender stereotypes will impede women's progress. This theory presumes, third, that organizational systems and structures work as well for women as they do for men, in spite of the fact that women still do far more domestic work than do their male counterparts. And finally, this theory presumes patience, the implication being that women's equal representation at the top is just a matter of time.

*Women and Leadership in Higher Education*, pp. 23–39
Copyright © 2014 by Information Age Publishing

The trouble is that the pipeline has been a pipe dream. Since the theory achieved currency more than 30 years ago, the number of women at the top of their professions, the number of women in high positions of leadership and management, has remained dauntingly, depressingly low. The focus of this discussion is women and leadership in American higher education. But the barriers facing women in this context are similar to those facing women in other contexts. In fact, as the numbers below will attest, women in higher education generally do better than women in other occupations, most obviously business and government.

On one of the most basic measures of inequality, the numbers speak for themselves; in the second decade of the 21st century the gender wage gap is every bit as wide as it was in the first decade of the 21st century. Women continue to earn less than four fifths of what men earn (Institute for Women's Policy Research, 2013). Moreover, "if the five-decade trend is projected forward, it will take almost another five decades—until 2058—for women to reach pay equity" (Institute for Women's Policy Research, 2013, para. 2). Put differently, the pipeline in pay has not yet paid off, though it is projected to do so—if women will only be content to wait another half century.

As to women in positions of leadership, the figures are even less heartening. Women hold a mere 4.6% of *Fortune* 500 chief executive officer and *Fortune* 1000 positions (Catalyst, 2014). Women's representation is strikingly low not only at the very highest levels, but also at the levels immediately below. Women hold less than 15% of executive officer positions at *Fortune* 500 companies—and fully one quarter of these companies have no women serving in these positions at all (Rasmus, 2013). Women as board members fare only slightly better, constituting about 16% of corporate boards (Catalyst, 2013). Additionally, for the last few years these numbers have remained stagnant, or inched up only very slightly, as have the numbers of American women who are high earners—women hold just 8% of the top earning jobs in the country (Rasmus, 2013).

The numbers are better in government—but, again, they are far from what was originally envisioned when the pipeline became conventional wisdom. In 2014, women held just over 18% of the 535 seats in the U.S. Congress. And they held just over 23% of statewide elected executive offices. Additionally, only 13% of the 100 largest cities in the United States had women mayors (Center for American Women and Politics, 2014).

It is clear that the pipeline has failed dismally, dramatically, during the long period of its common currency to provide women with equity to men. This applies across the board, to women in virtually all American institutions, particularly at high levels of leadership and management.

The results of a study titled in fact, "Pipeline's Broken Promise," published in 2010 by Catalyst, concluded:

> The pipeline is in peril … women lag men in advancement and compensation from their very first professional jobs and are less satisfied with their careers overall…. It's not a matter of different aspirations. The findings hold even when considering only men and women who aspired to chief executive officer/senior executive level. It's not a matter of parenthood. The findings hold even when considering only men and women who did not have children. (Carter & Silva, 2010, pp. 2–3)

In short, the higher up one goes on any organizational ladder, the more likely it is to find men clustered at the top. It is true that the fashion now is the flattened hierarchy, with an emphasis on teamwork and empowerment. In this sense, women do have more of a say now than they did in the past. But if the progress promised by the pipeline is measured by the numbers of women in positions of leadership, the pipeline has fallen far short.

One of our own institutions, Harvard University, provides a vivid case in point. The university is, by no means, oblivious to the problem. It boasts a woman president, Drew Faust, and it expresses constant concern about the issue of equity for women in various forums, including in its own publications such as the *Harvard Gazette* and *Harvard Magazine*. For example, the former featured an article on a conference at the Harvard Business School geared toward its women graduates. One professor, Robin Ely, was quoted as saying that while the numbers of women who opt out of the workforce altogether is not large, so far as women's professional success is concerned, the problems remain, and they are major. Women, she said, are:

> Pushed out by organizations that demand a 24/7 work schedule, as well as … pulled out by a culture that promulgates a compelling—some might say guilt-inducing—image of motherhood that's hard to live up to while you're trying to hold a job. (Koch, 2013, para. 22)

Similarly, in an attempt to promote greater gender equity—at least on its own turf—the Harvard Business School made a concerted, extended attempt to alter its culture. In 2013, it concluded a 2-year experiment that changed its curriculum, its rules, and its social rituals, all in order to foster female success. Of course in so doing it admitted, if only tacitly, that the pipeline had been a failure. Year after year women who arrived at the business school with the same test scores and grades as men had fallen behind, even before their time at the school was completed. Moreover, attracting and retaining female professors had been a losing battle: In

2007 nine of the 28 female junior faculty left, three because they were denied tenure, the rest either because they chose not to apply for promotion or took a leave of absence as a way of bringing to a close their time at Harvard (Merrigan & White, 2010). In other words, even at relatively early stages of women's professional lives, the pipeline was leaking.

We hardly need add that the situation at other Harvard schools—the law school, for example—is little different. In 2013, female faculty members represented less than 20% of the total of 92 law professors and assistant professors. Moreover there were complaints from students that "there are a lot of clubs that have a very large percentage of male leadership, especially in law journals and organizations that lead into academia, which is already a very male dominated field" (Patel, 2013, para. 6). Indeed the situation at the law school was perceived to be so egregious that a new coalition was formed—"Shatter the Ceiling"—precisely to address some of the lingering, still festering issues (Patel, 2013, para. 1).

At Harvard, clearly, the inequities apply virtually across the board. The September-October 2013 issue of *Harvard Magazine* featured an article that made the situation plain; it was titled "Where the Women Aren't." Again, the focus of the piece was on women faculty, not on women administrators. But the point was the same: The pipeline was leaking or, at least, it was not doing what it was supposed to be doing with anything resembling all due speed. As of 2013, women constituted less than one quarter of the tenured faculty at Harvard and one quarter of the total faculty ranks. Moreover the gender composition of tenure-track faculty has stayed more or less the same for the last two decades—the most recent figures actually representing a decline, from about 40% to about 35% ("Where the Women Aren't," 2013). So much for the pipeline among faculty ranks.

But conventional wisdom is difficult to dislodge. In this instance it is clear that pipeline facts have failed to bring an end to pipeline fictions. The "pipeline" word is still being used in the best of circles, as if the experiences of the last 30 years have taught us little or even nothing. For example, while an article in the *Financial Times* in 2013 carried the headline that "fundamental change" regarding gender diversity in the boardroom could take "at least a generation" (Medland, 2013), the piece nevertheless took seriously the pipeline as the preferred solution. A British woman board consultant was quoted approvingly:

> We have made a fair bit of progress on the nonexecutive front, but it's very slow on the executive side because there just aren't enough women in the pipeline. If we want more female executives coming though we will have to start a lot earlier. (Medland, 2013, para. 15)

Of course what we already know, based on several decades of experience, is that having more women in the pipeline is, of itself, insufficient. Or, more precisely, it is insufficient if the goal of equity is to be realized within a timeframe that we, at least, consider acceptable.

The pipeline has, however, done something consequential. It has pre-empted protest. By promising women that their time will come, the pipeline has kept them quiet. Women on campus, like women in America everywhere else, have been socialized to accept the status quo, to believe that progress is inevitable if only we are prepared to be relentlessly patient.

## THE PIPELINE IN HIGHER EDUCATION

The pipeline theory in higher education implies that the more women students, the more women junior faculty, and the more women lower-level administrators, the more women will rise to the top. As White (2005) put it, ideally the end result is "many women flowing out of the 'pipeline' to swell the most senior ranks of the faculty and administrative leadership positions" (p. 22). The problem obviously is that while the numbers of women at the lower levels of the academy have continued to grow—notably among students at both the graduate and undergraduate levels—significant change, major change, continues to remain elusive.

Women—and people of color—continue to be underrepresented at the highest levels of higher education leadership. "Higher Ed Presidential Pipeline Slow to Change" ran the title of a 2013 article published in *The Higher Education Workplace*. The article reported that at a time when women constituted over half of undergraduate and master's degree students, they accounted for only a quarter of college presidents. Women are also underrepresented as chief academic officers (41%), executive vice presidents (36%), and academic deans (28%). In the most elite institutions, women have made dramatic progress, but racial and ethnic minorities still lag behind. Another 2013 headline summed it up: "At the Ivies, It's Still White at the Top" (Patton, 2013). Although five of the eight presidents of Ivy League institutions were women, only 10–20% of upper administrators were racial or ethnic minorities.

In explaining the underrepresentation of women in leadership roles, researchers stress multiple factors. One involves the lingering and largely unconscious bias that continues to confront women seeking leadership roles. A wide array of empirical studies has found that women lack the presumption of competence enjoyed by White men, and that they need to work harder to achieve the same results (Foschi, 1996; Ridgeway & England, 2007). One study published in 2012 points out the persistence of such bias, even among highly educated academics. Yale researchers Moss-Racusen, Dovidio, Brescoll, Graham, and Handelsman (2012) asked science faculty at six major research universities to evaluate an applicant for a lab manager's position. All of the professors received the same description of the applicant, but in half the descriptions the applicant was named John, and in the other half, Jennifer. John was rated more competent and more likely to be hired and mentored than Jennifer. Similarly, in studies of academic leaders, women frequently report needing to work twice as hard and be twice as good in order to be viewed as equal to men (Edwards, 2001; Gerdes, 2003; Tiao, 2006; Wolverton, Bower, & Hyle, 2008). Common complaints include not being listened to and not being taken as seriously as male colleagues (Tiao, 2006). Women of color are particularly likely to report having their competence and credentials questioned (Edwards, 2001; Edwards-Wilson, 2001). Many experience tokenism, finding themselves in situations where they are made aware of their unique status yet "feel compelled to behave as though this difference did not exist" (Edwards, 2001, p. 47).

A related problem is that women, particularly women of color, find that peers and superiors are relatively intolerant of their mistakes. Obviously this can be costly, for an unpopular decision in an unforgiving environment can waylay a career (García, 2008; Sturnick, 1999). Fearing that they will be more harshly judged, women tend to shy away from risks. They also internalize prevailing stereotypes and discount their own leadership potential. Lack of confidence and fear of failure can keep women from even aspiring to top positions (Madsen, 2008). As Sheryl Sandberg famously put it, women do not "lean in" (Sandberg, 2013).

Because many qualities traditionally associated with leadership are masculine, women confront a double bind and double standard (Catalyst, 2007). They can appear too assertive or not assertive enough, and what is assertive in a man can be seen as abrasive in a woman. Female leaders who make tough calls risk being stereotyped as cold, unfeeling, insensitive, hard-nosed, pushy, demanding, nasty, ironfisted, overbearing, and bitchy (Harter, 2009; Tiao, 2006).

A further problem involves in-group favoritism. Extensive research documents the preferences that individuals feel for members of their own groups. Loyalty, cooperation, favorable evaluations, and career opportunities all increase for in-group members (Brewer, 1998; Fiske, 2000; Reskin, 2000). Women in traditionally male-dominated settings often remain out of the loop of support available to their male colleagues (Hewlett, Marshall, & Sherbin, 2012; Ragins, 1999; Tiao, 2006). And, because the numbers of women in upper level academic administrative positions lag behind men, there are fewer female mentors and sponsors for aspiring colleagues (Madsen, 2008). Again, this shortage is particularly pronounced for women of color (Brown, 2005; Edwards, 2001).

A final barrier to women in academic leadership involves work-family conflicts. Colleges and universities are greedy institutions (Coser, 1974). The time demands of running complex organizations, coupled with evening and weekend events, pose challenges for any woman with significant caretaking commitments. Moreover, despite men's increasing assumption of family responsibilities, women continue to assume a disproportionate burden in the home, and to pay a price in the world outside it. They still spend over twice as much time on care of children as men, and over three times as much time on household tasks (Konigsberg, 2011; U.S. Department of Labor, 2012). Women also provide more than twice as much elder care, not only for their own parents but for their in-laws as well (Johnson & Wiener, 2006). These disproportionate burdens make it harder for women to assume academic leadership roles and to compile performance records that would equip them for such positions (Madsen, 2008).

## INDIVIDUAL STRATEGIES

What enables women to overcome these obstacles and rise to positions of authority, and what makes them effective once they get there? Do women lead differently than men? A growing array of studies of women who reach positions of academic leadership provides some answers to these questions.

A common finding is that female leaders in higher education tend to adopt a participatory, consultative leadership style (Bonebright, Cottledge, & Lonnquist, 2012; Madsen, 2008; Tiao, 2006). This finding is consistent with the research on female leaders more generally, which concludes that women have a more democratic decision-making approach than men (Eagly & Carli, 2007). As some presidents noted, because women "have been socialized to be concerned about relationships" (Nesbitt, 2007, p. 97), they tend to have a collaborative style well-suited to academic environments, which value nonhierarchical process-oriented leadership (Shinn, 2002). However, this style is not without its difficulties. To some audiences, this participatory approach can seem weak and indecisive (Sturnick, 1999). Women have sometimes responded by adopting more authoritative approaches (Jablonski, 1996; Young, 2004), or "androgynous" styles that combine traditionally masculine and feminine traits (Madsen, 2008). For many women, their goal is to appear assertive but not abrasive (Wenniger, 2001). To that end, they need to be what University of Michigan President Mary Sue Coleman has described as "relentlessly pleasant" (Babcock & Laschever, 2008, p. 253).

Many women in academic leadership positions also stress the need to adapt their style to whatever it is the situation demands (Madsen, 2008). As one women chief executive officer noted, "There is no one model of successful leadership that fits all circumstances" (Edwards-Wilson, 2001, p. 46). Another explained that an effective style must:

> Grow out of the needs of the times. If the house is on fire, you'd better be very directive. If you are going to revise the promotion and tenure guidelines, you had better be very participatory. If you have a style and somebody can say, "you're always going to do this," you're going to be a disaster because you don't have enough sense to read the situation and know what's required. (Madsen, 2008, p. 249)

This insight is consistent with research on leadership generally, which finds that individuals who are most successful have a repertoire of styles that can fit diverse contexts (Goleman, 2000).

In addition to that mix of styles, certain other qualities appear critical to academic leaders' success. High ethical standards are at the top of the list (Kouzes & Posner, 2003; Loston, 2001; Madsen, 2008; Nesbitt, 2008; Tiao, 2006). Women leaders speak of not losing sight of core values (Tiao, 2006), needing to be open and honest (Gellman-Danley, 2001), and serving as "models of integrity" (Madsen, 2008, p. 254). A related quality is the willingness to put the institution's interests first (Tiao, 2006). Successful presidents recognize that it is "not about you" (Madsen, 2008, p. 259). Obvious though this seems in principle, it can prove challenging in practice. Individuals often rise to positions of leadership because they have high needs for personal achievement. But once they are in such those positions, especially in higher education, they must subordinate those needs to those of the institution. This will often require using their power to empower others (Loston, 2001; Madsen, 2008).

Another critical leadership quality is a capacity for lifelong learning. Female presidents emphasize a willingness to do their homework, hear criticism, acknowledge mistakes, and reflect on failures (Madsen, 2008). Self-knowledge and a commitment to continuous personal development are essential to success (Madsen, 2008; Tiao, 2006). In *The Jossey-Bass Academic Administrator's Guide to Exemplary Leadership*, Kouzes and Posner (2003) put it bluntly: "The best leaders ... are the best learners" (p. 101). To increase their opportunities for learning, effective leaders also proactively seek mentors and sponsors. Advice and support from individuals who have held academic leadership positions is often necessary for career development (Brown, 2005; Gerdes, 2003; Hewlett, Marshall, & Sherbin, 2012; Madsen, 2008). By the same token, serving as mentors for the next generation of leaders is a professional responsibility (Brown, 2005; Madsen, 2008).

Another key leadership quality is judgment. For example, effective leaders pick their battles wisely (Tiao, 2006). As one woman put it, "You can't fight for every issue. It's demanding and exhausting and may distract you from issues that matter more…. Women choose their battles deliberately, cautiously, and carefully" (Cook, 2001, p. 97). Factors to consider are timing, the odds of winning, the price of losing, and the values at issue. Some presidents warned against seeking too much too soon. "Don't try to change things until you are in a position of strength" (Gerdes, 2003, p. 266), one leader advised. Women need to give others "the time to become accustomed to your ideas … you are in this for the long haul; be strategic with your influence and your energy" (Douglas, 2008, p. 32). Presidential power must be earned, not assumed and is a resource not to be squandered prematurely (McDaniel, 2001).

A case history in the value of incremental change is the failed campus coup at the University of Virginia. The board of trustees summarily forced the resignation of Teresa Sullivan on the grounds that she lacked "bold and proactive leadership" (Carey, 2012, para. 2) on controversial issues such as budgetary cuts and online education (Rice, 2012). But when the campus erupted in protest, the board was forced to retreat and reinstate Sullivan. What Sullivan had recognized and the trustees had not, was that, as she explained to a *New York Times* reporter, "this was an institution steeped in tradition. People love the tradition, and they would not react well to sudden change" (Rice, 2012, para. 28). Clearly the trustees had also not reckoned with all the different stakeholders that now have an impact on what happens in higher education. The days when boards, or for that matter presidents themselves, can arbitrarily make decisions, without taking into account an array of others, both inside and outside the institution, are over.

Exercising good judgment also requires good listening. As one president put it, "Being able to just sit and listen is more than half of communicating. It is the hardest thing we do. It's much more tiring than talking" (Douglas, 2008, p. 32). Another similarly noted that hearing people is critical and that "you can only do that if you are quiet enough to listen to what they are saying" (Madsen, 2008, p. 260). Good listening skills are also the foundation of other key leadership abilities such as forming alliances, facilitating teamwork, and building consensus (McDaniel, 2001; Tiao, 2006).

Finally, a striking number of female leaders mentioned a quality that seldom figures in leadership texts. Donna Shalala, who has held three academic presidencies, as well as a U.S. Cabinet position, put it bluntly. "You have to have a good sense of humor" (Shinn, 2002, p. 19). Other leaders agreed. Humor can go a long way in relieving tension and stress (McCorkle & Oldenburger, 2001; Nesbitt, 2001; Tiao, 2006; Wolverton et al., 2009). It can also communicate difficult truths (McCorkle & Olden-burger, 2001). The ability to laugh at oneself is especially critical (Gerdes, 2003). Of course in higher education, as in every other context, leaders need cultural sensitivity. They should be aware of the power dynamics of a situation, and avoid using humor in ways that would raise hackles and alienate potential supporters (McCorkle & Ollenburger, 2001).

## INSTITUTIONAL STRATEGIES

As this overview suggests, we do not believe that progress is inevitable in the foreseeable future. Women continue to confront unconscious biases and structural barriers that impede their progress to leadership levels. What, then, can institutions of higher education do to accelerate prog-ress?

The first, and most essential step, is to recognize the problem and to hold administrators accountable for addressing it. A wide array of research finds that the most important factor in ensuring equal access to leadership opportunities is a commitment to that objective, which is reflected in workplace priorities, policies, and reward structures (Catalyst, 1998, 1999; Klenke, 1996; Mattis, 2000). This, in turn, requires account-ability. Decision makers need to be held responsible for results as well as for practices that influence those results, such as evaluation, career devel-opment, mentoring, and work/family accommodation.

Commitment from the top is critical. Campus leaders need to acknowl-edge the importance of diversity and equity, to assess progress in achiev-ing them, and to hold individuals at every level of the organization accountable for improvement. Inclusive search processes are part of the answer. One model is the Rooney Rule, applicable to search processes in professional football. The National Football League requires teams to pledge to include a minority candidate among the finalists for each coaching and general manager position and to conduct an on-site inter-view with that finalist (Hack, 2003). During the first seven years after the rule was adopted in 2003, the number of Black head coaches in the National Football League increased from 6% to 22% (Bransom, 2012). Search committees also need to broaden the pool from which they con-sider candidates. The practice of looking only to academic officers as presidential candidates not only puts women at a disadvantage, it also preempts access to "new ideas, new viewpoints, and innovative ways of addressing new challenges" (Kirwan, 2008, p. 5). To make significant progress, academic administrations need concrete assessments of results. On this point, conventional wisdom is right: Workplaces get what they measure. Campuses should compile information on recruitment, hiring, promotion, and retention, broken down by sex, as well as race and ethnicity. Surveys of current and former employees can also provide valuable information on equity and quality-of-life issues. Decision makers need to know whether men and women are advancing in equal numbers and whether they feel equally well supported in career development. Where possible, campuses should assess their own progress in comparison with similar organizations.

Any serious commitment to expand women's leadership opportunities requires a similarly serious commitment to address work/family conflicts that stand in the way of advancement. Best practices and model programs are readily available on matters such as flexible and reduced schedules, telecommuting, leave policies, and childcare assistance. Such options are critical in retaining potential leaders. In surveys of high-achieving women, between two thirds and four fifths of respondents identify work/family issues as a major part of the problem and the solution for women's advancement (Hewlett & Luce, 2005). Most of these women rate schedule flexibility as more important than compensation. Institutions of higher education also need to insure that women who seek temporary accommodations do not pay a permanent price. Stepping out should not mean stepping down. Individuals on reduced or flexible schedules should not lose opportunities for challenging assignments or eventual promotion. Work/life policies need to be monitored to ensure that options are available in practice as well as in principle, and that women at the highest leadership level feel able to take advantage of them. In short, if employers want the most able and diverse leadership candidates possible, the working environment needs to attract and retain them.

Mentoring and sponsoring initiatives are also critical. Where informal relationships are lacking, formal programs can help fill the gap. Of course, relationships that are assigned are seldom as effective as those that are chosen. But some access to advice and support may be better than none. At the very least, structured programs can keep talented but unassertive women from falling through the cracks, and remove concerns about appearances of favoritism or sexual impropriety that sometimes inhibit mentoring relationships. Well-designed initiatives that evaluate and reward mentoring activities can improve participants' skills, satisfaction, and retention rates. The only systematic large-scale study to date has found that mentoring programs are correlated with modest gains in female representation in managerial positions and that White women benefit most (Kalev, Dobbin, & Kelly, 2006). Academic institutions could also do more to recognize the importance of diversity in their curricular and research priorities. At a minimum, this will require greater integration of diversity-related issues in core courses. Professional and MBA programs could also increase research support for scholars and continuing education for practitioners, on gender equity issues. Decision makers need to know much more about what works in the world, and academic institutions are uniquely positioned to help fill the gap.

Higher education has a corresponding responsibility to model equal opportunity. College campuses are gatekeepers to positions of leadership in American society, and their own institutions ought to reflect the diversity of the society they seek to serve. Campuses cannot simply wait for the pipeline to deliver that diversity. They must act affirmatively and proactively to promote gender equity in practice as well as principle.

Finally, we might point to President Shirley Tilghman of Princeton as something of an exemplar of a woman leader in higher education. From day one of her presidency she did her level best to address existing inequities. One of her first acts as president was to appoint Amy Gutmann as provost—this in spite of the fact that many of those associated with Princeton, past and present, considered one woman at the top of this previously all-male bastion quite sufficient. One of Tilghman's more recent acts was to form a steering committee on undergraduate women's leadership, headed by Nan Keohane, the former president of Duke University and author of the chapter that follows. What she and others on the Princeton campus had noticed was that there was a problem not only at the end of the pipeline, but at the beginning. Among undergraduates at Princeton there was disparity between men and women in visible positions of campus leadership. Further, women undergraduates were winning fewer academic prizes and post graduate fellowships than men. There was, in other words, a problem pertaining to women and leadership at every point in the pipeline. But, as the comparative data attested, the problem was by no means confined to Princeton. In fact, many of the patterns at Princeton were replicated on the campuses of peer universities (Princeton University, 2011).

All this suggests, of course, that remedies are required at every point in the pipeline. If the pipeline is to avoid being discredited entirely, it must become less a convenient fiction than a realistic mechanism for creating change. This will, however, require individual and institutional strategies that are much more forward leaning than what we generally have now. Only an assertive, yes, even an aggressive approach will move women in higher education along more quickly than the glacial pace to which we seem, unfortunately, to have become accustomed.

## CONCLUSION

We would be remiss in the end if we failed to place the issue of women and leadership not only in broader professional and institutional contexts, but in a broader political context as well. It is no accident that the pipeline has failed to live up to its promise precisely during a time in which anything resembling a vibrant women's movement has receded into history. By and large women are not organizing on their own behalf. By and large they are not protesting inequity on anything other than on an occasional individual level. And by and large they are lacking the support and critical mass that historically has been required to create significant change. Of itself this does not necessarily spell doom. The strategies sketched out above hold promise for making the pipeline flow more freely. But it does suggest that in the absence of broader political support, other kinds of support—personal, professional, and institutional—are that much more important. In fact, it becomes critical if we are to be spared the unhappy task of writing a chapter similar to this one 10 or 20 years from now.

## REFERENCES

Babcock, L., & Laschever, S. (2008). *Ask for it: How women can use the power of negotiation to get what they really want.* New York, NY: Bantam Dell.

Bonebright, D. A., Cottledge, A. D., & Lonnquist, P. (2012). Developing women leaders on campus: A human resources-women's center partnership at the University of Minnesota. *Advances in Developing Human Resources, 14*(1), 79–95.

Branson, D. M. (2012). Initiatives to place women on corporate boards of directors—A global snapshot. *Journal of Corporate Law, 37*(4), 793–814.

Brewer, M. B., & Brown, R. J. (1998). Intergroup relations. In D. T. Gilbert, S. T. Fiske, & G. Lindzey (Eds.), *The handbook of social psychology* (4th ed., Vol. 2, pp. 554-594). New York, NY: McGraw-Hill.

Brown, T. M. (2005). Mentorship and the female college president. *Sex Roles, 52*(9/10), 659–666. Retrieved from http://digitalcommons.uncfsu.edu/cgi/viewcontent.cgi?article=1000&context=swk_faculty_wp

Carey, K. (2012, June 12). The decline and fall of a public university: How status anxiety doomed the University of Virginia. *New Republic.* Retrieved from http://www.newrepublic.com/blog/plank/104204/university-of-virginia-teresa-sullivan

Carter, N. M., & Silva, C. (2010). *Pipeline's broken promise.* New York, NY: Catalyst.

Catalyst. (1998). *Advancing women in business—The Catalyst guide.* San Francisco, CA: Jossey-Bass.

Catalyst. (1999). *Women of color in corporate management: Opportunities and barriers.* New York, NY: Catalyst.

Catalyst. (2007). *The double-bind dilemma for women in leadership: Damned if you do, doomed if you don't.* Retrieved from http://www.catalyst.org/knowledge/double-bind-dilemma-women-leadership-damned-if-you-do-doomed-if-you-dont-0

Catalyst. (2013). *Catalyst, quick take: Women on boards.* New York, NY: Author.

Catalyst. (2014, January 15). Women CEOs of the Fortune 1000 [Web log post]. Retrieved from http://www.catalyst.org/knowledge/women-ceos-fortune-1000

Center for American Women and Politics. (2014). *Women in elective office 2014* [fact sheet]. Retrieved from http://www.cawp.rutgers.edu/fast_facts/levels_of_office/documents/elective.pdf

Cook, S. G. (2001). How women administrators choose their battles. In M. D. Wenniger & M. H. Conroy (Eds.), *Gender equity or bust! On the road to campus leadership with women in higher education* (pp. 96–100). San Francisco, CA: Jossey-Bass.

Coser, L. A. (1974). *Greedy institutions: Patterns of undivided commitment.* New York, NY: Free Press.

Douglass, B. (2009). Having fun. In M. Wolverton, B. L. Bower, & A. E. Hyle (Eds.) *Women at the top: What women university and college presidents say about effective leadership* (pp. 21–35). Sterling, VA: Stylus.

Eagly, A. H., & Carli L. L. (2007). *Through the labyrinth: The truth about how women become leaders.* Boston, MA: Harvard Business School Press.

Edwards, J. M. (2001). Assorted adaptations by African-American administrators. In M. D. Wenniger & M. H. Conroy (Eds.), *Gender equity or bust! On the road to campus leadership with women in higher education* (pp. 46–50). San Francisco, CA: Jossey-Bass.

Edwards-Wilson, R. (2001). You go, girl! African American female presidents lead with style. In M. D. Wenniger & M. H. Conroy (Eds.), *Gender equity or bust! On the road to campus leadership with women in higher education* (pp. 43–46). San Francisco, CA: Jossey-Bass.

Fiske, S. T. (2000). Stereotyping, prejudice, and discrimination at the seam between the centuries: Evolution, culture, mind, and brain. *European Journal of Social Psychology, 30*(3), 299–322. Retrieved from http://www2.psych.ubc.ca/~schaller/Psyc591Readings/Fiske2000.pdf

Foschi, M. (1996). Double standards in the evaluation of men and women. *Social Psychology Quarterly, 59*(2), 237–254.

García, M. (2009). Moving forward. In M. Wolverton, B. L. Bower, & A. E. Hyle (Eds.), *Women at the top: What women university and college presidents say about effective leadership* (pp. 37–53). Sterling, VA: Stylus.

Gellman-Danley, B. (2001). Women and campus politics: Don't do it *their* way! In M. D. Wenniger & M. H. Conroy (Eds.), *Gender equity or bust! On the road to campus leadership with women in higher education* (pp. 100–105). San Francisco, CA: Jossey-Bass.

Gerdes, E. P. (2003). Do it your way: Advice from senior academic women. *Innovative Higher Education, 27*(4), 253–275.

Goleman, D. (2000, March/April). Leadership that gets results. *Harvard Business Review, 78*(2), 78–90.

Hack, D. (2003, December 9). The NFL spells out new hiring guidelines. *The New York Times*, p. D3.

Harter, C. C. (2009). Still standing. In M. Wolverton, B. L. Bower, & A. E. Hyle (Eds.), *Women at the top: What women university and college presidents say about effective leadership* (pp. 55–70). Sterling, VA: Stylus.

Hewlett, S. A., Marshall, M., & Sherbin, L. (with Adachi, B.) (2012). *Sponsor effect 2.0: Road maps for sponsors and protégés*. New York, NY: Center for Talent Innovation.

Hewlett, S. A., & Luce, C. B. (2005). Off-ramps and on-ramps: Keeping talented women on the road to success. *Harvard Business Review, 83*(3), 43–54.

Higher Ed Presidential Pipeline Slow to Change. (2013). *The higher education workplace*. Retrieved from http://www.cupahr.org/diversity/files/ Higher%20Ed%20Presidential%20Pipeline%20slow%20to%20change.pdf

Institute for Women's Policy Research. (2013, September 18). Most women today will not see equal pay during their work lives [Press Release]. Retrieved from http://www.iwpr.org/press-room/press-releases/most-women-working-today-will-not-see-equal-pay-during-their-working-lives

Jablonski, M. (1996). The leadership challenge for women presidents. *Initiatives, 57*(4), 1–10.

Johnson, R. W., & Weiner, J. M. (2006, February). *A profile of frail older Americans and their caregivers, Urban Institute* (Occasional Paper No. 8). Retrieved from http://www.urban.org/UploadedPDF/311284_older_americans.pdf

Kalev, A., Dobbin, F., & Kelly, E. (2006). Best practices or best guesses? Assessing the efficacy of corporate Affirmative Action and diversity policies. *American Sociological Review, 71*(4), 589–617.

Kirwan, W. E. (2008). Diversifying: The American college presidency. *The Presidency, 11*(Supplement), 4.

Klenke, K. (1996). *Women and leadership: A contextual perspective*. New York, NY: Springer.

Koch, K. (2013, April 5). Sisterhood of the traveling pantsuit. *Harvard Gazette*. Retrieved from http://news.harvard.edu/gazette/story/2013/04/sisterhood-of-the-traveling-pantsuit/

Konigsberg, R. D. (2011, August 8). Chore wars. *Time*. Retrieved from http://content.time.com/time/magazine/article/0,9171,2084582,00.html

Kouzes, J. M., & Posner, B. Z. (2003). *The Jossey-Bass academic administrator's guide to exemplary leadership*. San Francisco, CA: Jossey-Bass.

Loston, A. W. (2001). Leadership survival strategies in the vacuum of upheaval. In M. D. Wenniger & M. H. Conroy (Eds.), *Gender equity or bust! On the road to campus leadership with women in higher education* (pp. 268–276). San Francisco, CA: Jossey-Bass.

Madsen, S. (2008). *On becoming a woman leader: Learning from the experiences of university presidents*. San Francisco, CA: Jossey-Bass.

Mattis, M. C. (2000). Women entrepreneurs in the United States. In M. J. Davidson & R. J. Burke (Eds.), *Women in management* (pp. 53–68). Thousand Oaks, CA: SAGE.

McCorkle, S., & Ollenburger, J. (2001). Humor as a management tool. In M. D. Wenniger & M. H. Conroy (Eds.), *Gender equity or bust! On the road to campus leadership with women in higher education* (pp. 279–281). San Francisco, CA: Jossey-Bass.

McDaniel, T. (2001). Special caveats for new women presidents. In M. D. Wenniger & M. H. Conroy (Eds.), *Gender equity or bust! On the road to campus leader-*

*ship with women in higher education* (pp. 132-135). San Francisco, CA: Jossey-Bass.

Medland, D. (2013, February 21). Fundamental change could take 'at least a generation.' *Financial Times*. Retrieved from http://www.ft.com/intl/cms/s/0/9be82ad4-7438-11e2-80a7-00144feabdc0.html#axzz2tWOVETLE

Merrigan, T., & White, W. (2010, April 14). Harvard Business School grapples with gender imbalance. *Harvard Crimson*. Retrieved from http://www.thecrimson.com/article/2010/4/14/faculty-school-business-women/

Moss-Racusin, C. A., Dovidio, J. F., Brescoll, V. L., Graham, M. J., & Handelsman, J. (2012). Science faculty's subtle gender biases favor male students. *Proceedings of the National Academy of Sciences of the United States of America, 109*(41), 16474–16479. doi:10.1073/pnas.1211286109

Nesbitt, M. T. (2009). A perfect fit. In M. Wolverton, B. L. Bower, & A. E. Hyle (Eds.), *Women at the top: What women university and college presidents say about effective leadership* (pp. 87–99). Sterling, VA: Stylus.

Patel, D. A. (2013, March 28). Law school coalition aims to mitigate campus gender disparities. *Harvard Crimson*. Retrieved from http://www.thecrimson.com/article/2013/3/28/hls-coalition-gender-disparities/#

Patton, S. (2013, June 9). At the ivies, it's still White at the top. *The Chronicle of Higher Education*. Retrieved from http://chronicle.com/article/At-the-Ivies-Its-Still-White/139643/

Princeton University, Steering Committee on Undergraduate Women's Leadership. (2011). *Report of the steering committee on undergraduate women's leadership*. Retrieved from http://www.princeton.edu/reports/2011/leadership/download/

Ragins, B. R. (1999). Gender and mentoring relationships: A review and research agenda for the next decade. In G. Powell (Ed.), *Handbook of gender and work* (pp. 347–370), Thousand Oaks, CA: SAGE.

Rasmus, G. (2013, July 9). Fortune 500 company names new CEO, gender inequality still exists. *The Jane Dough*. Retrieved from http://www.thejanedough.com/fortune-500-company-names-new-female-ceo-gender-inequality-still-exists/

Reskin, B. (2002). Rethinking employment discrimination and its remedies. In M. F. Guillén, R. Collins, P. England, & M. Meyer (Eds.) *The new economic sociology: Developments in an emerging field* (pp. 218–244). New York, NY: Russell Sage.

Rice, A. (2012, September 11). Anatomy of a campus coup. *New York Times Magazine*. Retrieved from http://www.nytimes.com/2012/09/16/magazine/teresa-sullivan-uva-ouster.html?pagewanted=all&_r=0

Ridgeway, C. L., & England, P. (2007). Sociological approaches to sex discrimination in employment. In F. Crosby, M. Stockdale, & A. Ropp (Eds.), *Sex discrimination in the workplace* (pp. 189–212). Malden, MA: Blackwell.

Sandberg, S. (2013). *Lean in: Women, work, and the will to lead*. New York, NY: Alfred Knopf.

Shinn, S. (2002, July/August). At the top of her game. *BizEd*. Retrieved from http://www.e-digitaleditions.com/i/63429/2

Sturnick, J. (1999). Women who lead: Persevering in the face of skepticism. *The Presidency, 2*(2), 28–33.

Tiao, N. (2006). *Senior women leaders in higher education: Overcoming barriers to success* (Doctoral dissertation). Retrieved from http://commons.emich.edu/theses/

U.S. Department of Labor, Bureau of Labor Statistics. (2012). American time use survey [Press Release]. Retrieved from http://www.bls.gov/news.release/pdf/atus.pdf

Wenniger, M. D. (2001). Tips to circumvent alien gatekeepers. In M. D. Wenniger & M. H. Conroy (Eds.), *Gender equity or bust! On the road to campus leadership with women in higher education* (pp. 114–116). San Francisco, CA: Jossey-Bass.

Where the women aren't. (2013, September/October). *Harvard Magazine.* Retrieved from http://harvardmagazine.com/2013/09/where-the-women-aren-t

White, J. (2005). Pipelines to pathways: New directions for improving the status of women on campus. *Liberal Education, 91*(1), 22–27. Retrieved from http://www.aacu.org/liberaleducation/le-wi05/le-wi05feature2.cfm

Wolverton, M., Bower, B. L., & Hyle, A. E. (2009). *Women at the top: What women university and college presidents say about effective leadership.* Sterling, VA: Stylus.

Young, P. (2004). Leadership and gender in higher education: A case study. *Journal of Further and Higher Education, 28*(1), 95–106.

CHAPTER 3

# LEADERSHIP OUT FRONT AND BEHIND THE SCENES

## Young Women's Ambitions for Leadership Today

**Nannerl O. Keohane**

In the literature related to women and leadership, the concept of a "pipe-line"—as presented in the previous chapter by Barbara Kellerman and Deborah Rhode—is often used to denote the group of women who hold potential for taking on positions of leadership. We refer to "leaks" or "blockages" in the pipeline to mean diversions or obstacles that cause previously ambitious young women to exit the pipeline and take up lives that do not include significant leadership responsibilities or professional accomplishment at the highest levels. However, as we learn more about what young women today say they want to do with their lives, we need to think more comprehensively about what this pipeline includes and how well the metaphor describes the situation.

This chapter will draw upon the findings of the Princeton University Steering Committee on Undergraduate Women's Leadership (Princeton University, 2011), as well as those of a similar committee at Duke University a decade earlier, for evidence about the concerns of female students and their preferences for areas of involvement in leadership. With these

*Women and Leadership in Higher Education,* pp. 41–55
Copyright © 2014 by Information Age Publishing
All rights of reproduction in any form reserved.

data in mind, we can broaden our understanding of the leadership hopes and ambitions of young college women today.

To tackle this subject productively, we need to think more carefully about our key term, *leadership*. We may all think we know leadership when we see it, but as many observers have noted, there are almost as many definitions of leadership as there are leaders (or scholars of leadership). In my book, *Thinking About Leadership,* I used this definition: "Leaders define or clarify goals for a group of individuals, and bring together the energies of members of that group to pursue those goals" (Keohane, 2010, p. 23).

In this chapter I want to juxtapose two kinds of leadership: "out front" and "behind the scenes." Over the centuries, men have generally been the visible, out-front leaders, with women most often providing the subtle, behind-the-scenes leadership. In the past few decades this scenario has changed dramatically, as more and more women in many fields have stepped up for leadership out front. What about the future?

To explore this question, I will first consider briefly the kinds of leadership that women have always provided and the leadership positions women now hold that were essentially inaccessible in the past. I will then share some of the data, conclusions, and recommendations included in the Princeton University (2011) and Duke University (2003) reports mentioned previously. Finally, I will speculate about the implications of these reports for the future of women's leadership in higher education. What kinds of steps might we take to support, encourage, and inspire young women as they consider leadership roles in the years ahead?

## WOMEN'S LEADERSHIP: PAST AND PRESENT

Throughout human history, leadership has been closely associated with masculinity. Very few women before the 20th century exercised institutional authority over men and women. In most societies throughout history, people have simply assumed that women were incapable of authoritative leadership. Yet despite this stubborn linkage between leadership and maleness, some women in almost every society and era have proven themselves capable of providing leadership.

Certain situations have been especially conducive for women's leadership: all-female settings such as girls' schools, women's colleges or convents, and occasions when dynasty trumps gender, allowing Cleopatra or Elizabeth I of England to be a ruling monarch. Similarly, in situations when men were temporarily absent—for example, in wartime when men were away fighting—women have had ample opportunities to lead. Women have also led social movements around causes for which their interests are especially involved; think of the settlement house campaign, the feminist movement, and the battle for women's suffrage.

More frequently, women have been leaders in informal situations. Women have led families and family businesses. Women across history have provided leadership in volunteer endeavors such as education, religious activities, care for the sick and wounded, cultural affairs, and charity for the poor. Although this is a more low-profile type of leadership than being a king or a prime minister, it is essential to the flourishing of human communities.

In stark contrast to this record of a few queens, abbesses, and heads of school, since 1950 we have seen dozens of women in the most authoritative positions in the world. Women have been elected president or prime minister of countries across the continents. Women have served in legislatures around the world, and as corporate chief executive officers, university presidents, generals, and judges.

Projecting that same trajectory forward, it is easy to assume that the future will be one in which all top leadership posts finally become gender neutral, with women as likely as men to hold them. Sometimes we think this is the obvious path, and the only question is how long it will take. As Rhode (2003) noted: "At current rates of change, it will be almost three centuries before women are as likely as men to become top managers in major corporations or achieve equal representation in the U.S. Congress" (p. 7). However glacial the pace, we may assume that eventually leadership opportunities for women will equal those of men; societies will arrive at that point inevitably, given how things are moving. One might call this path *convergence toward parity*.

The major problem with this scenario is that women who are ambitious for leadership still face formidable obstacles, and there is no guarantee that the obstacles will disappear in the years ahead. The barriers to women in authority today are more subtle than those faced by Queen Elizabeth I of England, but they are surprisingly stubborn. In their book *Through the Labyrinth*, Eagly and Carli (2007) used the ancient female image of the labyrinth to describe the multiple obstacles women face on the path to top leadership. Finding a way through the maze to the central prize of top leadership is a challenging task for men as well as women; however, but women encounter additional cul-de-sacs and dead ends that men generally do not face.

## OBSTACLES TO WOMEN'S LEADERSHIP

The first obstacle to women's leadership that usually comes to mind is the conflicting responsibilities of home and family. Women in almost all societies still have primary (if not sole) responsibility for child care and home-making. This commitment is deeply rewarding for many women. It is dauntingly difficult to combine responsibility for home and children and a high-powered leadership job, unless one enjoys an egalitarian partnership in the home, has enough money to pay for child care and housekeeping, and can locate these essential services. Few organizations (or nation-states) have workplace policies that support family-friendly lifestyles, including high quality, reliable, affordable child care, flexible work schedules, and support for anyone caring for a sick child or aging parent.

Discussions of blockages in the pipeline often focus (for good reason) on these formidable conflicting responsibilities of time and commitment—family commitments versus the demands of work. However, other obstacles are more relevant for understanding the attitudes of undergraduate women.

For students and adults, gender stereotypes keep getting in the way of being judged simply on the basis of one's accomplishments. Women are supposed to be nurturing, but those who are kind and sensitive may be judged not tough enough to make hard decisions. Women who demonstrate that they are up to such challenges may be described as "shrill" or "bitchy." According to Eagly and Carli (2007), the social science evidence that supports this generalization is clear. This "catch-22" clearly plagued Hillary Rodham Clinton in her campaign for the presidency in 2008, as it has countless women across the years.

Women also have fewer opportunities to be mentored. Some senior male professors or corporate leaders try to advance the careers of young women, but male bosses often find it easier to mentor young men. Some senior women leaders are disinclined to mentor younger women, and those who do can become overwhelmed if there are only a few mentors for the many junior women seeking mentoring.

As if all of this were not enough, the most insidious obstacle on the path to top leadership for women may be the influence of popular culture—a formidable force in shaping expectations for young people. Contemporary culture seldom suggests a high-powered career as an appropriate ambition for a person of the female sex. Advertisements, websites, and TV shows regularly portray young women as sexy and provocative. Rarely are women shown making decisions, behind a desk in the corner office, or in a lab coat or military uniform. The ambitions of girls and women are discouraged when they are taught to be deferential to males and not compete with them for resources, including power and recognition. Women internalize these stereotypes, which leads them to question their own abilities. For all these reasons—expectations of primary responsibility for domestic duties, gender stereotypes, absence of mentors, and the powerful influence of popular culture—women ambitious for out-front leadership today face significant obstacles that do not confront their male peers.

Discussing the pipeline in terms of obstacles or blockages, however, assumes that significant numbers of women are ambitious for top leadership. It assumes that young women enter the pipeline eagerly and then exit it only when obstacles to forward movement become too difficult to overcome. In an essay entitled "You've Come a Long Way, Baby—and You've Got Miles to Go," Kellerman (2003) saw no reason to assume that women would continue to move into demanding positions of top leadership at the same rate as they did in the late 20th century. She asks readers to consider the possibility that most women really do not *want* such jobs. As she stated: "Work at the top of the greasy pole takes time, saps energy, and is usually all-consuming," so "maybe the trade-offs high positions entail are ones that many women do not want to make" (Kellerman, 2003, p. 55). Maybe, in other words, there are fewer women senators or chief executive officers because women do not want what men have.

If Kellerman is right, then we could expect that as women see what such positions entail, fewer will decide that high profile leadership is where their ambitions lie, and the numbers of women in such posts will recede from a current high-water mark toward something closer to the world of the mid-20th century. Women have proven that they can succeed in high-powered, visible leadership posts. They have seen the promised land of top leadership; however, most women, in this scenario, will decide that such lives are not for them. They will instead choose more traditionally female occupations and pursuits. Rather than *convergence toward parity,* this alternative option might be referred to as the *differential ambitions* scenario.

I would argue that neither of these scenarios—convergence toward parity nor differential ambitions—fully captures what is likely to be a complex future for women's leadership. To understand the mindset and aspirations of the next generation of women, it is helpful to know something about their attitudes as college undergraduates.

## AMBITIONS OF YOUNG WOMEN FOR LEADERSHIP TODAY: THE PRINCETON STUDY

At the request of President Shirley Tilghman, I chaired a steering committee on undergraduate women's leadership, which was assembled in 2009 to mark the 40th anniversary of undergraduate coeducation at Princeton. The work of the committee provided an unusual opportunity to explore the ambitions of young women *before* they confront the specific obstacles to high-powered achievement that arise because of the tensions between work and family. Our findings thus allow us to consider the ambitions of young women making decisions for themselves as individuals, without (in most cases) having taken on significant responsibility for the care of other people.

The rationale for the formation of the steering committee included the fact that since 2002 Princeton had no female Rhodes Scholars. Furthermore, in September 2009 eight men and no women stood for election as president of the class of 2013. The small number of women in the most visible leadership positions on campus, including president of student government, editor of *The Princetonian* (student newspaper), class presidents, and heads of the most prominent extracurricular organizations, was also of concern.

Our 18-member committee included male and female students, faculty, and staff (some of them graduates of the university). In addition to working through five subcommittees, we met regularly as a full committee, discussing the findings of our research as well as formulating conclusions and recommendations. The final report, issued in March 2011, was made available to all interested readers (see http://www.princeton.edu/leadership/).

Our committee was charged by President Tilghman, in part, with determining "whether women undergraduates are ... seeking opportunities for leadership at the same rate and in the same manner as their male colleagues" (Princeton University, 2011, p. 110). In a nutshell, the answer to this question was "No." Women undergraduates at Princeton today are not seeking leadership opportunities at the same rate, or in the same manner, as young men.

To shed light on undergraduate leadership at Princeton, the Steering Committee held focus groups with students of many different backgrounds, student-life administrators, and alumnae. We conducted informal interviews with many others, including faculty members. We administered a survey to the members of the first-year class, asking these new students about their intentions to seek leadership roles at Princeton. The first part of the survey was distributed before the students arrived at Princeton in September 2010; the second part was distributed in November, after they had become acclimated to Princeton's culture and expectations. The Steering Committee established a website inviting members of the community to respond to a set of questions or share their observations with us. More than 200 students, faculty, staff and alumni/ae responded in three months. Student members made field trips to learn about women's leadership on other campuses. The Princeton Alumni Council organized a set of regional discussions of this issue. We commissioned a literature review by a social science graduate student and shared references with one another. These details are provided so that readers can be assured that the points discussed below are based on systematic data, not just casual impressions shared by committee members.

Members of the committee wrestled regularly with questions about what kind of leadership matters on campus, and why. Our steering committee learned that many undergraduate women are vigorously engaged in extracurricular activities at Princeton. Our key findings related to *what kinds* of activities appealed to them, and leadership in *which posts*. Many recent alumnae and female students told us that they were not interested in very visible leadership positions like student government president or class president; they were more comfortable leading behind the scenes, for example, as vice president or treasurer. Other women did not find traditional organizations such as student government or the campus newspaper appealing places to become involved, preferring to lead in an organization committed to a cause they care about (e.g., the environment, education reform, tutoring underprivileged kids in Trenton, a dance club, or an a cappella group).

The evidence supporting this conclusion is compelling. Over the 10 academic years between 2001–2002 and 2010–2011, 33 of the 40 class presidents were male (83%), as were 86 of 100 presidents of eating clubs (a major Princeton institution). On the other hand, when we examined top officeholders in other student organizations, generally less prominent, 28 of 50 (56%) were female (Princeton University, 2011). During this decade, only one woman had served as undergraduate student government president, and only two as editors-in-chief of the *Princetonian* (Princeton University, 2011). Our survey also indicated statistically significant differences, consistent with these data, in the types of leadership that appealed to male and female undergraduates and in how individuals in each group thought about power.

When we asked young women about this pattern, they told us that they preferred to put their efforts where they could make a difference in a cause they cared about, rather than advancing their own resumes or having a big title; in other words, female students sought "high-impact" rather than "high-profile" jobs. In this, they gave different answers than their male peers. They also behaved differently than the alumnae of 40 years ago at the outset of coeducation at Princeton. There is ample evidence from the history of the university as well as recollections of older alumnae that the women in the 1970s and 1980s were feisty pioneers determined to prove that they belonged at Princeton against considerable skepticism and opposition (Princeton University, 2011, pp. 25–27). Those women ran for and were elected to the highest offices and took visible leadership in traditional campus organizations; they showed very different tendencies than the female students of the last 10–15 years (Princeton University, 2011).

Thus our committee discovered that "There are differences—subtle but real—between the ways most Princeton female undergraduates and most male undergraduates approach their college years, and in the ways they navigate Princeton when they arrive" (Princeton University, 2011, p. 4). Some evidence exists, in other words, for the *differential ambitions* hypothesis, but not simply because of the all-consuming nature of top leadership jobs in traditional organizations. Both men and women regularly told us that "despite being less likely than men to stand as candidates for a presidency or other visible posts, undergraduate women do a large proportion of the important work in the organizations to which they belong" (Princeton University, 2011, p. 5).

An additional finding of this study was that "sometimes women who have expressed interest in more prominent posts have been actively discouraged by other students" (Princeton University, 2011, p. 5), especially male peers who assert that such posts are more appropriately held by men. And through our focus groups and surveys we learned (as have many social scientists researching similar subjects) that "women consistently undersell themselves, and sometimes make self-deprecating remarks in situations where men might stress their own accomplishments" (Princeton University, 2011, p. 5). These findings highlight the significant obstacles to parity in leadership, even when women are interested in demanding jobs.

Given the interest expressed by these female students in leadership "behind the scenes," and in top posts in alternative organizations, the findings of our Princeton study complicate the familiar "pipeline" image. This evidence suggests that we should not think in terms of a single strand of potential leaders flowing in the same direction, toward the corner office in a traditional institution, whether student government or a corporation, a newspaper editorship, government post, or the presidency of a university. Although the ambition for highly visible posts remains pertinent for some young women, others prefer a different outcome, whether a less prominent post with significant responsibilities or a demanding top job in a nontraditional organization, including innovative organizations that they themselves create or found.

As Bowen and Bok (1998) found in studying the "flow of talent" in higher education, there is no rigid pipeline here. Instead, a pattern diverging and sometimes reconverging—a pattern like that of rivers on flat land—does a better job of describing the ambitions of undergraduate women today.

## RESEARCH ON OTHER CAMPUSES

Members of our Princeton Steering Committee were, of course, quite interested in learning whether the patterns we saw were unique to Princeton or were also reflected on other campuses. Our subcommittee on this topic received informal reports from 10 other institutions, including several Ivy League institutions, other strong research universities, and a few selective liberal arts colleges. We discovered that:

> Princeton is not alone in the underrepresentation of women in student government leadership. Our peers report similar gender imbalances in the top elected positions on their respective campuses. Just as we observe here, women are overrepresented in the less visible leadership positions—both offices below the presidential level in traditionally prominent organizations, and leadership (including presidencies) in less prominent organizations. (Princeton University, 2011, p. 90)

On these peer campuses women dominate as leaders in community service, social justice, and (to a lesser extent) the arts. We also heard perceptions of lower levels of self-confidence among women, compared with their male peers.

Although these generalizations about other campuses are not based on systematic research, it is striking to learn that some of the attitudes and behaviors in campus leadership that we have found at Princeton were present elsewhere. It is important to note, however, that we have no comparative data from public research universities, less selective institutions, or community colleges. Anecdotal reports indicate that the patterns are reversed in some public institutions and community colleges, with women holding more traditional leadership posts than men. It would be very useful to pursue this topic to learn whether the phenomenon we have identified is reflected beyond one set of private research universities and liberal arts colleges.

We also know, from campus visits and personal experience, that the patterns we found are not reflected in the experience of women's colleges. At a women's college, women hold all the student leadership posts on campus—in the most traditional as well as "cause-related" organizations, president to committee chairs. There appears to be no dearth of women in these colleges who are eager and ready to hold such jobs.

As president of Duke University, a decade before the Princeton Report was issued, I had charged a similar committee to explore the status of women on campus. I chaired this steering committee for the women's initiative at Duke, with the able colleagueship of Professor Susan Roth, who led an Executive Committee that oversaw our research efforts. Like the Princeton committee, the Duke group worked through subcommittees and conducted numerous focus groups, interviews, and conversations. Our goal was to improve the climate for women at Duke generally and to take steps that would benefit everyone at Duke, men as well as women. The final report, issued in the fall of 2003, can be found online at (http://today.duke.edu/showcase/reports/WomensInitiativeReport.pdf).

Although the committee discussed the situations of women in every part of Duke, the section on undergraduate women students attracted most of the attention. One of our sophomore female respondents used a memorable phrase "effortless perfection" (Duke University, 2003, p. 12) to describe the social environment she experienced as a woman at Duke. This term was adopted by the media and clearly resonated with students on other campuses. The point of the phrase was that undergraduate women were expected to be smart (without threatening their male peers), beautiful (without ever seeming to take any trouble about it), academically accomplished (without appearing to work too hard), charming, and serenely self-confident. In reality, behind this public face many Duke undergraduate women expressed a lack of self-confidence about their ability to live up to the standard they believed was being set by other students. Duke women also told the committee that they wanted more opportunities "for close relationships with peers or adults in an environment that would encourage them to resist conformity, and help create experiences affirming women's autonomy and self-determination" (Duke University, 2003, p. 14).

The Duke Women's Initiative was not specifically focused on leadership. However, committee discussions of student campus leadership "revealed somewhat separate tracks for men and women, with women more likely found in community service, arts, and sororities, and men more likely found in student government and fraternities" (Duke University, 2003, p. 13). Thus, the basic pattern we saw at Duke was similar to the findings of the Princeton research a decade later.

## RECOMMENDATIONS AND IMPLEMENTATION

What lessons can be drawn from these reports for the future of women's leadership in higher education? Given that the dilemmas of childcare and family responsibilities are not at issue for most undergraduates, what do the findings of these two campus studies tell us about young women's ambitions for leadership today? What might be done to help them accomplish their goals and to ensure that young women provide significant leadership in higher education in the future?

If we focus first on the disinclination of these young women to seek visible and demanding leadership posts in traditional organizations, gender stereotypes and the impact of popular culture would appear to be the most pertinent obstacles. As noted, these factors can lead to a decline in self-confidence and an inability to envision oneself in a demanding post. One way to tackle these problems is through supportive and thoughtful mentoring. And indeed, in our research at Princeton, this was one of the most prominent recurring themes. Many alumnae told us that they wished they had had "good advice, close connections with peers and others who understand life at Princeton, and relationships with people at different stages of life whom one knows and can trust" (Princeton University, 2011, p. 98). We heard the same sentiments from women students. Although both students and alumnae welcomed supportive mentoring by men, they also noted "the importance of female faculty and staff as role models for female achievement" (p. 89) and expressed a desire for more meaningful connections with older women students (Princeton University, 2011).

Therefore, one of the committee's central recommendations was mentoring for academic achievement, success in social and extracurricular life, professional accomplishment, and leadership on campus. When we discussed mentoring for leadership on campus, the committee's recommendations noted that this involved "finding a voice, feeling comfortable with exercising authority, understanding how to set or influence an agenda, and learning how to run a meeting, pick one's battles, handle discouraging or offensive remarks, network, strategize, and build coalitions" (Princeton University, 2011, p. 99). Such suggestions clearly resonated with women students at Princeton. Two creative and innovative programs for women mentoring women were developed within months of the publication of the report: one initiated by the staff in one of the residential colleges, and one launched by student leaders themselves with support from the Women's Center.

Our committee also recommended a more coherent program of leadership training at Princeton, for both women and men. Although a number of such programs existed on campus, they needed to be more widely known through sharing best practices and expanding opportunities. Again, students eagerly picked up this idea and a leadership training program was instituted within the first year after the report was issued, with support from the Offices of Student Affairs and Campus Life. As opportunities for mentoring and training become more common, we believe that more women will emboldened to put themselves forward for offices they might not previously have considered.

At Duke, the major recommendation in our section on undergraduates was for a "sustained women's leadership program" (Duke University, 2003, p. 15). Mindful of the impressive history of the Duke Woman's College during the first three quarters of the 20th century, we hoped that "undergraduate women who participate will receive some of the benefits of a single-sex educational experience embedded within their otherwise coeducational campus life" (Duke University, 2003, p. 15). And, indeed, this is precisely what has happened. The Baldwin Scholars Program has given dozens of students each year an opportunity to experience connections with other women on campus, both students and faculty, as well as to participate in academic seminars, residential programs, internships, and training (Duke University, n.d). Outside evaluations of the Baldwin Scholars Program after its first five years attested strongly to its effectiveness in increasing the self-confidence, academic achievement, leadership opportunities, and general satisfaction with the Duke experience for the women who were involved.

Programs based on the Baldwin Scholars model are being formed on other campuses as well. One excellent example is the Sophie Newcomb Program at Tulane University (n.d.) which, like the Duke program, is deliberately inspired by the history of the women's college within the university. Such programs exemplify the value of offering single-sex experiences within the larger coeducational university, providing participants the best of both worlds.

The other key finding of the Princeton research was that many female undergraduates are ambitious for very demanding top posts in organizations devoted to causes they care about. In addition to mentoring and leadership training, our report also recommended that we recognize the importance of leadership in various types of causes, activities, and sectors of human life, and not assign value only to leadership in traditional organizations. We should do this not in a second-hand or apologetic fashion, but understanding that many women care about a range of causes and human concerns, and they want to give their time and energy to tackling them as directly as they can. Many men care about these things as well; however, it appears that women today are more likely than their male peers, as undergraduates, to put their efforts into work of this kind. Perhaps this is because of the idealistic desire to "make a difference," to establish their identity or character in a culture where women are sometimes regarded as less serious or less substantive than men, and/or to test out the potential value of a career in the field of their choice after they graduate.

The commitment to a cause that marked the choices of many of these young women is an admirable factor in itself, and surely our world would be much impoverished if this motivation were to disappear. There can also be distinctive rewards in working behind the scenes to make sure the purposes of an organization are fulfilled. Successful organizations depend on good, dedicated leaders in second- and third-rank posts, not just at the very top. Commanding vast resources, wielding significant power, proving that something rarely undertaken by members of one's class or gender or ethnic group can be done—all these can be admirable (or occasionally, questionable) motives for leadership. Yet, they are not the only motives or ambitions that we should acknowledge. We should build our plans and expectations for the future on a more capacious conception of leadership than this.

Those of us on the Princeton Steering Committee who had assumed that the more prominent roles were the only crucial indicators of women's success in leadership—and the best preparation for demanding leadership roles in life after Princeton—learned through our research how important it is to value all kinds of leadership. But members of the committee were also in agreement, by the end of the process, that high-profile leadership positions in traditional organizations provide unique opportunities for gaining significant skills and accomplishing broad priorities. There are still good reasons to focus on such positions in thinking about women's leadership, given the crucial significance of such posts in so many sectors of human activity, including higher education. Such positions ought not to be held so predominantly by men, on campus or in the larger world.

## CONCLUSION

We cannot yet know, of course, how the young women at Princeton and Duke will fare as leaders in the world after graduation. We cannot simply assume that their recorded attitudes toward leadership will remain the same in the "real world," when they are confronted with the demands and rewards of a professional career, public leadership, or volunteer activities. However, it seems plausible that their basic understanding of leadership as a multifaceted form of human behavior expressed in varied contexts and in the service of diverse goals will not be greatly altered. It is this conception that we should keep in mind as we ponder the probable future of leadership in higher education.

In the final section of our Princeton report, we envisioned a world in which both male and female undergraduates, and men and women more generally, would take on both kinds of leadership posts, out front and behind the scenes, high profile and supportive, both in politics and business, and also in the arts and diverse nonprofit activities—including higher education. Leadership of both kinds is important in getting the world's work done, and these types should not so frequently be divided along gender lines. Women should have opportunities for top-level leadership in higher education as in every other field and be encouraged to see such posts as relevant and important for their lives. The remaining obstacles to such leadership should be systematically tackled by those of us who know how important it is for these women to succeed. Men should also take their share of the crucial work of leadership behind the scenes.

Dealing with the requirements of one kind of leadership can often help a leader be more effective in the other.

Fortunately, there will be pioneering leaders of both sexes in the years ahead, providing role models in many different kinds of leadership. There will also be visionaries, including scholars developing new political and social theories, as well as those who contribute through rhetoric, fiction, poetry, and art. These will be the guides as our daughters and granddaughters, their husbands and partners, our students and their students in the years ahead, fill out the scenario of women's leadership.

In her great feminist classic *The Second Sex*, Simone de Beauvoir (2011) reminds us that it is very hard to anticipate clearly things we have not yet seen. As Beauvoir stated: "Let us beware lest our lack of imagination impoverish the future" (p. 765). She noted:

> The free woman is just being born.... Her "worlds of ideas" are not necessarily different from men's, because she will free herself by assimilating them; to know how singular she will remain and how important these singularities will be, one would have to make some foolhardy predictions. What is beyond doubt is that until now women's possibilities have been stifled and lost to humanity, and in her and everyone's interest it is high time she be left to take her own chances. (p. 751)

When we try to anticipate the future trajectory of some trend or movement, including women's leadership in higher education, it is wise to keep Beauvoir's counsel in mind. Visionary strategic thinking and clear definitions of what counts as success are essential to the accomplishment of any major goal. Yet we should also avoid impoverishing the future by prematurely closing off diverse options for development.

Because countless women and men in the intervening decades have worked hard to make the path easier for women, our possibilities as leaders are no longer "lost to humanity" (Beauvoir, 2011, p. 751). But these gifts are still stifled, to some extent, and we are operating with models of leadership designed primarily by and for men, models passed down for millennia. It is surely high time that we as women be left to take our own chances as leaders in every field, including higher education—with support from our partners, families, colleagues, peers, and from society as a whole.

## REFERENCES

Bowen, W. G., & Bok, D. (1998). *The shape of the river: Long-term consequences of considering race in college and university admissions*. Princeton, NJ: Princeton University Press.

de Beauvoir, S. (2011). *The second sex* (C. Borde & S. Malovany-Chevallier, Trans.). New York, NY: Vintage, Random House.

Duke University. (n.d.). Baldwin Scholars Program. Retrieved from the Duke University website: http://baldwinscholars.duke.edu/

Duke University, Steering Committee for the Women's Initiative. (2003). *Report of the steering committee for the women's initiative at Duke University.* Retrieved from http://today.duke.edu/showcase/reports/WomensInitiativeReport.pdf

Eagly, A. H., & Carli, L. L. (2007). *Through the labyrinth: The truth about how women become leaders.* Boston, MA: Harvard Business School.

Kellerman, B. (2003). You've come a long way, baby—And you've got miles to go. In D. Rhode (Ed.), *The difference "difference" makes: Women and leadership* (pp. 53–58). Palo Alto, CA: Stanford University Press.

Keohane, N. O. (2010). *Thinking about leadership.* Princeton, NJ: Princeton University Press.

Princeton University, Steering Committee on Undergraduate Women's Leadership. (2011). *Report of the steering committee on undergraduate women's leadership.* Retrieved from http://www.princeton.edu/reports/2011/leadership/documents/SCUWL_Report_Final.pdf

Rhode, D. (Ed.). (2003). The difference "difference" makes. In *The difference "difference" makes: Women and leadership* (pp. 3–50). Palo Alto, CA: Stanford University Press.

Tulane University. (n.d.). Sophie Newcomb Scholars Program. Retrieved from the Tulane University website: https://tulane.edu/newcomb/scholars/

# PART II

## STRATEGIES FOR WOMEN'S LEADERSHIP DEVELOPMENT

# CHAPTER 4

# AMERICAN COUNCIL ON EDUCATION'S *IDEALS* FOR WOMEN LEADERS

## Identify, Develop, Encourage, Advance, Link, and Support

**Leah Witcher Jackson Teague and Kim Bobby**

The individuals who lead institutions of higher education in the 21st century hold one of the most important roles in shaping the future of societies. Within the context of the United States, research indicates that a strong system of higher education is a significant contributor to the country's ability to compete in the global marketplace (Center on Internationalization and Global Engagement, 2011). Colleges and universities must generate new knowledge, create new discoveries, and educate a workforce capable of supporting innovation and economic development. Yet institutional leaders face unprecedented challenges in achieving their missions even as the nation looks to its colleges and universities to provide an educated citizenry for the future.

Juxtaposed with these realities is the growing recognition that innovation and productivity are fostered by a diverse and inclusive leadership and workforce (Forbes Insights, 2011); however, at the highest levels of leadership across higher education, diversity is sorely lacking. The overall

*Women and Leadership in Higher Education*, pp. 59–76
Copyright © 2014 by Information Age Publishing
All rights of reproduction in any form reserved.

percentage of women leading colleges and universities remains disproportionately low despite the fact that the majority of students served by
those colleges and universities are women. Women are most likely to head
associate colleges (33%), followed by baccalaureate colleges (23%), master's colleges and universities (23%), and lastly, doctorate-granting (22%)
institutions (American Council on Education, 2012a). Women presidents
have not yet reached parity nor have women achieved the one-third representation in leadership roles that is necessary, according to researchers
(Tarr-Whelan, 2009; The White House Project, 2009), to bring about substantive change for them and the organizations they serve.

The American Council on Education (ACE) has worked for the past 40
years on the national level to influence women's equity, diversity, and
advancement in higher education. Based in close proximity to the
nation's leaders in Washington, DC, ACE works through its Inclusive
Excellence Group (IEG) to focus on programs, resources, and research
designed to foster greater diversity and inclusion in higher education
leadership. Programs for women leaders supported by the Inclusive
Excellence Group adhere to a set of principles represented by the acro-
nym IDEALS: Identify, Develop, Encourage, Assist, Link, and Support.

Each year the IEG hosts multi-day regional and national leadership
development forums for mid- and senior-level female administrators
interested in advancing within the ranks of higher education leadership
(Baltodano, Carlson, Witcher Jackson, & Mitchell, 2012). Additionally,
IEG's efforts to provide broad-based leadership development training are
greatly leveraged through the extensive use of volunteer state networks of
women leaders throughout the country (Baltodano et al., 2012). Each
state network is led by a governing board of women administrators in that
state and is guided by IEG and a group of women presidents of colleges
and universities as well as other experienced women leaders known as the
Women's Network Executive Council (WNEC). Collectively, these state
networks provide leadership development programming for more than
8,000 women each year.

Among the initiatives supported by ACE, the WNEC is also leading an
effort titled the "Moving the Needle" initiative that seeks to raise national
awareness of the importance of gender parity and to suggest practices
and models designed to help achieve gender parity in senior leadership
positions. As part of the Moving the Needle initiative, Inclusive Excellence Group and WNEC recently conducted a survey to gather information about leadership development programs available to women who
aspire to advance into senior-level administrative roles. This chapter first
presents an overview of ACE's historic commitment to advancing women
in higher education administration and then discusses the organization's

leadership development programs as well as other related initiatives, including the recent survey project and Moving the Needle initiative.

## ACE'S HISTORIC COMMITMENT TO
## THE ADVANCEMENT OF WOMEN LEADERS

Across the decades since the founding of ACE in 1918, the organization has guided the development of numerous reports, committees, and commissions to address the needs and concerns of women within the field of higher education. ACE's involvement in the advancement of women in higher education began in earnest in 1951, when, under the direction of ACE president Arthur Adams, ACE sponsored its first national conference devoted entirely to the topic of women (Elliott, 2014). Adams also established the Commission on Women. Dissertation research by Elliott (2014) on ACE's Office of Women in Higher Education notes: "Adams always claimed the work was not to provide women with *special privileges*, but to more adequately contribute to society" (p. 190). Adams' public support for the role of women in society "engrained in ACE's culture a pattern of advocacy for women's agendas, research, and advancement" (p. 190).

The decades of the 1960s and 1970s brought new challenges and opportunities to women in higher education as the political and cultural climate of the United States changed radically. Even though the Commission on Women was terminated for budgetary reasons in 1962 shortly after Adams' retirement, some of its work continued through the financial support of the Carnegie Corporation and others (Elliott, 2014). In September 1970, ACE issued its Special Report, *Discrimination against Women in Colleges*; this document, along with the enactment of Title VII and Title IX, laid the foundation for ACE's modern efforts to advance women in higher education administration (Elliott, 2014).

Led by president Roger W. Heyns, who was conscious of changing political tides and new constituencies, ACE in 1972 devoted its 55th annual meeting to the theme, "Women in Higher Education," and more formally began its work to support the advancement of women. At the urging of two women on the ACE board of directors, the board adopted two initiatives: (1) reestablish the lapsed Commission on Women in Higher Education (Burns Phillips, 2008), and (2) "open an office at ACE exclusively attending to women's needs in higher education" (Elliott, 2014, p. 212). During the early years of the Office of Women in Higher Education (OWHE), under the direction of its first four leaders (Nancy Schlossberg, Donna Shavlik, Emily Taylor, and Judith Touchstone), the office formulated what would become its primary mission at that time: to identify and encourage women who were ready for administrative leadership (Elliott, 2014).

One of the most significant contributions of ACE through the OWHE was the creation of the ACE Women's Network for the advancement of women in higher education. In 1976–1977 the Carnegie Corporation of New York provided supportive funding to launch the National Identification Program (NIP), the predecessor to the ACE Women's Network. The initial Carnegie grant funded the development of state planning committees with representation reflecting the state's higher education structure; each planning committee was led by a woman holding a senior-level administrative position at a college or university in that state. Working with a panel of advisors that involved both men and women leaders within the state, the planning committee and state coordinator were expected to create effective strategies to identify and advance women into senior leadership positions within the state's colleges and universities. In 1977, three states (California, New York, and Florida) took the lead in creating state networks. Within a year, those states were joined by Wisconsin, Texas, Massachusetts, Illinois, Michigan, Minnesota, Pennsylvania, Ohio, and Indiana; New Jersey followed shortly thereafter. Five years later, the ACE Women's Network became a state-based, national program (ACE, 2013b). This system of volunteer state networks, currently known as ACE's Women's Network but operating autonomously of ACE, remains central to the culture of ACE's commitment to the advancement of women.

Also during the 1970s, the OWHE began hosting forums, with its first symposium in 1974 titled "Women Considering Careers in Higher Education." Additionally, the OWHE recognized the need to conduct research and produce data to disseminate nationally regarding women's advancement. Over time, providing relevant and current research became a hallmark of the OWHE, resulting in the publication of many seminal works on women in the presidency as well as other reports reaffirming the inclusion of women and girls in all human rights endeavors (Elliott, 2014).

During the 1990s and 2000s, under the leadership of its next three directors (Judith Sturnick, Claire Van Ummerson, and Donna Burns Phillips), the OWHE focused its vision while simultaneously expanding its reach. The office reenergized the state networks, added regional forums, cosponsored summits for women of color, and launched an Alfred P. Sloan-funded project titled "Creating Options: Models for Flexible Faculty Career Pathways," which promoted a national dialog on behalf of women faculty regarding flexible career policies and programs for tenured and tenure-track faculty (Elliott, 2014).

In 2011, ACE reorganized its divisions and merged its work for the advancement of women and underrepresented diverse leaders. As a result, the OWHE and the Center for Advancement of Racial and Ethnic Equity merged into one group, the Inclusive Excellence Group (IEG), and the work to support and advance women leaders continued. Currently, IEG retains its commitment to the advancement of women in higher education administration by primarily focusing on three programmatic areas: (1) the national system of state networks, known as the Women's Network; (2) regional and national women's leadership development conferences; and (3) the Moving the Needle initiative. Each of these areas is described in the sections that follow.

## ACE WOMEN'S NETWORK

The system of volunteer state networks that began in 1977 with funding from the Carnegie Corporation of New York remains central to the culture of ACE's commitment to the advancement of women. The program, now known as the ACE Women's Network, operates autonomously of ACE and continues to help train and promote women to administrative positions, working purposefully to support the advancement of women from underrepresented profiles.

The activities of the various state networks are aligned across the country through their affiliation with ACE's Inclusive Excellence Group and Women's Network Executive Council (WNEC), and together the state networks and WNEC constitute the ACE Women's Network. WNEC, composed of women executives who serve as both mentors to the state coordinators and advisors to the IEG staff, articulated the following vision for the ACE Women's Network: "[To] be recognized as the premier vehicle for connecting women at all levels of higher education, providing support to further professional development and advancement, and transforming higher education locally, nationally, and globally" (ACE, 2013b, p. 8). WNEC established core principles and developed formal expectations for the state networks. Over the past 37 years, each state network developed organizational structures that best fit the specific needs of its particular state. Nonetheless, the state network structure of a planning board, a state coordinator, institutional representatives from higher education institutions in the particular state, and the support of college presidents remains the hallmark of the ACE Women's Network.

Each state network, within the ACE Women's Network, operates autonomously but draws from the resources of ACE's IEG to facilitate the networking and leadership development of women interested in pursuing leadership opportunities in higher education. As part of the Women's Network, each state network adopts the IDEALS core principles in supporting women leaders in higher education:

- **I**dentify women leaders
- **D**evelop their leadership abilities
- **E**ncourage the use of those abilities
- **A**dvance women's careers
- **L**ink them to other women and mentors
- **S**upport women in mid- and executive-level positions throughout their careers

The state networks, now active in 42 of the 50 states, conduct a wide variety of programs and initiatives in response to the needs of women in their states. Collectively, the programming of the state networks reaches approximately 8,000 women per year. Most state networks conduct state-wide or regional conferences annually, providing professional development and networking opportunities for women at all levels in higher education administration. Many states present awards to women leaders, enhancing public awareness of their contributions. Several states have sponsored student leadership conferences for women, and others include women students in meetings and awards programs. Some of the state networks have sought to advance women's leadership by hosting receptions for women legislators, women college presidents, and women board members. Similarly, some state networks have targeted specific audiences (e.g., deans, department chairs, and vice-presidents) with workshops and seminars. Many states have partnerships with other women's organizations, collaborating to meet shared goals.

## ACE'S WOMEN'S LEADERSHIP DEVELOPMENT FORUMS

The National Women's Leadership Forums, first offered in 1977, continue to be a signature program for supporting women's advancement across higher education. These three-day leadership programs target women administrators (typically deans and higher-level positions) who are aspiring to a presidency, vice presidency, or major deanship. The interactive programs, held in June and December, foster discussions with women presidents and executive search firm consultants who help participants develop effective career strategies. Over the years, between one-fourth and one-third of National Forum alumnae have reported advancing into senior-level positions (Elliot, 2014). While the Forums provide participants the information, resources, and confidence to return to their positions and think about professional advancement, they also serve as an effective opportunity for networking and problem solving among the participants.

IEG also offers two Regional Women's Leadership Forums aimed at emerging leaders. Midlevel administrators enter these three-day forums prepared to hone leadership skills such as fundraising, strategic planning, career mapping, and media relations. Until 2011, attendance at each forum was capped at 25 to 35 participants to allow for significant interaction and individual attention. Participants also meet with search firms to prepare for a potential interview process. In 2012, ACE had its highest number of participants with a total of 86 women attending three regional forums and a combined 86 attendees at the two national forums.

Accepting its first applicants in 2012, ACE's newest leadership development program, the Spectrum Executive Leadership Program, is geared toward women and administrators of color who are interested in pursuing presidential positions in the near term. The program guides participants in developing a successful search strategy and managing the transition into the presidency. This highly interactive program combines face-to-face and virtual meetings over several months, in addition to facilitating candid conversations with search firm executives and sitting presidents from diverse institutions and backgrounds. The program served three cohorts, and with additional sponsorship the program could be offered again in the future. The IEG recognizes that preparing women for leadership addresses only part of the needed action steps. More women must actually secure top academic leadership positions.

## MOVING THE NEEDLE INITIATIVE

Soon after the release of The White House Project Report in 2009, the Office of Women in Higher Education (now IEG) and its advisory council, WNEC, reached out to other like-minded higher education, non-profit, government, and corporate organizations with similar goals for realizing the advancement of women to the highest ranks. Madlyn Hanes, vice president for Commonwealth Campuses for Pennsylvania State University and one of the founders of the Moving the Needle initiative, recounted the motivation behind the initial invitation: "The case supporting the benefits, including a much-improved ROI, to organizations where women hold the highest leadership posts is compelling. Nevertheless, the juxtaposition in perception and actuality is startling" (M. Hanes, personal communication, January 30, 2014). More effort was needed, Hanes continued, "to enlighten and empower higher educators and higher education decision- and policymakers to effect gender parity in the senior-most ranks of higher education institutions and leadership of their governing boards."

The philosophy behind the "Moving the Needle" collaboration is the belief that networking key organizations and individuals can more effectively leverage their mutual interests and resources. The ambitious goal of this initiative is to raise national awareness about the importance of parity in higher education leadership and to create a sense of urgency and suggest practices and models for achieving gender parity through deliberate action by higher education decision and policymakers. Through a series of invitational roundtables discussed below, ACE has fostered discussion among key stakeholders and made recommendations on a national scale. As Hanes recognized, "The good that comes from the collaborative temperament of women leaders is a powerful and prevailing value proposition" (M. Hanes, personal communication, January 30, 2014). The roundtable discussions began a commitment to effect change that continues to be palpable.

## Moving the Needle Roundtable #1

The Moving the Needle initiative began in the spring of 2010 at the invitation of ACE president Molly Corbett Broad. Twenty-six university presidents and other executives from leading higher education associations and related organizations gathered in Washington, DC, on Tuesday, May 18, 2010 for a roundtable discussion to explore the reasons for the stalled progress of advancing women into higher education leadership roles. The gathering was titled: *Moving the Needle: Developing a 21st Century Agenda for Women's Leadership.*

Molly Corbett Broad opened the meeting by explaining that while women represented the majority of college graduates and were well represented in entry and midlevel administrative positions, they lacked proportionate representation in higher level positions (ACE, 2010). At the time, only 23% of the chief executive officers, 38% of the chief academic officers, and 36% of the academic deans in higher education were women. The rate of women advancing through the traditional "pipeline" from faculty to midlevel administrative positions to executive leadership positions had leveled off, resulting in significant underrepresentation in comparison to men assuming senior-leadership roles. The goals for the 2010 roundtable were: (1) to discuss major obstacles to women's advancement to top leadership positions; and (2) to identify purposeful strategies for increasing opportunities for women and inspiring them to seek presidential positions (ACE, 2010).

The coauthors of The White House Project Report, Lucie Lapovsky and Marie Wilson, opened the 2010 Roundtable program by presenting the highlights of their recently released research findings that benchmarked women's leadership in 10 sectors across the United States. As presented in the opening chapter of this volume, at that time only 18% of top leadership positions across the 10 sectors were held by women; within academe, 23% of the presidents were women. Lapovsky and Wilson affirmed the work of ACE and the participants for being the first group to strategically address concerns raised in the report (ACE, 2010).

The common themes that emerged during general and group discussions throughout the day mirrored findings in The White House Report (2009). The participants noted in particular the finding that the majority of Americans believed that parity already existed between men and women in this country, perhaps contributing to a sense of complacency that was inhibiting needed progress within higher education systems. In reality, the research findings documented, women significantly lagged behind men on numerous key indicators. Participants concurred that concerted efforts were needed to heighten a sense of urgency to identify and develop women leaders and to advance them into top leadership positions. Deloitte and General Electric, corporations that placed a high priority on the leadership development of women, were cited as possible models from the business sector. Specifically mentioned was General Electric's successful program that selected and mentored 200 women toward senior-level positions (ACE, 2010). Given that colleges and universities train and influence both future leaders and the workforce, participants advocated that higher education institutions should have a stronger commitment to diversity and promoting women's leadership than the business community.

When those assembled discussed the barriers to women in higher education, participants noted that men comprise the overwhelming majority of members of the governing boards of higher education (Catalyst, 2007). Because governing boards select or approve the highest level executive positions, the recruiting, selection, and hiring processes of executive administrators are controlled by men. Participants voiced concern that governing boards often have preconceived notions about women candidates, including their potential failings or weaknesses. For example, hiring authorities sometimes view women as being ill-prepared to deal with athletics, budget, fund-raising, spousal roles, and endowments. However, ACE's 2007 survey on the characteristics and career path of college presidents (King & Gomez, 2008) indicated that most of these areas mentioned as concerns for women candidates were precisely the areas for which all new presidents (the vast majority of whom were men) felt insufficiently prepared. Participants also expressed concern that without appropriate attention to such biases, conscious or otherwise, women would continue to be disadvantaged in the hiring proNScess for leadership positions. The Association of Governing Boards was identified as an important partner in helping to address this barrier, as were search firms.

The group also spent substantial time discussing a second highlighted barrier to women—that women themselves may not aspire to top leadership roles. Participants viewed the rising generation of women as less inclined to seek promotion or advancement, a conclusion confirmed in an ACE 2009 survey that found fewer women than men holding roles as chief academic officers aspiring to the presidency (Eckel, Cook, & King, 2009). Although the group did not suggest that younger women were void of ambition, concern was expressed about their lack of career aspiration. Consistent with the findings of the Princeton study (Princeton University, Steering Committee on Undergraduate Women's Leadership, 2011) discussed in Chapter 3 of this volume, female leaders were viewed as more committed to living fulfilled, worthwhile lives with satisfying careers than aspiring to presidential roles. One participant in the 2009 ACE survey commented: "I have noticed how young women look up to the women in these positions and say, 'I don't see joy'" (ACE, 2010, p. 5). Roundtable participants agreed that efforts were needed to encourage women to aspire to top leadership positions. The group applauded ACE's production of a video depicting the extent to which currently sitting women presidents viewed their roles as very fulfilling.

Other ACE activities were discussed and affirmed as beneficial. Specifically acknowledged as important development programs for women were the system of state networks and the national and regional leadership development forums supported by ACE's OWHE (Baltodano et al., 2012). Also discussed was the joint ACE/Sloan project focusing on work-life balance of faculty. The goal of this project was to improve the lives of faculty by recommending practices within institutions that support work-life balance. Improved flexibility in workplace structures was identified as being important to encourage more women to seek advancement. Research from the business sector (Deloitte, 2011) has documented that improved flexibility has additional benefits such as reducing work/life conflict for men and women, enhancing productivity for managers as well as parents, and improving well-being and reducing absenteeism.

Although participants did not organize a collaborative or ongoing effort at the first roundtable, they created a list of recommendations for consideration and action by ACE. These recommendations were similar to the recommendations reiterated at the second and third roundtables as discussed below. All of the recommendations became part of the call to action that is summarized in the conclusion of this chapter.

## Moving the Needle Roundtable #2

The Moving the Needle initiative took a hiatus in 2011 while the ACE staff members focused their attention and energy on restructuring ACE's divisions and transferring the functions of the OWHE to the newly created IEG. The second Moving the Needle Roundtable convened on June 28, 2012, drawing together 37 women and men from leading associations and organizations with active women's leadership agendas. Much of the day was spent revisiting the challenges and roadblocks that had been discussed in 2010, with proposed solutions offered as summarized in Table 4.1 (ACE, 2012b).

During the months following the 2012 roundtable, the IEG took action on two of the specific recommendations. First, assisted by WNEC, the IEG conducted an environmental scan of women's leadership programs in spring 2013. The purpose of this scan was to (1) ascertain the breadth and scope of leadership programs available to women faculty and administra-

**Table 4.1.   Moving the Needle Roundtable #2 Discussion Points**

| *Challenges or Roadblocks for Women* | *Suggestions From Roundtables* |
|---|---|
| • Underrepresentation of women on governing boards and search committees responsible for recruiting and hiring senior administrators | • Partner with the Association of Governing Boards and search firms to raise awareness of the full parameters of the issues.<br>• Encourage further research and publication of the benefits of increased diversity on boards and in leadership teams. |
| • The influence of biases (often unconscious) that affect recruiting and hiring decisions | • Raise awareness of possible biases adversely affecting female candidates.<br>• Encourage broader thinking in terms of candidates' experiences and skills as well as transferability of past experiences and responsibilities into the new position. |
| • Women's lack of confidence or hesitancy to self-promote<br>• Women's loyalty to current institution | • Encourage mentoring, coaching, and sponsoring.<br>• Establish more leadership development programming. |
| • Women's lack of relevant experience in key leadership areas (e.g., finance and budgeting, fundraising, athletics) | • Encourage women to recognize the transferability of their past experiences and responsibilities into the desired position.<br>• Advise women on how to gain needed or helpful experience (e.g., through volunteer and other opportunities). |
| • Unwillingness or inability to move to another location, often related to spouse or other family situations | • Promote models of family-friendly and flexible-work policies. |

tors in higher education, and (2) identify other key stakeholders and program representatives who should be invited to participate in a national effort to realize the advancement of women. The environmental scan was conducted in two phases. First, in March 2013, a survey was sent to individuals representing 66 organizations and/or institutions believed to have leadership development programs specifically designed for women in higher education. The survey closed in June 2013, with only a 17% response rate. To ensure that sufficient information was collected, phase two of data collection began. The IEG staff mined the internet, gathering information about programs from organizations that had not responded to the survey, plus other identified organizations. Of the 77 organizations reviewed, 31 had leadership programs for women in higher education, collectively serving at least 850 participants annually. The intended participants in these programs served women ranging from faculty ranks through those holding senior-level administrative roles.

The second activity organized by the IEG in response to the recommendations that emerged from the 2012 roundtable was to plan the first-ever ACE's annual meeting session dedicated to women's advancement in higher education. The 2013 session was a collaboration between ACE's WNEC and Higher Education Resource Services (HERS). Approximately 120 attendees participated in a session titled *The Pathway from Our Perspective: Can We Move the Needle Beyond 26%?* During the interactive presentation, a panel of university presidents and senior administrators provided information from the 2012 ACE survey on the American College President related to gender inequities; attendees then discussed strategies for advancing women into senior leadership roles. Panel participants Josefina Baltodano (founding executive director of the Executive Leadership Academy in the Center for Studies in Higher Education at University of California, Berkley) and Judith White (Executive Director of HERS) later described the collaborative session as a historic event that served as a platform for developing stronger voices and meaningful dialog (J. Baltodano & J. White, personal communication, February 11, 2014).

## Moving the Needle Roundtable #3

After the success of the WNEC/HERS joint session at the annual ACE meeting in March 2013, IEG and WNEC organized a third roundtable. The goal for the 2013 roundtable was to move beyond talking about the issues to developing practices and models and setting concrete aspirational goals for increasing the number of women in senior leadership positions in higher education. The invitation list for the third roundtable included all the representatives of higher education-related institutions

who had attended either of the first two roundtable in addition to representatives from other organizations identified through the survey
described above.

The 46 attendees began the June 18, 2013 roundtable by reviewing the
2012 ACE survey on the American College President, which identified little change since the previous report had been released 5 years earlier. In
2011, 26% of college and university presidencies were held by women, an
increase from 23% in 2006 and 13% in 1986. However, at doctoral-granting institutions, only 22% of the presidents were women (ACE, 2012a).
After reviewing the 2012 survey results, the group received reports on the
two action items that arose from the 2012 roundtable (the environmental
scan of leadership programs and the joint session at ACE's 2013 annual
meeting). Since the accumulation of information for the environmental
scan was still ongoing at the time of the 2013 roundtable, participants
encouraged continued work by the IEG and the creation of a database
from the gathered information. Based upon the success of the joint session at the 2013 ACE annual meeting, participants strongly recommended future sessions dedicated to the advancement of women at each
ACE annual meeting.

The 2013 roundtable participants affirmed that the issues and barriers
discussed in the previous roundtables needed continued attention, and
subsequent discussion focused primarily on devising a plan of action and
identifying the resources required to sustain the effort. A strong consensus
emerged that the time had come to move beyond talking about the need
for a national effort to raise awareness to taking decisive steps to arouse a
national sense of urgency regarding the importance of greater diversity in
executive positions. Participants urged IEG and WNEC to take the lead in
developing a plan with a call to action and concrete aspirational goals for
increasing the number of women in senior leadership positions in higher
education. The assembled group agreed to participate in an innovative collaboration involving a broad spectrum of organizations and leaders. Recognizing that both resources and staff would be required to advance this
initiative, one suggestion involved identifying a retired president who
could provide leadership to orchestrate a successful campaign. The group
also recommended the creation of a recognition program to highlight successes or to solicit positive endorsements from institutions with demonstrated commitment to, and success in, advancing women (ACE, 2013a).

## Moving the Needle Call to Action

Based on the discussions and recommendations from all three roundtables, WNEC set about to develop a plan for increasing the number of

women in senior leadership positions in higher education. WNEC (2014) proclaimed a bold vision of increasing the percentage of women in the senior-most leadership positions at higher education institutions to at least 50% by the year 2030. The announced mission was to create parity for women holding, or aspiring to hold, leadership positions in the academy through collaborative partnerships. Recognizing the ambition of the vision, the Moving the Needle value statement acknowledged the necessity of collaboration:

> Today, 26% of college and university presidencies are held by women. Progress has been at best incremental and taken a decade to move the needle three percentage points. The vision of parity necessitates creating a national imperative for advancing women's leadership and a carefully crafted national agenda to guide its implementation. In short, there must be a renewed effort to achieve in two decades what amounts to doubling the progress realized over many decades. No single organization can accomplish this alone; collaboration among like-minded organizations can and will make the difference. (WNEC, 2014)

Accompanying the aforementioned statements of vision, mission, and value, the following four goals were approved by WNEC (2014) for presentation to the planned June 2014 meeting of strategic partners:

1. ***Generate a national sense of urgency elevating the need for advancing women in higher education.*** Research has well established that organizations truly embracing diversity and inclusion are not only more profitable but also more productive and innovative (Catalyst, 2007, 2011; Colorado Women's College, 2013; Deloitte, 2011; Desvaux, Devillard, & Sancier-Sultan, 2011; Forbes Insights, 2011; Herring, 2009). A diverse set of experiences, perspectives, and backgrounds is crucial to encourage different perspectives and foster innovation that is particularly important at higher education institutions responsible for educating and training future leaders, workers, and citizens. These findings recognize that gender diversity in organizations' top offices and in the boardroom is not just a matter of social justice and advancement but a smart business move as well. Until the decision-makers acknowledge and embrace the connection between diversity and success, the development and implementation of diversity strategies will languish. There is a need to raise awareness of the significant benefits of gender parity and to increase visibility of the importance of accomplishing parity in leadership positions.

2. ***Encourage governing boards and other higher education decision- and policymaking bodies to consider practices for recruiting and***

*hiring women to chief executive offices.* The significant number of presidential retirements projected in the short term creates an opportunity to increase the diversity of the next generation of presidents as well as other senior leadership positions. With the Association of Governing Boards (2010a, 2010b) reporting that men on the governing boards outnumber women by more than two to one, those who will select the next generation of leaders genuinely must be committed to recruiting highly qualified and diverse candidates and their actions must evidence a sincere desire for a more inclusive culture enriched by diverse backgrounds and experiences. Recommended policies and practices need to be suggested to encourage institutions to recruit highly qualified women of all races and color to create a richly diverse pool of candidates for senior leadership positions. Additional recommended practices need to be suggested to ensure that through the interview and selection process all candidates are given fair and due consideration regardless of their gender or ethnicity.

3.  *Achieve women's advancement to mid-level and senior-level positions in higher education administration by building capacities in women and in institutions.* Since the majority of presidents and senior leaders come from within academia, ensuring that women and persons of color are increasingly represented in mid-level administrative positions is essential to the goal of increasing the diversity among senior leaders. With the significant drop-off of women faculty from instructor and lecturers (55%), and assistant professors (49%) to full professors (29%), the pool from which many senior administrators are chosen—tenured faculty—is disproportionately small (National Center for Education Statistics, 2012). More women need to be identified and encouraged to prepare for and seek entry and midlevel administrative positions. Additionally, research shows that work-life balance policies can not only benefit those who aspire to leadership positions, but also strengthen the institutions. Benefits reaped by organizations with workplace flexibility include reduced work/life conflict for men and women, enhanced productivity for managers (male or female, with children or without), and improved well-being and reduced absenteeism for all employees (Deloitte, 2011). Recommended practices and programs can identify, encourage, and support women in faculty and entry and midlevel administrative positions as they seek administrative positions and gain leadership experiences.

4.  *Suggest practices and models that recognize success in advancing women in higher education.* Research has affirmed that public recognition of good or exemplary performance encourages such per-

formance by inspiring people to do more, thereby driving greater levels of discretionary effort. Recognition of an organization's success and sharing practices and models further motivates its people to participate. Awareness can be raised across the higher education community by publicizing institutional success stories and practice, perhaps through an annual program that recognizes high-achieving colleges and universities (WNEC, 2014).

Based upon the discussions and recommendations from all three roundtables, WNEC assembled recommended actions steps for each of the four goals (WNEC, 2014). These action steps will serve as the foundation for the work of the groups tasked with achieving the stated goals. At a gathering of strategic partners in June 2014, the work of the initiative began. WNEC will present the vision, mission, value statements, and goals discussed above. Participants had the opportunity to join one of the groups formed to develop strategies and implement action steps for each of the four goals. Those assembled also had the opportunity to join the Moving the Needle initiative and to encourage synergy across interested parties, igniting a national sense of urgency to embrace the need for and the benefits of advancing women into senior leadership positions across higher education.

## CONCLUSION

Leading an institution of higher education for any and all leaders is not only a difficult task but also a responsibility that is critically important to the development of future citizens and leaders. Leadership development programs dedicated to the advancement of women are more essential than ever to meet the complex challenges facing today's higher education leaders. As Madlyn Hanes stated, "Leadership programs are effective venues for aspiring, newly inducted, and experienced women leaders. They provide a welcoming environment to share concerns, solve problems, and assess the ever-changing higher education landscape" (M. Haynes, personal communication, January 30, 2014). Haynes added that leadership programs also create important networking and mentorship opportunities that are critical to women's career advancement.

Molly Corbett Broad, President of ACE, included in the top initiatives of ACE a commitment to "developing the next generation of leaders who will take on those presidential positions and help sustain the preeminence of American higher education" (DiSalvio, 2013). ACE's leadership programming offered through the IEG maintains a focus on the unique issues facing women and other underrepresented leaders from diverse backgrounds that will transform the landscape of leadership in higher education.

## REFERENCES

American Council on Education. (2010, May). *Moving the needle: Developing a 21st century agenda for women's leadership, a spectrum initiative event.* Notes from Moving the Needle Roundtable. Washington, DC: Author.

American Council on Education. (2012a). *The American college president 2012.* Washington, DC: Author.

American Council on Education. (2012b, June). *Moving the needle together: Advancing women in higher education leadership.* Notes from Moving the Needle Roundtable. Washington, DC: Author.

American Council on Education. (2013a, June). *Working together to move the needle: Advancing women in higher education leadership.* Notes from Moving the Needle Roundtable. Washington, DC: Author

American Council on Education. (2013b). *2013 ACE Women's Network handbook.* Retrieved from http://www.acenet.edu/news-room/Documents/ACE-State-Coordinators-Handbook.pdf

Association of Governing Board of Universities and Colleges. (2010a). *Policies, practices, and composition of governing boards of independent colleges and universities.* Retrieved from http://agb.org/sites/agb.org/files/u3/2010IndependentBoardComposition Survey%20Summary.pdf

Association of Governing Board of Universities and Colleges. (2010b). *Policies, practices, and composition of governing boards of public colleges, universities and systems.* Retrieved from http://agb.org/sites/agb.org/files/u3/2010PublicBoardCompositionSurveySummary.pdf

Baltodano, J. C., Carlson, S., Witcher Jackson, L., & Mitchell, W. (2012). Networking to leadership in higher education: National and state-based programs and networks for developing women. *Advances in Developing Human Resources, 14*(1), 62–78.

Burns Phillips, D. (2008). *A brief history of the Office of Women in Higher Education.* Washington, DC: Office of Women in Higher Education.

Catalyst. (2007). *The bottom line: Corporate performance and women's representation on boards.* New York, NY: Catalyst.

Catalyst. (2011). *The bottom line: Connecting corporate performance and women's representation on boards (2004–2008).* New York, NY: Catalyst.

Center on Internationalization and Global Engagement, American Council on Education. (2011). *Strength through global leadership and engagement: U.S. higher education in the 21st century.* Washington, DC: American Council on Education.

Colorado Women's College. (2013). *Benchmarking women's leadership in the United States 2013.* Denver, CO: Colorado Women's College.

Deloitte Touche Tohmatsu Limited. (2011). *Only skin deep? Re-examining the business case for diversity.* Retrieved from http://www.deloitte.com/assets/Dcom-Australia/Local%20Assets/Documents/Services/Consulting/

Human%20Capital/Diversity/
Deloitte_Only_skin_deep_12_September_2011.pdf

Desvaux, G., Devillard, S., & Sancier-Sultan. S. (2011). *Women at the top of corporations: Making it happen.* Paris, France: McKinsey & Company. Retrieved from http://www.mckinsey.com/features/women_matter

DiSalvio, P. (2013, July 9). New directions for higher education: Q&A with ACE's Molly Corbett Broad on attainment. *The New England Journal of Higher Education.* Retrieved from nebhe.org/thejournal/new-directions-for-higher-education-qa-with-aces-molly-corbett-broad-on-raising-attainment/

Eckel, P., Cook, B., & King, J. (2009). *The CAO census: A national profile of chief academic officers.* American Council on Education. Washington, DC: American Council on Education.

Elliott, J. D. (2014). *The American Council on Education's Office of Women in Higher Education: A case study of evolution and decline 1973-2011* (Unpublished doctoral dissertation). George Washington University, Washington, DC.

Forbes Insights. (2011). *Global diversity and inclusion fostering innovation through a diverse workforce.* Retrieved from http://images.forbes.com/forbesinsights/StudyPDFs/Innovation_Through_Diversity.pdf

Herring, C. (2009). Does diversity pay? Race, gender, and the business case for diversity *American Sociological Review, 74*(2), 208–224.

King, J. E., & Gomez, G. G. (2008). *On the pathway to the presidency: Characteristics of higher education's senior leadership.* Washington, DC: American Council on Education.

National Center for Education Statistics, U.S. Department of Education. (2012). *Digest of education statistics (NCES Publication No. 2012–001).* Retrieved from http://nces.ed.gov/pubs2012/2012001.pdf

Princeton University, Steering Committee on Undergraduate Women's Leadership. (2011). Report of the steering committee on undergraduate women's leadership. Retrieved from http://www.princeton.edu/reports/2011/leadership/documents/SCUWL_Report_Final.pdf

Tarr-Whelan, L. (2009). *Women lead the way: Your guide to stepping up to leadership and changing the world.* San Francisco, CA: Barrett-Koehler.

The White House Project. (2009). *The White House Project: Benchmarking women's leadership.* New York, NY: Author.

Women's Network Executive Council. (2014, March). Unpublished mission statement approved at WNEC meeting.

CHAPTER 5

# HERS AT 50

## Curriculum and Connections
## for Empowering the Next Generation
## of Women Leaders in Higher Education

### Judith S. White

The development of a new generation of women for senior posts in higher education is of utmost importance to meet the need for attaining a diverse cadre of leaders, capable of responding to the challenges of a rapidly changing environment. Institutions of all types will continue to struggle with demands for greater outcomes in an era of fewer resources; indeed, many institutions will be forced to reinvent themselves to meet these demands (Fusch & Mrig, 2011). The new conditions of work for leaders in the academy will require a broader range of skills and capacities than was needed to succeed in earlier generations. In addition, much evidence indicates that broader diversity among decision-makers aids productivity. Specifically, recent studies have shown a record of better performance by organizations that have a larger number of women leaders than do their peers (Joy, Carter, Wagner, & Narayanan, 2007). The current plateau in the percentage of college and university presidencies held by women mandates that higher education act quickly to develop and support more women to assume these roles (Cook & Kim, 2012). This chapter will contribute to meeting the current leadership development

*Women and Leadership in Higher Education*, pp. 77–95
Copyright © 2014 by Information Age Publishing
77

challenge by outlining a variety of best practices identified by Higher Education Resource Services (HERS) during over 40 years of experience in women's leadership development programming. Additionally, new approaches are suggested based on recent research with women in executive roles in the academy as well as surveys and interviews with women at earlier career stages.

Since 1976 HERS Institutes have offered an intensive residential leadership development curriculum for women faculty and administrators. The programs enroll a total of 200 participants per year in the three institute locations: Bryn Mawr College, Wellesley College, and the University of Denver. Over 5,000 women from approximately 1,200 campuses in the United States and other nations have participated. For the past seven years, HERS has been involved in a continuous process of assessing and revising the curriculum of its signature HERS Institutes.

Responding to a general sense that women's progress toward achieving a greater share of executive roles had stalled, in 2006 the HERS Board undertook a review of the HERS Institute curriculum (White, 2012a). The original findings in 2006 indicated that both executive women leaders surveyed by the board and HERS Institute participants from a wide range of mid- to senior-level positions were experiencing more difficult working conditions on their campuses. New topics and pedagogical approaches added in 2006–2008 provided broader skills for addressing current conditions and planning for future advancement. Having implemented these curriculum changes in the previous two years, HERS faculty and staff were in a position to respond quickly to the new challenges facing campuses in the aftermath of the fall 2008 global financial crisis. By the spring of 2011, HERS had completed a significant revision of its HERS Institutes, with modifications made to the curriculum, pedagogy, and formats.

In 2012, to mark the 40th anniversary of the founding of HERS, the board undertook several new initiatives to begin exploring how the HERS Institutes might be extended and new programs added. These initiatives included a Summit of Women Presidents, a research collaboration with the University of Colorado at Colorado Springs and the Center for Creative Leadership studying senior women leaders, and new outreach events with HERS alumnae and other partners who were providing women's leadership development programs. The initiatives offered opportunities for assessing the challenges ahead for women leaders in higher education and the new range of skills and capacities that would be needed. These results have prompted the HERS Board to take bold action in planning for the next decade. As part of the organization's new strategic plan, *HERS at 50* (2013b), the board has adopted a broad new mission statement and a set of initiatives to create and sustain a community of women leaders, keeping the HERS Institutes as a central enterprise but moving far beyond what HERS has done before.

## HERS CURRICULUM FOR INSTITUTIONAL LEADERSHIP

The HERS organization began in 1972, growing out of the efforts of two different groups of women administrators, one in New England and the other in the Philadelphia area. Both groups recognized that the moment was right for giving attention to developing more women leaders for higher education. In that year, Title IX of the Higher Education Reauthorization Act was passed. Under Title IX, institutions accepting federal assistance were obligated to provide equitable educational opportunities regardless of sex. Fulfilling this obligation would mean an end to rules that barred admission for female students at many colleges and universities or in specific academic programs on some campuses. The HERS founders anticipated that the new law would act as a spur to employ and advance women faculty and administrators to serve as role models on campus. With funding from a small grant, the New England group launched HERS as a project to identify and support women who might be candidates for positions of higher education leadership. In 1976, the group in the Philadelphia area received funding to start the first HERS Institute, a month-long residential program at Bryn Mawr College. As described in a 2012 article in *Advances in Developing Human Resources* titled "HERS Institutes: Curriculum for Advancing Women Leaders in Higher Education," the curriculum from the beginning featured the dual mission of HERS: advancing women leaders *and* enhancing gender equity through institutional change (White, 2012a).

"Preparing the Individual for Institutional Leadership" was the overarching goal of the original HERS Bryn Mawr Summer Institute, as described by Secor's (1984) chapter on the history of HERS, published in *New Directions for Higher Education*. To support that goal, curricular sessions focused on broad areas of institutional practice: "academic governance, human relations skills, finance and budgeting, administrative uses of computing, management and leadership, as well as professional development for leadership in the academic setting" (White, 2012a, p. 13). The HERS Administrative Skills Program was launched at Wellesley College in 1978. It was offered in a different format, meeting in five two-day sessions across the academic year, and also provided an institutional perspective to women who were generally quite focused on department-level responsibilities. As described by Speizer (1984), three interrelated themes provided broad understanding of the institution as a whole: "Planning and Fiscal Management, Managing in Organizations, and Professional Development" (White, 2012a, p. 13).

The faculty organizing and presenting the curriculum at both HERS programs were experienced women administrators from across the spectrum of institutional responsibilities. Their professional expertise and examples drawn from their daily activities served to provide first-hand illustrations of leadership challenges. The faculty were also encouraged to share personal stories as guidance for the younger women participating in the Institutes. The participants represented a wide variety of institutional roles. The largest percentage of each class was from the faculty; this group was complemented by participants from student life, development, finance, administrative services, and other operational units (White, 2012a). The diverse background of participants and faculty thus contributed to the range of institutional perspectives on the institute topics. Pre-institute assignments reflected the goal of gaining a broad view of campus life. In addition to assignments to interview cabinet officers to learn about the view from the highest levels of administration, each participant was required to conduct an analysis of her own position within this new perspective. The goal for each woman was to determine "opportunities for professional growth, impact, and advancement" (White, 2012a, p. 14).

## REVISING HERS CURRICULUM FOR
## WOMEN LEADERS IN A NEW ERA

Thirty years after the launch of the first HERS Institute, the HERS organization experienced a change in leadership and legal structure. In anticipation of the retirement of the founding director, a group of HERS Institute faculty who had been serving as an advisory board began the process of incorporation. With the hiring of a new president/executive director in 2005, HERS shifted from being a sponsored program overseen through offices at the sites of the institutes (Bryn Mawr College, Wellesley College, and the University of Denver) to being an independent non-profit with a board of directors (White, 2012a). This transition presented the opportunity for a significant review of the HERS programming. A review was both timely and urgent, given compelling research (e.g., Valian, 1998) that indicated the movement of women into senior roles in higher education had slowed in the previous decade. The HERS Board was eager to learn more about how campus leaders would explain this situation and what they might suggest so that HERS could address the causes in its Institutes.

HERS undertook a series of intensive interviews with senior leaders, 25 current or former presidents (19 women and 5 men), and 5 academic search consultants specializing in presidential appointments (White,

2012a, p. 15). Their responses were sobering. In the view of those interviewed, too little had changed in terms of stereotypes about women's capacities and their appropriateness for leadership roles; in particular, reports included lingering doubts about women's expertise in dealing with money and difficult decisions. To senior women, these attitudes were particularly challenging given the increasingly high demands faced by all leaders in higher education. Many reported the sense that campus stakeholders were more likely to be hostile rather than supportive of senior leaders (White, 2012a). An additional challenge and disappointment, reported by the senior women, was their experience in trying to mentor younger women on their campuses toward administrative leadership roles. Many of the women faculty and administrators they approached resisted the suggestion of moving into senior-level roles.

With the responses from senior leadership in hand, the next stage of the inquiries turned to conversations with participants of the 2006 HERS Institutes. HERS staff asked these mid-career and more experienced women faculty and administrators about their views of working conditions on their home campuses and their perceptions of the possibilities for advancing into senior roles. Interestingly, these women often began by noting the achievement of unprecedented opportunities for women on their campuses. They were especially aware of the number of women in administrative posts—a contrast to their experience either earlier in their careers or while in graduate school. But even with these changes, the 2006 institute participants agreed with the earlier reports that the most-senior roles were rarely held by women. And, as might have been predicted from the reports from senior women, these younger women did not generally aspire to those positions themselves. Their reasons for this choice were not, however, related to their perceptions of explicit gender-bias. Instead they saw more difficult and demanding positions taking away time from family commitments. Without clearer reasons to justify this trade-off, they were unlikely to pursue positions with broader institutional responsibility.

In revising its curriculum, HERS thus faced a dual challenge. The Institutes needed to address the compelling need to bolster and prepare women for top positions in the academy. Yet HERS staff also needed to recognize and support younger administrators in leading effectively where they were—equipping all to cope with ever-more demanding conditions while also preparing those who wished to move up, to do so. Notably while not expressing a desire for "higher roles," the early- and mid-career women in the HERS Institutes did clearly see themselves as making important contributions to changes on their campuses. They were eager to share more of what they were undertaking in their own work and proposed that more time in the Institutes be devoted to learning from other participants as well as from the senior women on the faculty. This desire to lead and contribute in their current positions became the pivotal focus of the new curriculum revisions: HERS would shift more attention to the steps these women were already taking that connected them to the challenges and the accomplishments of senior leadership.

Consequently, *HERS Strategic Directions, 2006–2010* (HERS, 2006) set compound goals for the new curriculum. Going forward, the Institutes—including the new program at the University of Denver—would incorporate recommendations from the senior leaders about more attention to the environment for higher education and the multiple constituencies influencing campus policies and funding. The revisions also included suggestions to expand the curriculum related to budgeting and higher education finance. At the same time, rather than emphasizing the expectation of advancement to the highest positions of leadership, HERS faculty—guided by the evaluations of institute participants—focused on means for all to lead, at all levels, under the increasingly demanding conditions facing colleges and universities. The revised curriculum highlighted negotiation and conflict management, and incorporated analysis of off-campus issues buffeting institutions.

The overarching principle of this new curriculum was to provide a *continuous path* approach: Institute participants were encouraged to exercise their leadership while increasing their institutional impact in each role (White, 2012a). A central feature of this approach was the introduction of The HERS Leadership Project. Each participant was asked to identify a project through which she would make a specific contribution on her campus; during the institute individuals worked with a group of colleagues to apply elements of the curriculum to the challenges of their projects and develop strategies for implementing them. Participants were then invited to chart their leadership development plans in order to incorporate their goals for this project and possible roles in which they could have broader impact for the future. Finally, the participants were asked to examine their core values as leaders in higher education and to examine whether these commitments were worth taking on the obstacles they perceived to characterize more senior roles. The goal in these curricular revisions was to prepare these women to return to their campuses both more confident about their ability to lead and also clearer about the contributions they wanted to make.

## REVISING HERS INSTITUTES FOR
## WOMEN LEADERS IN TURBULENT TIMES

The revisions to the HERS curriculum in 2006–2008 laid a strong foundation for what would be the most significant changes yet in the nearly 40-year history of the program. The challenges posed by the global financial crisis of 2008 required that HERS faculty help institute participants to respond quickly to unprecedented demands. Faced with the startlingly swift disruptions coming to many campuses in 2008–2011, the women faculty and administrators in the HERS Institutes needed to understand the larger environmental context. They also sought informed solutions for addressing budget cuts and impending enrollment shortfalls. Despite the difficult circumstances, most HERS participants were eager to face current realities and to take up the challenges. During the next two years, HERS participants and faculty committed themselves to exploring how they might reframe the unsettled times that followed 2008 as an opportunity for institutional renewal. Simultaneously, the HERS staff and board also accepted responsibility for reinventing HERS to serve better both participants and their institutions. During 2009–2011, HERS Institutes initiated two more curricular revisions to address the challenging work ahead.

In 2009, HERS faculty began using new Curricular Themes to bring together a broad framework for meeting the challenges emerging from the new economic and political circumstances.

- Understanding the New Environment for Higher Education
- Planning and Leading Change in the Academy
- Managing and Investing Strategic Resources
- Engaging Individual and Institutional Diversity
- Mapping Your Leadership Development

Questions related to these themes ran through all presentations and assignments. At the same time, HERS faculty encouraged participants to use the Leadership Projects as individual case studies for exploring challenges and posing potential responses. Guest presenters during this period included women presidents who had led their institutions through periods of crisis; they brought strategies for rallying colleagues during turbulent times, especially by directing attention to improvement rather than simply recovery. HERS participants were also challenged to realize how much experience and creativity they could contribute to short-term responses and to the long-term reshaping of higher education.

In 2010–2011, the HERS staff made a significant change in the format of its programming. Responding to the reality of changing demands for time and funding, the three HERS Institutes would all be offered in a new shorter schedule, each delivering a 12-day curriculum (White, 2012a). The Summer Institute would be offered as a two-week residency in two locations, one at Bryn Mawr College and the other at the University of Denver. The year-long institute at Wellesley College was reformatted to be offered in four three-day sessions, rather than in five weekends. All the Institutes incorporated the same five critical themes. Now all HERS Institute participants would have one curriculum that was designed to develop their capacities for facing crisis and leading institutional renewal.

## HERS 2012: WOMEN LEADERS SHAPING THE DECADE AHEAD

In 2012, after 5 years of intense inquiry and curricular revision, HERS took time to celebrate the 40th anniversary of the founding of the HERS organization and to reflect on the progress for women in the past 40 years, as well as the challenges in the decade ahead. The board marked the period by approving several new initiatives for 2012–2013, all designed to explore how HERS might extend and expand the outreach of the institutes. Over the years, HERS had consistently involved senior women leaders as faculty and as advisors for HERS Institutes; however, women at this stage of their careers had never been a focus of HERS programs. In 2012 HERS convened a Summit of Women Presidents and Chancellors and launched a collaborative research project studying career paths of senior women leaders. While HERS had always encouraged institute alumnae to share their HERS experience through programs on their own campuses, these activities had not been directly supported by HERS staff. As part of the 40th anniversary celebrations, HERS reached out to the over 5,000 institute alumnae, inviting them to reconnect through reunion events held during each of the three Institutes and encouraging them to hold events on their own campuses. In newsletter features, HERS staff gave special recognition to several campuses where alumnae had initiated HERS-influenced women's leadership programs. Taking new initiative to partner with other organizations committed to women's leadership development, HERS developed sponsorship agreements and for the first time presented at joint conference events. Finally HERS staff began exploring how it might move beyond the long-standing practice of offering an online newsletter and collecting institute assignments via the website, to using learning management tools and social media to create better connections among HERS Institute participants and alumnae. All of these initiatives would provide more information regarding how HERS might continue changing in order to help women leaders take central roles in renewing their institutions and shaping the vision for broader transformation of higher education.

## HERS 2012 Summit for Women Presidents and Chancellors

A central event of the 40th anniversary year was the first HERS Summit of Women Presidents and Chancellors, held in April 2012. The theme of the gathering was "Shaping the Decade Ahead: Vision, Values, and

Actions." The goals for the three-day program were to acknowledge the turbulent conditions in which these women were working and to explore the ways in which they were taking action to shape directions of change rather merely responding to a continuing crisis. Seventy-five participants, most of whom were women presidents and chancellors, along with women leaders from national organizations and foundations, gathered to reflect on values and actions needed to respond to the challenges of the next 10 years. What values originally compelled their commitment to higher education leadership? What values would be required to lead changes for the future?

The transformations these senior women leaders advocated, and in many cases were already initiating, include four major shifts in recent practice in higher education:

- Restructure institutions and systems
- Reengage multiple constituencies
- Reinvest our own resources and seek more public support
- Redefine/redesign our leadership models (White, 2012b).

As the summit participants discussed their values, it was clear that these changes in practice are, in actuality, new ways of pursuing their original values. The overarching theme throughout the HERS Summit conversations was the critical role of higher education in serving individuals and communities through the transformative power of learning. These female leaders were firmly committed to learning, changing, and serving (White, 2012b). The values they added for addressing the future define a less conventional leadership model. Instead of *seizing* the day, these women are approaching the decade ahead with a more collaborative spirit. Along with courage and innovation, they also called for inclusion and a generous spirit (White, 2012b).

## HERS Institutes 2012

The theme of the HERS Summit became a central part of the curriculum of the 2012 HERS Institutes. What would it mean for these 200 institute participants to join with women presidents in *shaping the decade ahead*? HERS faculty duplicated the activities from the HERS Summit at the three HERS Institutes of 2012. What were the participants' values? How might they act on them?

It became clear that the 200 HERS Institute participants, like leaders at the HERS Summit, were also motivated by making a difference for others (HERS, 2012b). They expressed strong commitments to access and success for a wide range of students; similarly, they pursue their research and service with the goal of improving lives for individuals and broader communities. In coming to the HERS Institutes, the participants reported that they sought to learn new possibilities for making a difference through wider institutional impacts.

With the goal of a wider impact in mind, HERS staff linked the institute conversations about transformations needed in higher education to the Leadership Projects that participants were planning to implement on their own campuses. Were the immediate challenges faced by these participants related to the large shifts in higher education? Could this perspective help shape how they were responding? Would they describe themselves as leading with creativity, risk-taking, and generosity? What would they see as the most important values, skills, and capacities for shaping the decade ahead? The content of the HERS leadership project proposals revealed a range of responses to these questions (HERS, 2012a). Many participants provided examples of how the projects they were undertaking illustrated larger shifts in institutional structures and practices cited by the summit leaders. But others described themselves as still experiencing the changes on their campuses through a lens of reacting rather than leading. Across the three Institutes, responses from the 200 participants indicated a decided mix of confusion, fear, and excitement. *Stamina* sometimes joined *creativity* on their list of necessary values for the future (HERS, 2012b).

These women, nonetheless, were also eager to acquire the skills they would need to lead in these challenging times. From the current HERS Institute curriculum the participants could gain much, including the capacity to analyze institutional structures, to engage multiple stakeholders, and to assess financial risks and opportunities. They could come away with deepened understandings; they could be part of a larger national movement with connections to supportive HERS alumnae at all levels. But given the challenges ahead, was there more that HERS could be doing to support women participating in HERS Institutes, as well as other women leaders in higher education?

## HERS STRATEGIC PLANNING: SHAPING HERS FOR THE DECADE AHEAD

In 2013, the HERS Board undertook a strategic planning process to determine how the HERS organization might provide better support for women leaders through the HERS Institutes and the HERS alumnae networks and to move beyond with other activities. Central to this assessment was information gathered during the multiple projects initiated the year before. From these responses, the board needed to understand the responses to two questions: What would be the most important changes that HERS could undertake to encourage more women of all backgrounds to seek leadership roles—including the most senior positions? What strategies could HERS offer to support them as they undertake the transformative actions outlined by the women leaders at the HERS Summit 2012?

## Lessons From Senior Women in the Post-2008 Era

One explanation posited for the lower-than-desired number of women in college and university presidencies was the reluctance of women to seek positions in which working conditions had become even more difficult since the 2008 financial crisis. If indeed that was the case, what might HERS and other women's leadership programs add to their curriculum or advocate in other ways that could prepare and support more women for executive challenges? One of the HERS 40th anniversary initiatives had set out to explore these questions through the experiences of the generation of women currently in senior leadership roles in higher education. This effort was a collaborative research project with the University of Colorado at Colorado Springs (UCCS) and the Center for Creative Leadership (CCL), in which 35 women presidents and senior officers (provosts, vice presidents) were interviewed about their leadership paths. The primary research question was: What factors had motivated their seeking or avoiding senior leadership positions, and what factors had facilitated or blocked their progress to such roles?

The timing for this effort was linked both to the need for new leadership and to the opportunities for filling that need with more women. The most recent report on senior leadership in higher education, ACE's *The American College President, 2012* (Cook & Kim, 2012), indicated that the percentage of presidencies held by women had increased only slightly in the previous five years, from 23% to 26%. The percentage of chief executives of color, women and men, had decreased from 14% to 13%. At the same time, the report confirmed that more than half of the current presidents or chancellors expected to be retiring by 2020 (Cook & Kim, 2012). The decade ahead will provide unprecedented opportunities for advancing more women and more men from underrepresented groups into executive positions. This could be the decade for creating the critical mass of leaders from different backgrounds necessary for a significant shift in the culture of U.S. higher education.

Because the ACE report, *On the Pathway to the Presidency* (King & Gomez, 2008), had suggested that many cabinet-level officers were often not interested in pursuing positions as president or chancellor, a critical goal of the HERS (2013c) research was to understand what might be deterring some women from interest in these roles. With this question in mind, 21 of the 35 women interviewed as part of this study were in cabinet-level roles of provosts, vice presidents, or "chief officers" in various fields. The interviewees represented a variety of geographic regions and sectors of higher education. Their mean age was 57.5 years, and their time in current positions ranged from one year to over 10 years. Fifteen of the interviewees were women of color; this overrepresentation in the sample was deliberate in order to allow these voices to be heard.

A preliminary report of the research findings was presented to the HERS Board in 2013. It (HERS, 2013c) identified several themes that were familiar from earlier conversations with women presidents at the HERS Summit, especially their passion for making a difference and the importance that passion had in motivating their willingness to face the demands of their roles. After discussion with the HERS Board members, who are themselves women presidents and vice-presidents, the HERS staff selected three lessons that would have priority for revising curriculum and shaping strategic directions for HERS: political alliance-building, institutional support for family commitments, and more attention to advancing women of color from cabinet to chief executive positions.

**Political Alliance Building.** The research-project interviews confirmed that gendered expectations continue to shape the leadership of senior women (HERS, 2013c). These interviewees report a mix of stereotyped responses that make the political demands of their jobs especially challenging for them as women leaders. As Jamieson (1995) described the "double bind" phenomenon, women face the conflicting assignment of being "tough" enough to handle their jobs while still being "caring" (p. 120). The consequences of not achieving and sustaining that precarious balance can be swift and dangerous. These women have no magic answers, but they suggest humor in public—as well as finding confidantes with whom to share frustrations in private (HERS, 2013c). Additionally, they gave examples of seeking opportunities to reframe expectations so as to create a different climate for themselves and others. But the interviews also suggested a more systematic approach, best articulated as the need for women to build stronger public allies. These women appeared less likely than men to use their networks to rally defenders and mobilize support to counter political attacks. While the curriculum of HERS and other women's leadership programs address political skills for championing issues, it is clear that women's leadership networks need more focus on helping women develop political alliances and the expectation of public support in crisis situations.

**Institutional Support for Family Commitments.** In these interviews (HERS, 2013c), as in the conversations at the HERS Summit, these women presidents and senior leaders noted that the most draining dimension of their work was being pressed to curtail time with their families. They rarely use the language of striving to achieve balance, given that the expectation of balance was not viewed as one they could meet. Those most satisfied sought to prioritize family and personal events within their busy public schedules. These women were deeply grateful for the support they receive from their partners and children; many described the ways their families share the values they pursue in creating opportunities through education. At the same time, these women leaders rarely reported seeking campus support for their family commitments. They offered few suggestions for what institutional or public policy changes might make work roles more flexible. Without new models of support, the challenge of combining responsibilities for work and family will persist. Advocates for women's leadership will need to engage these senior leaders in more deliberate efforts to move the family issue to the center of policy discussions. In short, making appropriate changes in the area of both work and family demands will be critical for supporting the next generation of women leaders.

**More Attention to Advancing Women of Color From Cabinet to Chief Executive.** A central question of this study (HERS, 2013c) concerned the interest of cabinet-level officers in advancing to presidencies. Of those holding the provost position, some shared the view expressed in ACE's (King & Gomez, 2008) *On the Pathway to the Presidency* report that a presidency would take them away from their primary concern about faculty, teaching, and scholarship; others did not. Other vice presidents in the study, however, consistently reported interest in the chief executive role. Women of color in this group (HERS, 2013c), who were often in a nonacademic officer role (finance, advancement, diversity), reported being interested in pursuing presidencies. They noted, however, that coming from roles other than the provost position, added to their race, lowered their statistical likelihood of succeeding in presidential searches. During this exceptional period of executive openings in higher education, bringing the expertise and perspective of women of color into the cadre of new leaders will require deliberate cultivation and sponsorship.

## Lessons from Women in Earlier Career Stages as They Face the Future

Improving the conditions for succession and success for women in senior positions will contribute to better prospects for the next generation of women leaders. At the same time, stories from the HERS research project and many years of experience with HERS participants suggest that most women take their first steps towards the most senior roles with a focus on the immediate challenges of the position they hold. With this in mind, HERS took advantage of new outreach activity during 2012–2013 to conduct a survey and interviews to understand the views and needs of women in earlier career stages. The survey was administered during a joint HERS/ACE Women's Network conference session at the March 2013 annual meeting of the ACE (White, 2013). Because the 40 women responding in the HERS/ACE workshop survey were likely to be in advanced career stages, HERS commissioned an independent organization to conduct 40 interviews that included a larger sampling of women in earlier career stages (Keen Independent Research, 2013). All participants in the survey and the interviews were asked about potential obstacles in their career journeys and for suggestions on how HERS, ACE, and other women's leadership development programs might help facilitate their advancement into senior positions.

Again three lessons emerged that would influence HERS strategic planning: affirmation of the need for the fundamentals of the HERS curriculum, new perspectives from the youngest women in the studies, and suggestions for curriculum and connections that reach beyond what HERS or other women's leadership programs are offering today (Keen Independent Research, 2013; White, 2013).

**Curriculum of Leadership Fundamentals.** Women responding to both the survey and the interviews expressed interest in developing expertise in areas fundamental to leading in higher education today: negotiation, budgeting, reading institutional cultures, and leading change. They wanted more skills in media, board interaction, and lobbying. They also desired more information and advice about handling many of the topics that have brought women presidents into very difficult situations in recent years: athletics, donor relations, ethics, and finance. Likewise, these women were clear that they wanted help in managing work and family balance issues, though most framed the need as one of personal skills rather than as structural change requiring political activity and alliances.

**More Guidance for Next-Generation Career Paths.** Within the group of younger respondents, new requests and new possibilities emerged (Keen Independent Research, 2013). Many of the women in these interviews noted that they were in non-tenure-track positions; they needed to raise funds to cover their research positions or they knew their teaching assignments might be eliminated. Their situations indicated two important shifts from the conditions of earlier eras, with crucial consequences for women's career opportunities. First, the faculty appointments that have in the past been the most frequent career pipeline to senior leadership are less available. Second, the faculty responsibilities that once afforded both important experience and some career stability are now being uncoupled from the core institutional structure. These changes exemplify the restructuring of faculty roles away from a model of asking a tenure-track faculty to combine teaching, research, and service and toward a "next model" in which different employees take on these roles in a variety of non-faculty or non-tenure-track appointments (Finkelstein & Schuster, 2011).

Clearly many of these younger women are most interested in finding more support for regularized faculty appointments. At the same time, however, others asked for assistance in planning careers as "consultants"—being part of higher education but perhaps not anchored in a specific institution (Keen Independent Research, 2013). In preparing for a more entrepreneurial approach to their development, these women are actually seeking the same skills and capacities that will be necessary for all leaders as institutions seek to restructure, reach out to new constituencies, and better align their budgets to program priorities. These women in this "next model" generation need guidance from more experienced leaders so that they can find ways to be part of the transformative changes ahead rather than being pushed out by them.

**Continuous Women's Leadership Connections**. The obstacles and challenges reported in the HERS/ACE survey and the independent HERS interviews varied, but painfully consistent was the urgent need for support. Much of what was reported had to do with the lack of direction or encouragement from supervisors or colleagues. For some, this resulted in feeling an extreme sense of isolation. Others more obliquely referred to needing help they cannot—or do not—get on campus (White, 2013). To counter this void in preparation and recognition, these women reported looking to women's leadership development programs to provide the connections, skills, and advice needed to achieve transitions. They reported a desire for structured connections to other women, and particularly to women who can provide counsel for addressing their current challenges. They also identified a desire for mentoring for advancement to the next levels of responsibility and authority.

What was most important about these responses, however, was the way in which these women repeatedly requested that support be available not in one format but in multiple forms. Many expressed eagerness to be nominated for HERS and other residential programs, but more of them urged national organizations to partner and multiply opportunities in more locations. Some suggested local and regional programs on partnering campuses. Others proposed that women's leadership programs ally with national associations to present workshops "at every conference." Still others want women's leadership programs to use websites and social media to provide continuous resources online. More than one respondent suggested a phone or website "hot line" to offer emergency advice on difficult situations or especially promising opportunities. In the new world of constant and changing challenges, these women want "just-in-time" mentoring in order to keep themselves effective and resilient (Keen Independent Research, 2013; White, 2013).

## HERS AT 50: CURRICULUM AND CONNECTIONS FOR EMPOWERING WOMEN LEADERS

As indicated in these studies, women leaders desire both the fundamental skills that the HERS Institute curriculum has provided and as well the development of key new skills to navigate the turbulent trends in higher education. Beyond enhanced skills, it is also clear that women leaders in today's environment require connections to thrive. They need to share skills, approaches, and comradeship. This is true for the women in the most senior positions, where political alliances can help them with restructuring institutional capacity and creating collaborations for support. It is true as well for women in many other roles leading transformative change across each institution.

Indeed the HERS studies reveal a fundamental imperative much broader than curriculum revision or new programs for advancing senior women, critical as these changes may be (HERS, 2013c; Keen Independent Research, 2013; White, 2013). The greatest need and challenge for women's leadership development—as in higher education itself—is access. Not enough women have access to skills, perspective, connections, and critical advice. Particularly acute is the need for leadership development for women faculty and administrators of color and for women working in institutions that serve minority and first-generation college students. Clearly no one group can address this great need alone. But the HERS Board is committed to making a significant contribution to meeting this need in the critical decade to come. In order for HERS to achieve this ambitious goal, the HERS staff, faculty, and board must accept their own challenge of reinventing the organization in order to learn, change, and serve.

## NEW MISSION: CREATING AND SUSTAINING A COMMUNITY OF WOMEN LEADERS

Since HERS was founded in 1972, its mission has been expressed in terms of "advancing women leaders" and "advocating gender equity" (HERS, 2013a, p. 2). These phrases captured the organization's dual mission as HERS Institutes offered a leadership development curriculum to over 5,000 women faculty and administrators and prepared them to return to over 1,200 campuses as leaders of institutional change.

In October 2013, looking to its golden anniversary in 2022, the HERS Board adopted a broad mission statement for its new strategic plan, *HERS at 50*:

> Higher Education Resource Services (HERS) is dedicated to creating and sustaining a community of women leaders through leadership development programs and other strategies with a special focus on gender equity within the broader commitment to achieving equality and excellence in higher education. (HERS, 2013b, p. 1)

To advance a community of women leaders in the decade ahead, HERS will hone—and reach extensively beyond—its signature residential Institutes. Six areas of activity have been identified as key to achieving the new mission through a combination of curriculum and connections:

- HERS Institutes will continue to offer an evolving curriculum for developing skills and perspective, while the program also advocates and models the enterprise of creating community among women leaders.
- HERS alumnae will facilitate programs for others, to help create and sustain a community of women leaders.
- HERS Board, faculty, and staff will recruit, coach, and support women from diverse backgrounds for the highest executive roles.
- HERS will expand its partnerships with national associations in order to offer workshops and seminars on a local and regional basis.
- HERS will use social media and its website to provide online resources and connections among women leaders in the higher education community.
- HERS will encourage the community of women leaders in higher education to raise their voices to support this transformation.

## CONCLUSION

Higher education faces the challenge of reshaping its systems and structures to provide equality and excellence for increasing numbers of students with a wide variety of needs. The creativity and broad perspective necessary for this work require a larger and more diverse cadre of leaders. Women must be empowered to move into leadership roles in much greater numbers than they hold today.

For four decades, HERS has provided an intensive curriculum and national network for women who could participate in its HERS Institutes.

Today as higher education is restructuring to meet greater demands, HERS is also undertaking a transformative change in the nature of its mission and organization. The new HERS keeps the residential leadership development program of its Institutes as a central feature. Through this program, and the addition of extensive outreach strategies, HERS will work to create and sustain a community of women leaders. As HERS looks toward its 50th anniversary in 2022, it is providing curriculum and connections for supporting today's women leaders and empowering a new generation for the future.

## ACKNOWLEDGMENT

Material in the sections "HERS Curriculum for Institutional Leadership," "Revising HERS Curriculum for Women Leaders in a New Era," and "Revising HERS Institutes for Women Leaders in Turbulent Times" was adapted from the article "HERS Institutes: Curriculum for Advancing Women Leaders in Higher Education," published in *Advances in Developing Human Resources* in February 2012. This content is used by permission of SAGE Publications.

## REFERENCES

Cook, B., & Kim, Y. (2012). *The American college president 2012*. Washington, DC: American Council on Education.

Finkelstein, M. J., & Schuster, J. H. (2011, April). A new higher education: The "next model" takes shape. *The TIAA CREF Institute: Advancing Higher Education*, 1–9. Retrieved from http://www1.tiaa-cref.org/institute/research/advancing_higher_ education/ahe_nextmodel04112.html

Fusch, D., & Mrig, A. (2011, June). Rethinking higher education's leadership crisis. *Academic Impressions: Higher Ed Impact*, 7–13.

Higher Education Resource Service. (2006). *HERS strategic directions: The goals, programs, audiences 2006-2010*. Denver, CO: Author.

Higher Education Resource Services. (2012a). *HERS leadership project proposals*. Denver, CO: Author.

Higher Education Resource Services. (2012b). *HERS values exercises responses*. Denver, CO: Author.

Higher Education Resource Services (2013a). *Director of HERS institutes leadership profile*. Denver, CO: Author.

Higher Education Resource Services. (2013b, October 21). *HERS strategic planning retreat: Action summary*. Denver, CO: Author.

Higher Education Resource Services. (2013c, March 2). *Women's leadership research project: Report to HERS board*. Denver, CO: Author.

Jamieson, K. H. (1995). *Beyond the double bind: Women and leadership*. New York, NY: Oxford University Press.

Joy, L., Carter, N. M., Wagner, H. M., & Narayanan, S. (2007, October). *The bottom line: Corporate performance and women's representation on boards. New York, NY: Catalyst.* Retrieved from http://www.catalyst.org/publication/200/the-bottom-line-corporate-performance-and-womens-representation-on-boards

Keen Independent Research (2013, September 6). *Preliminary research 2013 HERS strategic scan*. Denver, CO: Author.

King, J. E., & Gomez, G. G. (2008). *On the pathway to the presidency: Characteristics of higher education's senior leadership*. Washington, DC: American Council on Education.

Secor, C. (1984, March). Preparing the individual for institutional leadership: The summer institute. *New Directions for Higher Education, 1984*(45), 25–33.

Speizer, J. (1984, March). The administrative skills program: What have we learned? *New Directions for Higher Education, 1984*(45), 35–45.

Valian, V. (1998). *Why so slow? The advancement of women*. Cambridge, MA: M.I.T. Press.

White, J. S. (2012a, February). HERS Institutes: Curriculum for advancing women leaders in higher education. *Advances in Developing Human Resources, 14*(11), 11-27. doi: 10.1177/1523422311429732

White, J. S. (2012b, June 18). *Women leaders re-inventing higher education* [PowerPoint slides]. Keynote address at the HERS Bryn Mawr Summer Institute. Denver, CO: Author.

White, J. S. (2013, June 18). *The pathway from our perspective* [PowerPoint slides]. Presented at the Moving the Needle Initiative meeting of the American Council on Education, Washington, DC: Author.

CHAPTER 6

# DEVELOPING WOMEN'S LEADERSHIP

## An Innovative and Unique Approach to Raising Leadership Capacity

### Lorri L. Sulpizio

The study and understanding of women and leadership is at a tipping point. The literature and research on women and leadership has reflected many of the same ideas and perspectives for over a decade, and it is safe to say we are in need of new conversations about women's leadership issues and new perspectives and practices on developing women leaders. Despite efforts dedicated to supporting and developing women's leadership, progress seems to be slow, and women continue to report struggles within their workplace environment (Kellerman & Rhode, 2007). Even within higher education, a traditional female-friendly field, women face gender bias and structural barriers. It is readily apparent that women still face a large leadership struggle and often enter high-level roles with little practice, feeling ill-prepared. This leadership struggle not only often makes the workplace frustrating for women, it also negatively impacts women's self-confidence and their ability to develop their capacity to lead.

The challenges faced by women in leadership become important when we consider that, despite relevant progress in today's public sector, women still hold significantly fewer positions of formal authority com-

*Women and Leadership in Higher Education*, pp. 97–114
Copyright © 2014 by Information Age Publishing
All rights of reproduction in any form reserved.

pared to men as documented in this volume's foundational chapter. This concern includes the paucity of women in positions as business executives, positions in public government and politics, and positions in professions such as education, law, religion, and medicine (Kellerman & Rhode, 2007).

Higher education is one industry in which women seem to have found opportunities for advancement, and yet, despite roles such as department chair, program director, or dean, women still are largely underrepresented in the highest roles within higher education (Aleman & Renn, 2002; DiGeorgio-Lutz, 2002). Leadership development programs designed to meet the needs of women leaders are necessary in order to specifically address the challenges that women face within higher education.

At the Women's Leadership Academy (WLA) in the Department of Leadership Studies at the University of San Diego, comprehensive programs have been designed to develop women leaders using teaching methods that incorporate several theoretical perspectives and innovative approaches to leadership. The methods and curriculum of the programs are based on cross-sectional research from a variety of disciplines and industries. Additionally, over the past few years these programs have been refined based on the most current and relevant research, and they continue to be uniquely created for women leaders in order to address the challenges and reflect the experiences of women within the field of higher education. When working to develop women's leadership capacity, programs must create content that is based on traditional organizational and leadership theory while also incorporating forward-thinking practice, challenging women to examine their leadership identity and giving them opportunities to practice and develop the skills and strategies that facilitate the exercise of effective leadership.

For women attempting to take up a leadership role, they must not only be seen, but also to see themselves, as leaders. This requires an identity shift by the woman wanting to develop her leadership capacity, and recognition by others of her leadership efforts (Ibarra, Ely, & Kolb, 2013). To develop women's leadership, there are gender-specific considerations necessary for leadership development programs in order to effectively foster and promote women's emergence as leaders. Scholars of women's leadership development have suggested that women need to develop a leadership identity and create networks that will help propel them forward (Ely, Ibarra, & Kolb, 2011), while also expanding their understanding and use of voice as well as their ability to own their power and take up their authority (Sulpizio, 2010).

The WLA is situated within the Leadership Institute at the University of San Diego and strives to offer programs that encourage women to take on new leadership roles as well as attempting to develop the leadership effectiveness of current women leaders. The WLA has designed programs that develop and enhance women's leadership through an approach that is founded on four key principles. First, the programs are characterized by making a clear distinction between leadership and authority. Second, the content and curriculum is based on the acknowledgment of a pervasive organizational gender bias where double standards and a male-as-normative model of leadership create challenging environments for women. Third, instead of considering leadership styles as dichotomous and delineated concepts of male and female styles of leadership, leadership effectiveness is viewed as an integration and embodiment of *both* masculine and feminine leadership practice. And finally, content and curriculum are created by using the perspective of group dynamics, presenting a new leadership language for women to develop and practice leadership in ways most relevant and useful for them. This multifaceted approach permits a research-based blueprint to the topics most significant to women's leadership experience, such as voice and power.

Although the WLA offers programs of various lengths and designed to serve a wide array of target industries, the four principles outlined above are the foundation for all of the women's leadership development programs. Originally based on current and seminal gender and leadership development research, the programs themselves and the feedback and response of the participants have provided ongoing support for the continued use of these principles as key WLA program guidelines. Each of these principles is described more fully in later sections of this chapter, with the recommendation offered that all leadership programs aimed at developing women should incorporate similar elements. Whether the goal is to prepare women to advance into more senior positions or to help women thrive in the positions they currently occupy, the unique experience of women within organizations and the impact of gender on women's leadership must be a paramount consideration in shaping leadership development programs.

As we examine each of the four elements, it becomes clear that they are built upon and dependent on each other. For example, looking through the lens of group dynamics includes looking at the places where authority and power are manifested, while also helping to expose some of the more subtle gender biases that often surface in departments. Gaining a deeper understanding of leadership and authority helps women recognize the necessity of being able to lead with a balance of both masculine and feminine leadership styles in order to most successfully engage in leadership skills and strategies. What the WLA programs embody is an integrated philosophy about leadership development, incorporating the most relevant topics and current research for enhancing women's leadership capacity.

## GENDER, LEADERSHIP, AND AUTHORITY

Before a woman can begin to develop herself as a leader, create a leadership identity, or find and use her voice in the practice of leadership, she needs to understand the conceptual difference between leadership and authority. In both popular culture and academic literature, women in roles of formal authority are often discussed in the context of leadership, and a woman who holds a role of formal authority is referred to as a *leader*. Missing from this perspective is a clear distinction between a woman who occupies a role of authority, such as a dean, university president, or department chair, and someone who exercises leadership or mobilizes a group toward adaptive change (Heifetz, 1994). At the onset of women's leadership development, participants should understand the difference between the exercise of leadership—a process—and a role of authority.

Authority and leadership are closely related, often used interchangeably, and considered to be synonymous. However, scholars differentiate between authority and leadership, using the term *authority* to signify power that is conferred in exchange for a service and the term *leadership* to signify working toward change or an adaptive challenge (Heifetz, 1994; Kotter, 2001; Monroe, 2004). The difference that has evolved from this perspective treats authority as something someone *has* that can be acquired and maintained, and leadership as an activity, as something someone *does*. Leadership then is the act of addressing challenges and influencing others to collaboratively create positive change. The distinction between authority and leadership is significant, especially for women, in that having some form of authority may be a critical element to exercising leadership because of the power and resources that accompany roles of authority. From this perspective, formal authority roles are desirable because, while a person can certainly lead change without positional authority, the power associated with those roles provides leadership opportunity. Getting women into those positions at the top is an important step for women to have more opportunities for exercising leadership.

Additionally, the definition of authority as power conferred for a service has several implications for the development of women's leadership. First, some scholars note that many women have trouble with the concept of power (Freeman, Bourque, & Shelton, 2001) and suggest that women have typically been more comfortable when they use power in the service of others (Miller, 1982). The traditional conceptions of authority equate power with domination or control, not as the capacity to move people toward a common mission or purpose. Women are likely to struggle with the concept of coercive power and feel uncomfortable using their power over others, while feeling much more comfortable using their power in the service of others (Miller, 1982). In order for women to think about taking up their authority, they have to think about their relationship with power and explore how power influences their lives. This is done at the WLA through an explicit naming of power as a significant influence and then challenging the participants to think, talk, and write about the ways in which they do and do not own their own power.

In developing women leaders, the authority/leadership distinction can be viewed in two ways. First, in authority roles—often the highest-level roles within a department—there is the power to create change, initiate policy, and exert positive influence. As such, women should aspire to advance into these roles (Ely et al., 2011; Sandberg, 2012). And second, the power that accompanies authority roles may be uncomfortable for many women, given that some women struggle to own their power and, accordingly, struggle in taking up their authority within a group (Sulpizio, 2010). So the discussion at the onset of a WLA women's leadership program becomes focused on understanding the difference between leadership and authority, examining the impact of power dynamics, and helping women begin to understand their own relationship with authority and power. Doing so early in the program leads to an exploration of how women can most constructively use authority and power to exercise leadership.

Notably, even while research continues to point out that women are largely underrepresented from authority roles and infrequently hold those senior-level positions, viewing authority as distinct from leadership illustrates that women are doing leadership all the time. In fact, inspiring others to collectively and collaboratively address tough issues and work toward change is something most of the WLA's participants identify themselves as doing quite regularly. Whether women are engaging in leadership in their role as a faculty member, a mother, or a committee member, women have shown success in the leadership process, without necessarily holding a position of authority. This perspective suggests that it may not be leadership that women struggle with, but authority within an organizational structure.

One way to clarify this distinction between leadership and authority for the participants of WLA programs is to avoid using the term "leader" to describe someone in an assigned role of authority. Within the WLA programs, the core faculty and staff refer to those with positional power in an organization as the *authority*, and use the word *leadership* to describe the activity of mobilizing a group and influencing people to make positive change. This linguistic detail is an important way to begin framing the participants' understanding of leadership as an activity and is linked to helping them craft their own identity of being capable leaders.

When women begin to better understand the concepts of authority, leadership, and power, they can begin to explore how those three concepts influence and contribute to their ability to exercise leadership. Women's development programs can begin the process of helping participants find their voice and create a strong leadership identity through an exploration of how authority and power impact their ability to speak up, act courageously, engage with others, and navigate through difficult situations. Seeing leadership as an attainable process, one that the women are already engaging in, is a foundational element of women's leadership identity. As such, women can not only recognize authority roles as something they can aspire to and eventually attain, but also, they realize that leadership is something that can be done with or without a positional authority role. Establishing the thought pattern that anyone can lead is pivotal to women seeing themselves as capable of leadership.

## A GENDER BIAS

In addition to the distinction being made within the WLA programs between authority and leadership, another differentiating factor is the gendered lens on which the WLA programs are based. The WLA programming explicitly acknowledges the gender bias, attitudinal prejudices, and discrimination that still exists in organizations, including higher education, and often creates a difficult climate for women to take up their authority, own their power, advance within the department, and exercise leadership. The participants are told at the onset that this perspective is not one of feeling victimized; they are encouraged to acknowledge gender bias as a way to make sense of their experiences and be prepared for the challenges they might face as they navigate organizational life. These biases may take the form of cultural attitudes, workplace policies and practices, or patterns that favor men (Ely & Meyerson, 2000; Kolb & McGinn, 2009; Sandberg, 2012).

One of these gender biases is the male-as-normative model of leadership, where leadership behaviors are aligned with masculine associated traits such as decisiveness, assertiveness, and competition. The qualities associated with being female—relational, emotional, and passive—are incongruent with socially accepted leadership practice. In this way, women are in a double bind (Catalyst Knowledge Center, 2007), and they face a double standard (Ely et al., 2011). They must either be feminine and compromise their leadership capacity or adopt male-normative leadership characteristics, which requires them to abandon their femininity. As we will see later in the chapter, the challenge for women is to embrace their masculine self while existing from their feminine space, yet doing so is not easy to accomplish.

Additionally, certain qualities, when demonstrated in women, become received and interpreted as negative, yet those same qualities in a man are celebrated and acceptable. A woman in authority who exhibits confidence and assertiveness may be perceived as arrogant or abrasive, and a woman who displays a caring attitude may be perceived as emotional or soft. As women attempt to navigate organizational life, settle into their cultural environment, and advance into more senior-level roles, the double bind creates an uncomfortable workplace climate for women (Eagly, 2007).

Women also face a trade-off between being perceived as competent or likeable. Research has suggested that women are less liked by their colleagues and peers when they are successful and display high levels of competence (Ely et al., 2011; Turner, 2012). Conversely, when women conform to feminine stereotypes and behave in ways that are consistent with expectations, they are liked, but not well-respected (Heilman, Wallen, Fuchs, & Tamkins, 2004; Rudman & Glick, 2001).

The WLA presents the reality of the gender bias in order to create realistic awareness about the climate women must exist within. In many ways, doing so gives women the permission to express the struggles they have historically faced as they have attempted to take up their authority when working in a male-normed culture. Once women have permission to own and acknowledge the still-pervasive gender bias, they can begin to move forward in their leadership practice, developing themselves to their highest capacity both in roles of authority and with their exercise of leadership.

## INTEGRATING THE FEMININE AND MASCULINE

The focus of much of the literature around women and leadership highlights gender differences in leadership styles (Bass, 1981; Chemers, 1997; Eagly & Johnson, 1990; Loden, 1985; Rosener, 1990) and suggests that the female way of leading, or women's style of leadership, might be even more effective than traditional male styles (Eagly, Karau, & Makhijani, 1995; Helgesen, 1990; Lipman-Blumen, 1992). Numerous studies, blogs, and articles have continually highlighted a gender difference in leadership style, claiming that feminine leadership appears one way and masculine leadership appears another way. Women, as the feminine, struggle when attempting to take up authority and exercise leadership in an organizational climate that values masculine expression (Ely et al., 2011). When faced with gender bias and leadership double standards, women are left unclear as to the best way to express themselves, both verbally and nonverbally, as they work to engage in effective leadership behaviors. Some women claim that they feel the need to lead like a man, while others hold to their feminine self, only to be received negatively among colleagues (Kellerman & Rhode, 2007). In summary, with leadership often thought about as a masculinized concept that is associated with being decisive, assertive, and independent (Ely et al., 2011), many women struggle with finding their own leadership style.

Women's leadership development programs must determine how they will frame and present the discussion around leadership style and consider how women will begin to build their own leadership skills. Within the WLA, the discussion about gendered leadership styles is considered to be detrimental to women's leadership development. In short, suggesting that men lead one way and women lead another creates a dichotomous view of leadership expression that does not allow for a more robust and dynamic presentation of leadership behavior and practice.

While certain masculine and feminine traits (Gerzema & D'Antonio, 2013) are assigned to men and women, respectively, and while individuals may be predisposed to one or the other, both men and women have the capacity to embody both the masculine and feminine. The expression of gender is socially constructed and men and women learn early on what behaviors are acceptably aligned with their gender (Lorber, 2010; Lorber & Farrell, 1990). When we examine this social construction through the lens of a masculinized concept of leadership, it becomes clear that women would struggle in expressing feminine behaviors while trying to find success in the masculine environment that defines leadership. In many cases, women report feeling fraudulent and inauthentic when they abandon their feminine self in the effort to lead like a man and fit in with their organizational culture (Kellerman & Rhode, 2007; Sandberg, 2012).

The fraudulent feeling women experience is largely due to the masculine-dominated culture of organizations, higher education included. Ironically, while the masculine, capitalistic model continues to define organizations, scholars and practitioners have suggested a need for a paradigm shift in how organizations are viewed as being successful, moving away from a focus on finance and the bottom line and toward a mission of sustainability that responsibly values human and social capital. For this shift to occur, leadership will require openness, value care, and relationships, and people must be receptive to new ways of thinking (Hirschhorn, 1998; Senge, Scharmer, Jaworski, & Flowers, 2004), all qualities that have been credited to feminine ways of practicing leadership (Eagly & Johnson, 1990).

The challenge facing women's leadership development programs is to help participants explore and find their authentic self, while embracing and developing the capacity to exercise leadership from both a feminine and masculine expression. This requires avoiding the dichotomy of *either* masculine *or* feminine style, and moving toward an inclusive style that embraces both. Research in the area of women's leadership that continues to suggest and promote a gender difference in leadership style is asking the wrong question. Rather than asking how women lead differently than men, we need to be asking how women can lead comfortably from their authentic feminine self while also developing the capacity to engage in masculine-type actions when needed. Women need to move away from becoming someone they are not and move toward accepting who they are and developing the capacity of the other. The beneficial end result involves existing from a synergistic space where both the feminine and the masculine exist harmoniously within each individual.

The WLA aims to promote a balanced or integrated approach of masculine and feminine ways of expressing leadership style. The programs teach women that they must honor and align the feminine self that exists at the core of their being female with the needed masculine behaviors that also exist within every woman. For a woman to become a working member of the team, especially in a male-dominated environment, she must exhibit masculine competencies and use those competencies to connect with her male colleagues. Ideally, a woman would have both the freedom and self-confidence to do this while staying grounded in her feminine self. If a woman abandons her feminine self, she will be ineffective in her efforts and feel discomfort in trying to fake a masculine identity that does not belong to her. In order for women to authentically operate with a masculine expression, they must hold true to the feminine self, finding a harmonious balance between the two. When women attempt to be part of the masculine world within organizations without building up a strong feminine core, the woman's masculine actions end up as a compensation for her sense of self that is not developed. In this way, women might feel or be perceived as an imposter. By adopting a lead-like-a-man approach without embracing her feminine self, a woman risks abdicating from her true self and, in doing so, cannot exercise leadership with knowing and conviction.

Women's leadership theory has spent too much time criticizing the masculine nature of organization life and not enough time promoting women's ability to exist within, and express, multiple ways of being and doing. Finding a feminine and masculine balance does not assign certain leadership styles as either masculine or feminine; rather, it encourages women to own the core feminine expression and exist from that place, while being able to engage in the expression of the masculine when necessary. In doing this, a woman can exercise leadership authentically, feeling comfortable in who she is and in the skill set available to her at any given time.

The WLA programs explore the blending of leadership characteristics and finding a feminine and masculine balance with participants by challenging the women to reflect upon, consider, and acknowledge the thoughts, feelings, and expressions of their feminine and masculine selves. This is done through journaling, group work, and supported discussions. After establishing this individual perspective, the participants move on to exploring leadership through the lens of group dynamics.

## GROUP DYNAMICS METHODOLOGY

A central method utilized by the WLA at the University of San Diego is a unique and innovative methodology that is based on group dynamics theory. The purpose of utilizing this theory is to help participants learn how to work with emotion and knowledge, while understanding the changing and complex circumstances that impact how groups and organizations learn, work together, and develop. At the core of this theoretical lens is the assumption that group processes influence and drive individual behavior. As discussed above, the WLA programs operate with an assumption that gender creates a dynamic context within organizations for both men and women, that women have to face issues of gender bias, and that they must strive to balance masculine and feminine approaches to leadership. Additionally, women must work toward taking up their authority and engaging in a leadership practice within their departments, all of this occurring in an environment with many moving parts. The group dynamics theory perspective honors the intensity of the process that women experience; as such, group dynamics is a useful method for developing women's leadership.

The approach of teaching and developing leadership using a group dynamics approach is one of the unique ways the WLA engages in developing leaders. Few programs at other universities use this pedagogical method, which is common across the offerings of the University of San Diego's Department of Leadership Studies. Two key components that are critical to the success of this methodology are described in the following sections: group-as-whole theory and case-in-point perspective.

### Group-As-A-Whole Theory

Group-as-a-whole processes examine how a group member is related to the larger organization and how, when in groups, people behave on behalf of group or parts of the group; in other words, the actions of individuals are viewed as a product of the group's own life and mentality (Wells, 1985). This perspective is helpful for women attempting to understand their place within the group, as well as to gain a better understanding of their own behaviors, thought patterns, and interactions. When a woman has a clear understanding of the larger system or group, she is more aware of how to engage with others and, as such, gets clarity around how to best take up her authority and exercise leadership. Because of the many dynamics that a woman faces within a department or organization, having a sense of the big picture, or the group-as-a-whole, helps situate her within that group and may provide clues for leadership practice. An understanding of the elements of group-as-a-whole can help a woman navigate the complexities of her authority role.

In the role of authority and when exercising leadership to make lasting change, the individual involved has to be aware of subgroup and inter-group processes. For example, as a department head or dean, a woman must be aware of multiple elements with the department. At any time, her attention might be focused on one particular situation or subgroup; however, doing so does not mean the other groups cease to exist. In fact, group processes operate similar to radio stations—each is always operational. A person being tuned into 103.7 does not mean that 93.3 is not simultaneously broadcasting; rather, simply that one has chosen to focus on and amplify another station (Wells, 1985). Because these processes constantly occur within group life, members of the organization, especially those in authority roles, must decide which issues to give attention. In this way, a woman can use her power and authority to help direct her attention toward the processes viewed to be most necessary.

Taking a group-as-a-whole perspective also involves making certain assumptions that explain how individuals behave when in a group. Specifically, the theory maintains that people rely on certain defense mechanisms to deal with the tensions that exist from group participation (Gillette & McCollom, 1995). Because of the gender bias, women might feel overly defensive when engaging in certain situations. One example of this is *projection*, a defense mechanism by which individuals separate parts of themselves and project those parts onto another person (Wells, 1985). According to Wells (1985), projection is a defense mechanism that allows people to manage the anxiety that comes from wanting to hold onto what is good and let go of what is bad. For example, a woman might react with contempt and resentment toward another person who constantly speaks out in the group, viewing the speaker as arrogant or overly dominant. However, the woman may be reacting to her own unrecognized desire to speak out in the group or her own tendency to dominate in other situations. While projection serves as a method for reconciling tensions between good and bad, it also provides a basis for individuals to empathize and identify with each other (Wells, 1985). Helping women understand their projections and their manifestations in actions and behaviors is part of developing their ability to exercise leadership effectively. It is these deeper processes that women need to explore and better understand as they establish their leadership identity and increase their capacity to take up their authority, advance within the organization, and exercise leadership.

One critically important element of group-as-a-whole theory is the belief that unconscious processes drive individual behavior and create the group life (Gillette & McCollom, 1995). The theory asserts that many individual actions are based on unconscious assumptions, judgments, valences, and thought patterns. When working to develop women leaders using the group-as-a-whole perspective, one challenge is to uncover some of the unconscious patterns that dictate group identity and effectiveness. In the WLA's programs, the women attempt the difficult task of becoming more aware of the unconscious processes going on within them as well as parallel and simultaneous processes occurring within the other members of their group. The women are encouraged to reflect deeply on their own thoughts and reactions to discover ways to manage the tensions, resentments, and interpersonal issues that often disrupt group effectiveness. In owning those innermost thoughts and patterns, a woman can begin to construct herself into an authentically empowered individual who takes up her authority and engages with others in a way that facilitates leadership.

## Case-in-Point Methodology

One method for working with the group-as-a-whole theoretical lens is to incorporate case-in-point methodology (Daloz-Parks, 2005). This approach allows the women to use themselves, the other participants, and the teaching staff as a case study for examining real-life group dynamics. With this method, the feelings, experiences, and situations are genuine and current, creating an environment that is ripe for learning about the exercise of leadership. Within the WLA programming, the case-in-point pedagogical approach is used not only to help participants learn about leadership but also to provide opportunities to practice leadership within a contained and supported environment. With the scaffolding of the faculty and facilitators, women can take risks, challenge their comfort level, and explore the edge of their leadership self.

## Case-In-Point Methodology

Case-in-point methodology requires an ability to work in the here-and-now, connecting real-time behavior to the larger purpose of the leadership development program. This approach requires presence and awareness of actions, thoughts, and behaviors in real time. When working with case-in-point methodology, the members of the system attempt to study their own behavior as it unfolds. One goal of this methodology is to make issues related to leadership more alive so the learning experience becomes real, involving cognitive and emotional integration (Cox, 2007). This in-the-moment learning experience is a critical one for women who often have not had opportunities to practice leadership and experiment with how they take up their authority and engage with the group. Essentially, case-in-point learning assumes that the learning workshop or conference environment replicates and mirrors the functions of work systems and outside organizations, and that the learning environment can be used to create similar dynamics to what happens in the real world, allowing participants to practice exercising leadership. While this approach is both innovative and unique to learning about leadership, it comes with some risks—one being that the women may be resistant to the disequilibrium and vulnerability that results from their own behavior being used as learning material. Because this method is atypical from what women have experienced or come to expect from professional development programs, it is important that the learning environment is supported and guided by experienced facilitators.

In order to practice case-in-point teaching and learning, the individual involved with various situations must navigate back and forth from the dance floor to the balcony, to use a metaphor developed by Heifetz (1994). The leadership strategy of getting to the balcony is useful to understand both case-in-point methodology and working with the here-and-now. Assessing a situation from a balcony view allows a person to gain a perspective that includes the entire situation, not just the limited personal perspective from which many people operate. Being on the balcony requires a person to leave the *dance floor* (the action) and reflect on what might be happening from a more holistic perspective (Heifetz, 1994). This practice becomes difficult because, to exercise leadership, a person must balance simultaneously being on the dance floor with being on the balcony. This reflection-in-action (Schon, 1983) is an important skill for taking up authority and exercising leadership that is emphasized in the WLA programs in order to improve leadership capacity. Being able to apply reflection-in-action and move from the dance floor to the balcony is especially helpful for women in authority facing difficult problems that require leadership. The balcony perspective, which provides a big-picture perspective, can also aid women in acknowledging the gender biases that might be creating subtle obstacles as they take up their roles.

Just as in real-life situations, interactions on a dance floor may be fast and constantly moving or sometimes slow and calculated; however, the task for the women is to recognize patterns and analyze how the patterns affect the larger system and the overall purpose. The challenge becomes working in the here-and-now and staying tuned in to everything going on—both within the self and within the larger systemic setting. Creating a leadership development program in this manner creates a laboratory-like environment that provides the opportunity for women to experience the dynamic environment that they will face in their professional roles.

The balance between the balcony and the dance floor and developing the skill of reflection-in-action is a requirement of working in the here-and-now. Being able to reflect on and analyze processes in the present moment contributes to more thoughtful action that might better serve the group's purpose or address the problem that has arisen. In order to engage in this reflective and analytical process, the leader needs to be constantly present and able to interpret and reflect upon the system—both what is occurring and what is not occurring. Often, even those experienced with leadership remain on the balcony or dance floor for too long. Those staying on the balcony observe, attempting to reflect on others' actions and analyze the situation without ever taking the risk of getting involved. Those who become lost in the dance continue to make comments and interventions without ever taking the time to stop and reflect. Providing room to practice removing oneself, especially when situations get heated, is an important skill; being able to pull back and consider what might be going on allows for better assessment and understanding of complex situations (Daloz-Parks, 2005). Because women need this skill in the real-life application of their authority roles and leadership practice, the WLA programs create an environment that simulates that dynamic.

## THE LANGUAGE OF LEADERSHIP

Most of the concepts and ideas presented through WLA programs are new for the participants. The ideas and topics are framed in a way that introduces concepts in innovative and fresh ways. The result of this is a new language of leadership, a new way of framing and understanding the leadership process. Research suggests that women's leadership development must include establishing a leadership identity, understanding the concepts of leadership, and improving upon the skills necessary to exercise leadership effectively (Ely et al., 2011). To do this, women must have a leadership language that is used to make sense of the concepts, engage with others, and create shared meaning among people. Very specific terms are associated with the model and philosophy on which the WLA is based. The importance of the leadership/authority distinction was made earlier in this chapter. One element of that distinction involves the tasks and challenges that face a person, group, or organization. Leadership deals with adaptive challenges—problems that have no known solution and often require a change in value or attitude to successfully address (Heifetz, 1994). Authority, on the other hand, deals with technical problems—problems that have a routine or procedural solution. While those in authority are positioned to exercise leadership and address adaptive challenges, they do not always do so (Heifetz, 1994). According to Heifetz and Linsky (2002), one of the most common sources of leadership failures is the tendency to treat adaptive challenges as technical problems and use routine or procedural methods to address them. In the WLA programs, the women are introduced to these terms and encouraged to use them to explain and understand their own experiences and leadership challenges.

In addition to the broader concepts of technical and adaptive leadership, certain metaphors are a part of the leadership language and identify feelings, emotions, and system dynamics. These metaphors help create a picture and an association that can make analysis more clear or tangible. Just as the glass ceiling or labyrinth are common metaphors to describe women's experience in advancing through organizations (Eagly, 2007), metaphors can help frame and make meaning out of an experience. For example, a pressure cooker can be used to represent the system or group as a container, also representing the varying levels of heat that may exist at any point and time. Because systems can only take a certain amount of heat, part of exercising leadership is the ability to detect when the heat in the pressure cooker is too high and then to reduce the heat (i.e., manage the stress before an explosion occurs). Alternatively, too little heat, or no heat at all, might signify work avoidance, given that some level of heat accompanies most adaptive challenges (Daloz-Parks, 2005).

Two other metaphors commonly used to understand the experiences of exercising leadership are the harp and the barometer (Daloz-Parks, 2005). A harp represents a person's own tuning. Certain topics, issues, conversations, or people may pluck an individual's harp strings and make that person feel anxious or come alive. This response is often a clue that an issue is significant within us or that we feel connected to a topic of conversation. Feeling the harp strings become plucked may be a sign to intervene and get on the dance floor. Similarly, a barometer is an instrument that measures pressure in the atmosphere. Like the harp, using the self as a barometer can indicate appropriate times to intervene and speak up (Cox, 2007). This skill of using the self as an instrument requires a commitment and willingness for introspection and personal scrutiny. In addition, an intense connection to the experience of the group is demanded, yet also a simultaneous separation in order to be connected equally to the self (Smith, 1995). Those best at leadership demonstrate a knowing of both the self and the larger group. As the participants in WLA programs develop an ability to take up their authority and exercise leadership, they also face the difficult task of being aware of their harp strings and being able to use their selves as an instrument, two assignments that require much mental focus and organizational awareness.

Another word that is commonly used to reflect a powerful group dynamic and function of leadership is *holding* (Cox, 2007). Sometimes a person will be said to be holding something for the group. Group dynamics theory claims that a particular person *holds* an issue or an emotion on behalf of the rest of the group. For example, White women often hold the need to be nice or polite regardless of their feelings of anger or resentment. Recognizing what a person may be holding is important, because the issues people hold influence how they interact with the group and how the group receives them. Often, an important issue or dynamic will be held by a person due, in part, to other people's unwillingness to take up the issue or own their part in the issue. These dynamics affect the group's overall effectiveness and can often derail organizations from achieving their purposes. Understanding both the subtlety and the complexity of how individuals hold an issue on behalf of the group is important for exercising effective leadership.

## CONCLUSION

In order to increase women's leadership capacity and prepare women to advance into senior roles, as well as to find success and fulfillment in the roles they currently occupy, programs aimed at developing women leaders should integrate a multifaceted approach that blends leadership and gender theory. In order to keep the participants engaged and provide them with relevant and useful content, programs need to incorporate innovative methods for teaching leadership. Women must understand that the exercise of leadership is distinct from a role of authority, and while women may be underrepresented in the highest roles, women can certainly exercise leadership and create positive, lasting change from within their current and future positions. In order to improve upon leadership ability, women need to engage in the deeper and more dynamic work of exploring the self while learning about the larger systems found within groups and organizations. Additionally, women need to find their own leadership identity by existing from their feminine core while developing their ability for masculine expression.

The WLA at the University of San Diego has created a series of programs around women's leadership development that address the issues most relevant to women's leadership, while using uniquely innovative methods to train women to fulfill their leadership potential. At the WLA, women engage in exercises and activities that provide opportunities to practice the skills that are most difficult for women leaders—navigating through the prevalent gender biases, expressing themselves with synergistic feminine and masculine styles of leadership, and creating a leadership identity while managing the complexities of the dynamic environment.

Women must learn new leadership skills and practice them simultaneously, recognizing that leadership development is an ongoing process.

## REFERENCES

Aleman, A. M., & Renn, K. A. (2002). *Women in higher education: An encyclopedia*. Santa Barbara, CA: ABC-CLIO.

Bass, B. M. (1981). Women and leadership. In R. Stogdill (Ed.), *Handbook of leadership: A survey of theory and research* (2nd ed.). New York, NY: Free Press.

Catalyst Knowledge Center. (2007). *The double-bind dilemma for women in leadership: Damned if you do, doomed if you don't*. Retrieved from http://www.catalyst.org/knowledge/double-bind-dilemma-women-leadership-damned-if-you-do-doomed-if-you-dont-0

Chemers, M. (1997). *An integrative theory of leadership*. Mahwah, NJ: Erlbaum.

Cox, D. W. (2007, Summer). Leadership education using case-in-point teaching. *Academic Exchange Quarterly, 154–158.*

Daloz-Parks, S. (2005). *Leadership can be taught: A bold approach for a complex world*. Boston, MA: Harvard Business School Press.

DiGeorgio-Lutz, J. (Eds.). (2002). *Women in higher education: Empowering change*. Westport, CT: Praeger.

Eagly, A. H. (2007). Overcoming resistance to women leaders. In B. Kellerman & D. L. Rhode, (Eds.), *Women and leadership: The state of play and strategies for change* (pp. 127–148). San Francisco, CA: Jossey-Bass.

Eagly, A. H., & Johnson, B. T. (1990). Gender and leadership style: A meta-analysis. *Psychological Bulletin, 108*(2), 233–256.

Eagly, A. H., Karau, S. J., & Makhijani, M. G. (1995). Gender and the effectiveness of leaders: A meta-analysis. *Psychological Bulletin, 117*(1), 125–145.

Ely, R. J., Ibarra, H., & Kolb, D. M. (2011). Taking gender into account: Theory and design for women's leadership development programs. *Academy of Management Learning & Education, 10*(3), 474–493.

Ely, R. J., & Meyerson, D. E. (2000). Theories of gender: A new approach to organization analysis and change. *Research in Organizational Behavior, 22*, 103–153.

Freeman, S. J., Bourque, S. C., & Shelton, C. M. (Eds.). (2001). *Women on power: Leadership redefined*. Lillington, NC: Northeastern University Press.

Gerzema, J., & D'Antonio, M. (2013). *The Athena doctrine: How women (and the men who think like them) will rule the future*. San Francisco, CA: Jossey-Bass.

Gillette, J., & McCollom, M. (Eds.). (1995). *Groups in context: A new perspective on group dynamics*. Lanham, Maryland: University Press of America.

Heifetz, R. (1994). *Leadership without easy answers*. Boston, MA: Harvard Business School Press.

Heifetz, R. A., & Linsky, M. (2002). *Leadership on the line: Staying alive through the dangers of leading*. Boston, MA: Harvard Business School Press.

Heilman, M. E., Wallen, A. S., Fuchs, D., & Tamkins, M. M. (2004). Penalties for success: Reactions to women who succeed at male gender-type tasks. *Journal of Applied Psychology, 89*(3), 416–427.

Helgesen, S. (1990). *The female advantage: Women's ways of leadership*. New York, NY: Doubleday/Currency.

Hirschhorn, L. (1998). *Reworking authority: Leading and following in the post-modern organization*. Cambridge, MA: MIT Press.

Ibarra, H., Ely, R., & Kolb, D. (2013). Women rising: The unseen barriers. *Harvard Business Review, 91*(9), 61–66.

Kellerman, B. & Rhode, D. L. (Eds.). (2007). *Women and leadership: The state of play and strategies for change*. San Francisco, CA: Jossey-Bass.

Kolb, D. M., & McGinn, K. (2009). Beyond gender and negotiation to gendered negotiation. *Negotiation and Conflict Management Research, 2*(1), 1–16.

Kotter, J. (2001, December). What leaders and managers really do. *Best of Harvard Business Review*, 3–11.

Lipman-Blumen, J. (1992). Connective leadership: Female leadership styles in the 21st century workplace. *Sociological Perspectives, 35*(1), 183–203.

Loden, M. (1985). *Feminine leadership or how to succeed in business without being one of the boys*. New York, NY: Times Books.

Lorber, J. (2010). *Gender inequality: Feminist theories and politics*. New York, NY: Oxford University Press.

Lorber, J., & Farrell, S. A. (Eds.). (1990). *The social construction of gender*. Thousand Oaks, CA: Sage.

Miller, J. B. (1982). *Women and power. (Work-in-progress)*. Stone Center for Developmental Services and Studies, Wellesley College, Wellesley, MA.

Monroe, T. (2004). Boundaries and authority. In G. R. Goethals, G. J. Sorenson, & J. M. Burns, (Eds.) *Encyclopedia of leadership* (pp. 112–117). Thousand Oaks, CA: Sage.

Rosener, J. (1990). Ways women lead. *Harvard Business Review, 68*(6), 119–125.

Rudman, L., & Glick, P. (2001). Prescriptive gender stereotypes and backlash toward agentic women. *Journal of Social Issues, 57*(4), 743–762.

Sandberg, S. (2012). *Lean in: Women, work, and the will to lead*. New York, NY: Random House.

Schon, D. (1983). *The reflective practitioner: How professionals think in action*. New York, NY: Basic Books.

Senge, P., Scharmer, C. O., Jaworski, J., & Flowers, B. S. (2004). *Presence: An exploration of profound change in people, organizations, and society*. New York. NY: Doubleday.

Smith, K. K. (1995). On using the self as instrument: Lessons from a facilitator's experience. In J. Gillette & M. McCollom (Eds.), *Groups in context* (pp. 113–136). Lanham, MD: University Press of America.

Sulpizio, L. (2010). *Women and authority: Transitioning into a role of authority in a graduate level leadership class* (Doctoral dissertation). Retrieved from Dissertation Abstracts International. (3399838)

Turner, C. (2012). *Difference works*. Austin, TX: Live Oak Book.

Wells, L. (1985). The group-as-a-whole perspective and its theoretical roots. In A. D. Colman & M. H. Gellar (Eds.), *Group relations reader 2* (pp. 109–126). Florida: A. K. Rice.

# PART III

## WOMEN'S EXPERIENCES AND CONTRIBUTIONS IN HIGHER EDUCATION LEADERSHIP

# CHAPTER 7

# WOMEN'S CONTRIBUTIONS TO HIGHER EDUCATION LEADERSHIP AND THE ROAD AHEAD

**Adrianna Kezar**

> What do 20th century missionary Gladys Aylward, contemporary Bible teacher Joyce Meyer, former president and CEO of eBay, Meg Whitman, and the 2004 Nobel Peace Prize recipient Dr. Wangari Matthai have in common? They are all women who brought their personal passions, convictions, energies, and strength to their innovative efforts in the exercise of leadership. (Chandler, 2011, p. 1)

In recent years there has been a revolution in the way leadership is conceptualized and practiced. One of the main reasons for this shift is greater recognition of women's leadership, which previously was evident more often at the grassroots level. In addition, women moved into positions of authority, which are often associated with leadership. In the past, traditional notions of leadership based on hierarchy, acting alone, often through mandated or top-down power and influence strategies, served as both the model and enactment of leadership (Kezar, Carducci, & Contreras-McGavin, 2006). However, today's images of leaders emphasize collaboration, with leaders acting collectively in concert with others (Allan & Cherrey, 2000). Images of leadership reflect mutual

*Women and Leadership in Higher Education*, pp. 117–134

power and influence processes, attention to relationships and tasks, and democratic and participatory forms of decision making (Eagly & Johannesen-Schmidt, 2001; Gerzema & D'Antonio, 2013). Leadership is focused more on ethics and values than in past eras (Chandler, 2011). All of these changes have been shaped by research on women's leadership. While many have called this collective set of characteristics *women's ways of leading*, I see it as women's contribution to the practice of leadership. One of the major contributions of women leaders and their practice is a fundamental rethinking of what leadership is as a phenomenon and how effective leadership can be enacted. And increasingly, the approaches to leadership assumed by women are being seen as beneficial. For example, transformational leadership, which has been identified as one of the most successful forms of leadership, is practiced more frequently by women leaders (Chandler, 2011). Many of the other characteristics associated with women's leadership—the development of followers, strong interpersonal relationships, participative decision-making—have also been associated with more effective leadership (Melero, 2011). And the good news is that studies of the next generation of leaders demonstrate that they think about leadership differently from the past, with both men and women claiming that collaboration, relationship-building, partnering, ethics, communication, inclusion, and innovation are the most important qualities of leadership (Gerzema & D'Antonio, 2013; Penney & Neilson, 2010).

Despite acknowledgement by scholars that women have a different conceptualization of leadership, women leaders cannot enact their preferred leadership due to organizational and environmental constraints (Fine, 2009; Melero, 2011). Self-report studies of women's views of leadership sometimes do not match studies of their leadership behaviors. In other words, they view leadership in stereotypically female ways, but enact it in stereotypically male ways. This demonstrates that women often enact leadership in more traditional ways and similar to those reported by men, particularly studies from 1980–2000 (as summarized in Kezar et al., 2006). For many decades woman have had to negotiate their more collaborative and nonhierarchical beliefs and values with the reality of their organizations. However, it is important to note that the most recent studies of workplaces where women are present in leadership positions have found women leaders to be more willing to operate differently (e.g., using teams more, having more open communication, more employee participation in decision making, and more development of employees), as reported by Melero (2011).

In this chapter, I first outline the many contributions that women have made to leadership conceptualizations and practice—both in general and in higher education in particular. In the second half of the chapter, I examine the changing environment and global economy marked by increased competition and the marketization and corporatization of campus practices, which favors the traditional directive, top-down forms of leadership. While women have made great contributions to leadership, they are increasingly in an environment that does not favor the important approaches to leadership that they can bring. In short, although women's approaches to leadership are needed more than ever, I suggest that to be successful in this environment, women may need to implement a hybrid form of leadership that integrates the best of what women have brought to leadership, but blend it with strategies that have also been associated with men's leadership to be successful on today's campuses. This suggestion is similar to Jean Lipman-Blumen's (1996) proposed model of connective leadership and earlier work on androgynous leadership (Korabik, 1990; Park 1997; Powell & Butterfield, 1989; Roseman, 1986) noting that the most successful leaders are often those that combine stereotypically male and female approaches to leadership. Also, as we have seen from prior research, despite women having bold and new conceptualizations of leadership, they are often constrained in the ways they can enact this leadership. Furthering this concern about being able to enact women's preferred approach to leadership, we need to examine the current global economic context and the way it may impinge on how women practice their leadership (Fine, 2009).

Throughout the chapter, I will refer to women leaders or leadership as a term referencing research on women leaders. However, I do not mean to imply that all women leaders act in the same ways, but am referring instead to trends in some literature related to the ways women have approached leadership that have been documented in some studies. There are many women who utilize and enact traditional, hierarchical conceptualizations of leadership and some who blend the two approaches. There are others who act in ways that defy any of the commonly described forms of leadership. Thus, when I refer to women, I am speaking of a particular genre of studies and not trying to apply this to all women leaders. In addition, not all men utilize the practices of traditional forms of leadership and many practice forms of leadership described as the new contributions (e.g., collaboration or nonhierarchical) provided by women leaders. My goal is not to stereotype how various forms of leaders act, but to demonstrate new directions that have come into our current thinking about, and proven practices for, successful leadership. In fact, stereotyping of qualities associated with men and women only limits the approaches they can use in leadership and has typically negatively impacted women. Specifically, when women did not act in gender-defined ways, they may be looked at negatively by coworkers (Chandler, 2011).

## WOMEN'S CONTRIBUTION TO
## LEADERSHIP CONCEPTUALIZATION AND PRACTICE

While not exhaustive, this section attempts to describe some of the key areas where women's leadership has expanded our understanding of successful ways to lead or be part of a leadership process. I start most sections with a quote from the book *Woman at the Top*, which profiles women college presidents, describing their leadership approaches. The following are the main areas women have contributed to leadership: participatory decision-making, shared or team approach, collaboration, relational and inclusiveness orientation, harnessing multiple perspectives, empowerment, development/learning, inclusive, ethics, integrity, and common purpose. Many of these characteristics are related and overlap; in fact, these characteristics have been combined into leadership models such as the social change model of leadership (Astin & Leland, 1991); the team model (Bensimon & Neumann, 1993); and shared leadership (Pearce & Conger, 2002). Others refer to this new approach often associated with women's leadership as the postindustrial leadership approach (Rost, 1993). While I discuss these qualities separately, the models just listed are also helpful articulations of the way that these characteristics can be combined and acted in unison.

### Consultation, Democratic, and Participative

> A great leader constantly listens for and to multiple sources of information. He or she asks, what does this tell me about my organization, its culture, and its working? (Wolverton, Bower, & Hyer, 2009, p. 105)

In meta-analyses of studies of women leaders, researchers have found women to engage in more democratic and participative rather than autocratic and directive forms of decision making and leadership (Eagly & Johannesen-Schmidt, 2001). Women leaders are more likely to ask for input on decisions and to include others in decision-making processes than men. Even the most recent studies continue to find consultation and democratic decision making as one of the most significant differences between the way men and women lead (Brown & Lightfoot, 2012). Women were also able to read the situation and understand when a more participatory leadership style was needed (Eagly & Johannesen-Schmidt, 2001; Gerzema & D'Antonio, 2013). As leaders, women tend to not only reach out for input but to listen more as part of the leadership process (Nielsen & Huse, 2010).

## Shared or Team Leadership

Building a team is probably one of the most important things a president does. (Wolverton et al., 2009, p. 2)

Many studies of women leaders note how they tend to lead groups or teams by using a shared approach, rather than being a single leader (Fine, 2009). In these studies, women speak about the importance of building a team, seeking consensus, and drawing on all points of view as important to successful leadership process (Fine, 2009; Wolverton et al., 2009). This collective orientation to leadership is thought to emerge from women's consultative emphasis demonstrated through their democratic approach to decision-making. This leadership approach has emerged as one of the most fundamental differences in the ways they lead from men (Chandler, 2011; Pearce & Conger, 2002). The notion of shared leadership is also associated with less hierarchy, top-down, and position-based notions of leadership. Instead, for many women, leadership is seen as the characteristic of anyone within the organization who has the desire to create change. Therefore, part of the leader's role is to identify and connect various individuals with the potential to lead and to help develop them and empower them; both dimensions are described more fully below (Pearce & Conger, 2002).

## Collaboration

My leadership philosophy is to promote collaboration and team building. (Wolverton et al., 2009, p. 91)

Because women leaders typically see leadership as a shared process comprising a team or group, they are more likely to focus on collaboration, networks, and partnering as important dimensions of leadership (Dahlvig & Longman, 2010; Ferren & Stanton, 2004). Collaboration is defined as people working together toward a shared purpose. Through studies of women leaders, leadership skills associated with successful collaboration have included frequent interaction with coworkers, inclusion of individuals in decision making, fostering healthy relationships, encouraging networking and partnerships, and actively creating alliances (Allan & Cherrey, 2000; Safarik, 2003). Collaboration inherently involves many different individuals and begins to make the unit of analysis for leadership broader and more complex. It also suggests that leadership is a process.

## Relational and Inclusiveness Emphasis to Leadership

> Leadership is about relationships; working with people, getting people to work with you, you simply cannot do it all. (Wolverton et al., 2009, p. 97)

Most studies of leadership demonstrate the importance of both a task and relational orientation (Northouse, 2013). Leaders need to create change, but they also need to build relationships to make change happen in meaningful ways. Men have strongly been identified with a task orientation to leadership, even as research study after research study identifies both task and relationship building as key to successful leadership. It is important to note that both men and women score well on relational and task emphasis when looking across a host of studies (Ayman & Korbik, 2010). However, women's contribution to leadership has been to demonstrate what a relationship-based form of leadership looks like and to draw on relationships to create even more successful approaches to leadership (Safarik, 2003). For example, Bensimon and Neumann (1993) found that women leaders helped identify interpersonal conflicts in groups, as well as mend them. Women were more likely to play the role of emotional monitor that is essential for strong team functioning and leadership process (Bensimon & Neumann, 1993). Women leaders try to create an environment of trust and have authentic caring for others that translate into greater commitment among coworkers and better organizational outcomes (Brown & Light, 2012).

Women's attention to relationships results in greater inclusiveness among members of the leadership team and groups as well as members of the organization in general. Women leaders typically engage in many important practices that build inclusiveness, such as inviting participation, listening, and encouraging feedback (Kezar et al., 2006). Studies of women leaders have also found that they use their interpersonal skills and relationships to motivate coworkers rather than depending upon the positional power or authority more commonly used by men (Chandler, 2011). Women leaders tend to emphasize communication more than males and focus on bidirectional communication in which they encourage their followers or colleagues to test their opinions and views (Fine, 2009). One of the four components of transformational leadership is individualized relationships with followers (Northouse, 2013), and women routinely score higher on transformational leadership as well as this subcomponent of individualized consideration (Fine, 2009). In summary, this fleshing out of relationships into a deeper construct that includes trust, listening, bidirectional communication, authentic caring, individualized attention, inclusiveness, emotional monitoring, and other items is extremely important as building strong interpersonal relationships has been associated with more successful leadership in terms of organizational performance (Melero, 2011).

## Harnessing Multiple Perspectives

I prefer to talk about it openly so we can learn from each other's perspectives, to ask—what do you see that I don't see? (Wolverton et al., 2009, p. 75)

The inclusive orientation of women also leads employees within organizations to be more likely to share their perspective openly, particularly perspectives that may be outside the norm or deviate from traditional views. Having multiple perspectives emerge within a leadership process and having these views be engaged toward decision making has been identified in several studies as being related to cognitive complexity (Briskin, 2011; Kezar et al., 2006). While women are consultative and seek out perspectives, they also strive to ensure that multiple perspectives are obtained. Cognitive complexity (i.e., thinking that utilizes multiple views) has been associated with better decision making and organizational outcomes (Bensimon & Neumann, 1993). An example of this phenomenon is a study of governing boards; boards with women (or more women) on them tend to have more open debate and review of alternatives, which results in stronger decision-making (Nielsen & Huse, 2010).

## Empowerment

I share power. I don't have a problem with someone else representing me in the community or the provost making the decision in my absence. (Wolverton et al., 2009, p. 46)

Various studies of women leaders have demonstrated that they encourage empowerment among those that they work with (Kezar et al., 2006; Safarik, 2003; Wolverton et al., 2009). Empowerment is defined as the practice of sharing power and enabling other organizational members to act on issues they feel are important and relevant (Kezar et al., 2006). Various theories of shared or distributed leadership suggest that empowerment is a central component to enacting this process well (Spillane, 2007). As soon as the leadership process becomes collective, those individuals who are delegated responsibility will be more successful if they have power in order to conduct the work that has been distributed to them. Because women leaders tend to think about leadership more commonly as a collective or team process, empowerment is a natural outcome of being successful with this type of leadership (Kezar et al., 2006).

Organizationally, empowerment is typically achieved by breaking down hierarchical structures that contain power within only certain groups that hold positional authority through the creation of teams and the delegation of authority. More recent studies examining shared and distributed leadership have found that these two models are more successful when leaders empower others and make sure that they have the skills and ability to exercise the power they have been given (Pearce & Conger, 2003), which hints at women's next contribution.

## Development and Learning

> I firmly believe that if I do other people's work, I undermine them and certainly don't help them to grow. I don't help them to become a vital part of the organization which comes with growth. (Wolverton et al., 2009, p. 91)

Women leaders tend to emphasize and support learning among the individuals they work with as a central part of the leadership process. Day (2001) documented how women leaders provided the knowledge, skills, and ability for others within the organization to lead. In addition, women also focused on building support for groups of leaders so they had the networks, partnerships, and social capital to be successful (Day, 2001). As noted previously, those empowered to lead will fail if they lack the skills needed to successfully move an initiative forward, whether it is budget analysis, planning, or data interpretation skills (Kezar et al., 2006). While the support and development of people within an organization has always been important within various leadership models, the learning was usually in service to a particular goal of the organization or the leader. Alternatively, in more recent studies of women leaders, learning is understood to involve ongoing support as part of the leadership process. Women leaders also tend to monitor employee feedback and development more intensely than men (Melero, 2011). Notably, helping coworkers to learn has been associated with more successful leadership in terms of organizational performance (Melero, 2011).

## Ethics

> I have layed out a framework of ethical action—respect, trust, optimism, and intentionality and I use it with colleagues and it becomes a mutual commitment. (Wolverton et al., 2009, p. 118)

As women have assumed leadership positions, ethical approaches to leadership have grown in significance in the last 30 years—beginning with servant leadership and continuing with transformational and authentic forms of leadership (Northouse, 2013). More recent conceptualizations influenced by women leaders suggest that leadership is inherently tied to ethics and that change outcomes that are not ethical (e.g., convincing people to commit genocide) would not be considered leadership. Ethical leadership is defined as an attempt to act from the principles, beliefs, and values embedded in the leader's espoused system of ethics (Kezar et al., 2006). Many earlier conceptualizations of leadership focused on accomplishing goals with little examination of the process, including whether it utilized ethical means and outcomes. For example, if the leader was able to restructure an organization, leaving a third of the workforce without positions but cutting costs, this was seen as a wholesale good without consideration of the impact of the workers. Various studies have shown that women are more likely to be whistleblowers about unethical practices in organizations and to speak out against unethical behavior within organizations (Chandler, 2013). Women leaders who engage in change processes that better ensure stakeholder input and transparency practice associated ethicality (Collier & Esteban, 1999). Women's focus on collaboration, participation, and teams are all aligned with practices found in studies to be perceived as more ethical processes.

## Integrity

> Integrity has to do with knowing yourself, knowing your personality, and being true to yourself. No one trusts you just because you are the president. (Wolverton et al., 2009, p. 96)

In Northouse's (2013) most recent book synthesizing research on leadership, integrity is identified as one of the characteristics that has consistently emerged as an important quality for leaders. Integrity, which is acting congruently with one's espoused beliefs, is also emphasized among women leaders (Komives, Lucas, & McMahon, 1998). Self-awareness and reflection are often associated with the ability for leaders to enact integrity in their role (Astin & Leland, 1991). Women engage in processes of self reflection and awareness more often than men and are therefore able to identify lapses in integrity and remedy them more quickly (Wolverton et al., 2009). Studies of women leaders also suggest that not only do they value integrity but that they consider ways to ensure that they embody integrity (Kezar et al., 2006).

## Common Purpose

> It gives me great pride to know that what was once an institution to prepare young Indian people for assimilation is now an institution of the federal

government that prepares young people to be leaders in indigenous self-determination. And that I played a role in its transformation. (Wolverton et al., 2009, p. 132)

In addition to an ethical commitment to leadership, another important component that women have brought to leadership is a sense of common purpose or collective good (Komives et al., 1998; Safarik, 2003). In past conceptualizations of leadership, leadership vision and agenda often emerged from the leader as an individual. In more recent conceptualizations that draw upon women's approach to leadership, however, women seek input from the community about a vision for change. In addition, women leaders are more likely to create leadership that is aimed toward the common purpose or collective vision (Astin & Leland, 1991). While many studies of leadership in recent years have emphasized shared vision, it is usually the leader trying to convince followers to be part of a leader's vision. Studies of women leaders demonstrate that they tend to consult others extensively before developing a vision, leave the vision open for change, and think more broadly about their leadership as serving a common purpose rather than personal advancement or gain (Astin & Leland, 1991; Chandler, 2011). Various studies have shown that women tend to see power as the ability to make community and people's lives better rather than for personal gain or vision fulfillment (Astin & Leland, 1991; Chandler, 2011). Some studies have also examined this issue of common purpose in relationship to important social changes that women have led such as abolitionist, women's rights, peace movements, and other social causes that serve a broader common and often ethical goal (Chandler, 2011; Kezar et al., 2006). In summary, women have imprinted leadership with many new important qualities. In the next section, I consider these qualities in a changing global context.

## LEADERSHIP IN A MARKET AND CORPORATE ENVIRONMENT

The upside of this rough-and-ready culture is that it's extremely entrepreneurial; there are no holds barred. You can move an agenda faster here than you can in most academic cultures. (Wolverton et al., 2009, p. 61)

As noted in the introduction, women's leadership is enacted in a world that is often dominated by traditional male approaches to leadership and organization. Therefore, women have to navigate their own leadership preferences (e.g., being collaborative) within a world of hierarchical and top-down organizations and structures. An international study that included a focus on the millennial generation documented that they tend to view women's approaches to leadership as being preferable in the workplace

(Gerzema & D'Antonio, 2013), yet typically not represented within the organizations they are entering. Some of the key disconnects leaders see is organizations lacking integrity, not focused on the common good, little inclusion, lacking social responsibility, minimal coaching and development, and no shared leadership/ collaboration (Airini et al., 2011; Sherry & Neilson, 2010). The up-and-coming leaders say that organizational structures do not support a humane, collaborative, and inclusive form of leadership. They express concern about the driving goal of profit making and the ways that organizations emphasize goals over people. The academy, as well as other organizations, has changed in ways that make it hard to honor and enact what we now know is a beneficial approach to leadership and even preferred by today's next generation of leaders.

I am not arguing that women should be overwhelmed by these forces, but they need to be aware of them, carefully navigate them, and be appropriately responsive to the realities of this new environment into their approach. This section discusses how to think about blending women's approaches and contributions within the changing landscape of leadership by utilizing the connective leadership framework (Lipman-Blumen, 1996).

Until the last decade, some of the values that characterized college environments reflected women's approaches to leadership. Participatory and consultative forms of shared governance aligned with women's interests in garnering input for decision making. Many of the characteristics that made up the professional system of faculty—such as a focus on collegiality, emphasizing the importance of relationships, lack of hierarchy, and a sense of equality among people—reflect women's leadership. The traditional mission of higher education that was focused on contributing to the public good aligned with women's focus on a common or collective good. Thus, many of the characteristics of the academic organization would seem a strong fit for women's leadership.[1]

Unfortunately, as women are beginning to enter positions of authority on college campuses, the environment is changing markedly and is becoming much more corporate and market-driven in orientation, moving away from collegial and shared approaches to leadership. The pressure to compete comes from the global economy in which a more capitalist orientation is seen as preferable and essential for success in the coming decades (Slaughter & Rhoads, 2004). This trend has been epitomized on campuses through what has been termed academic capitalism, in which universities prioritize revenue generation activities at the expense of other activities (Slaughter & Rhoads, 2004; Zemsky, 2009). An example of this more market-driven culture on campuses is the need for leaders to focus on entrepreneurial activities in order to maximize profits from research ventures through patents and licensing by creating partnerships with industry. Another example is developing curriculum for businesses in an effort to seek revenue. Campuses are increasingly focusing on pursuing profits through technology transfer and lucrative partnerships and are deemphasizing the liberal arts and public service once important for the common or public good (Kezar, Chambers, & Burkhardt, 2005; Slaughter & Rhoads, 2004).

In addition to the profit-seeking motivation, a more corporate or market approach to management and leadership has also been embraced (Kezar et al., 2005; Slaughter & Rhoads, 2004; Zemsky, 2009). Within this corporate approach, leaders are encouraged to centralize power; develop top-down authority structures; cut costs; use corporate management practices such as outsourcing, benchmarking and metrics, marketing, and public relations; and exercise business oriented forms of accountability focused on the bottom line. Over the last 20 years, various studies have found that campuses have begun to move away from shared governance and participatory decision making, instead emphasizing these business management practices (Kezar et al., 2005; Slaughter & Rhoads, 2004). Several trends in higher education also demonstrate these corporate or marketization strategies. The move to a largely contingent or non-tenure-track faculty with semester-to-semester appointments is one of the major results of a new approach to management within colleges and universities. Over 70% of the faculty are now off the tenure track (Kezar & Sam, 2010).

The move to create more distance education programs that can be offered cheaply, but at a high price that maximizes profitability, is another example of the move to marketized management strategy (Kezar et al., 2005; Slaughter & Rhoads, 2004). Offering international programs to attract more students is increasingly viewed as a way to compete in the global marketplace for students (Slaughter & Rhoads, 2004). Institutional budgets being used for non-mission-central activities such as athletics, auxiliary services, marketing, and branding have been demonstrated to create a drain on instructional budgets and other key mission areas (Delta Cost Project, 2013; Kezar et al., 2005; Slaughter & Rhoads, 2004). Women's leadership contributions (i.e., new conceptualization of leadership) and success needs to be considered within this changing landscape.

While this emerging landscape is shaping future women's leadership, recent studies of women leaders suggest that some are not recognizing how to best navigate these new market and corporate conditions (Fine, 2009; Isaac, Griffin, & Carnes, 2010). Studies of failed women leaders identify that they do not anticipate the pressures and politics from influential board members, administrators, and faculty who have a strong connection with this new competitive, market environment. As a result, these women leaders' agendas are sidelined, they become embattled, and are unable to move their changes forward (Fine, 2003; Wolverton et al., 2009).

Therefore, if we examine the pressures that women will experience to lead in top-down, hierarchical ways focused on the bottom line, it seems important to think about ways women can lead that blend the approaches that they have fostered (such as collaboration and ethics) with an understanding of ways to navigate and work within the increasingly traditional leadership environment. The new generation of leaders, studied by Penney and Neilson (2010), identified these disconnects between leaders' personal beliefs and the organizations into which they were entering as employees, but noted they had no way to navigate the struggle. We need to do more to help future leaders think about this emerging struggle. Fortunately, there is research that addresses this challenge, which is described next.

One leadership model that attempts to blend the best of women's leadership approaches with traditional approaches to leadership is the connective leadership model developed by Jean Lipman-Blumen (1996). Lipman-Blumen argued that leadership needed to embrace a more complex and multifaceted approach in the 21st century, which she labeled as connective. The connective era is characterized by the global economy and greater cross-cultural interaction, with contradictory tensions pulling us toward greater global interdependence but also fragmentation based on our diversity. At a time when values dissonance and polarization could lead to paralysis or operating sub-optimally, successful leaders can reconcile differences and work across values systems and seemingly irreconcilable complex domains. The connective leadership model requires a blending of the various skills and approaches (i.e., collaboration as well as hierarchy) that could be seen across the leadership literature—including the most recent studies of women leaders, but also in earlier studies of more traditional and political forms of leadership.

According to Lipman-Blumen (1996), connective leadership is focused on three main areas (see in Table 7.1): *relational* (collaborative, contributory, the vicarious/mentoring); *direct* (powered, competitive, intrinsic); and *instrumental* (empowers, networking, and persuasion). Within the *relational* facet, the leader use collaboration and a contributory style by helping others to learn and succeed. Vicarious is encouraging and guiding others, often through mentoring. Within the *direct* area, intrinsic means relying on oneself to complete work. Competition is being driven by external standards of excellence and seeing each activity as a contest or forum for achievement. Power relates to using power wisely to get things done. Under the *instrumental* facet, personal means being charismatic and being able to motivate. The social style means harnessing networks and partnerships to get things done, and entrusters build strong relationships that can be utilized for support.

### Table 7.1.   Areas of Connective Leadership

| Elements of Connective Leadership | Subareas | Overarching Purpose |
|---|---|---|
| Relational | Vicarious – mentors<br>Contributory – helps<br>Collaborative – joins forces | Contributes to others tasks |
| Directive | Intrinsic – excels<br>Competitive – outperforms<br>Power – takes charge | Masters own tasks |
| Instrumental | Entrusting – empowers<br>Social – networks<br>Personal – persuades | Maximizes interactions |

Together these nine areas support contributing to others tasks (relational), mastering one's own task (direct), and maximizing interactions (instrumental). Lipman-Blumen (1996) emphasizes that although the model includes many political-oriented behaviors, they are ethically-oriented toward community benefits. She also advocates a politics of commonality as an alternative to the politics of difference favored by traditional, divisive leaders. Connective leaders try to build community among diverse groups in order to create a sense of belonging. Lipman-Blumen regards connected leaders as authentic and accountable. The leadership process itself encourages the widest possible set of individuals to join the leadership process. The model is also contingent, suggesting that different leadership situations will require different forms or balances between these three areas. Lipman-Blumen also notes how connective leadership blends in the qualities of other meta-models such as transactional/transformational leadership but moves away from the focus on the individual leader characteristic of transformational leadership to leadership teams. Connective leaders can be anyone, not just those in positions of authority, and can involve groups, not just individuals. A leader might recognize that he or she is not good at the instrumental dimension but brings in other leaders to help contribute this skill set. Lipman-Blumen notes that the instrumental path tends to be used least by leaders but is critical for success in this new era.

While Lipman-Blumen's (1996) book offers much greater detail than can be provided in this chapter, the main point is that women might be best guided into the future with a model that helps them blend multiple approaches to address the complex environment in which they exist. Using connective leadership, women are better able to determine when they might need to use traditional approaches but also how to counteract and circumvent them with this knowledge. Connective leadership does not necessarily suggest operating in traditional ways (using a directive style, for example), but instead recognizing that various styles exist and knowing how to communicate with leaders using different styles. This knowledge and skill would help women address the politics and unanticipated reactions that can lead to their failure to identify and appreciate market and corporate approaches in earlier studies noted above (Fine, 2009). Connective leadership is also about navigating the tensions of diversity, which women can do better if they are harnessing multiple approaches and even, when necessary, those with which they may be less comfortable. Notably, Lipman-Blumen's model is not the only approach at blending; Bensimon and Neumann's (1993) team leadership also involves blending the traditionally male and female approaches to leading. However, none of these models identifies the conflicting forces that women will have to contend with, which I address in this next section.

Within the context of higher education, women leaders in the future need to be able to balance traditional academic values and the new market values. Women might be better able to maintain those qualities associated with traditional campus approaches such as shared governance, a mission aimed at the public good, sharing power, and getting broad stakeholder input—qualities declining on campus but critical to future success. As a result of their alignment with traditional academic values, women leaders might be more skeptical of unethical choices like moving to a contingent faculty, distance education options that may not meet the same academic standards, or pursing questionable international partnerships. It is important for women to provide support for these traditional values that are being dismantled and build more support before these structures and processes are fully lost (Kezar et al., 2005). Given the race to pursue questionable objectives, it is important for women to raise their voices to slow these changes and to be the conscience of the campus.

Yet, there are ways that market values can enhance thinking of academic leaders. The traditional values that often prevent meaningful curricular and service changes that are in the best interest of students need examination. For example, for-profit higher education institutions are attune to measuring student outcomes and employment. Nonprofit or traditional higher education institutions have been slow to articulate and measure student outcomes. Market values tend to provide more attention to the students' interests and concerns, which could be a useful ethic for higher education leaders to absorb. Students have long been expressing concern about affordability, access, support structures, classroom climate, and other issues, but academic leaders are slow to respond. For-profit higher education tends to very proactively collect data on students and understand support systems or counseling they might need. The advantage of collecting and routinely reviewing data is that changes can be made such as extending hours for advising, providing online options for registration, and more customer-service friendly approaches to campus functions. Campus leaders are also often slow to respond to community or external needs; they may not develop the partnerships needed to increase student access, success, and employment. This is another area where for-profit and more entrepreneurial campuses have been strategic in thinking about ways to reach out to others in support of students. While there are other examples, higher education can benefit from many of the more market-oriented and entrepreneurial values if they are used in service of student learning and the collective good. In order to follow some of these new paths, women may consider using Lipman-Blumen's (1996) instrumental and direct styles to prod action. Women leaders can once again trail blaze in this next era by modeling how to blend academic and market values, leading in versatile and diverse ways.

## CONCLUSION

Leadership is a social construction that has changed over time—at times it has been coercive, others charismatic, and yet others political or managerial. In the most recent times, women have been pivotal in reshaping the views we now hold about leadership. Women have reshaped leadership conceptualizations and practice to include collaboration, collective action, non-positional actors, participatory decision-making, cognitive complexity, empowerment, inclusiveness, integrity, ethics, common purpose, and vision. This change is truly revolutionary in the history of the phenomenon of leadership. As we move forward in changing times, more alterations are likely to emerge. As Lipman-Blumen (1996) predicted, we are living in an era when leadership requires a complex integration of many different approaches to leading, but emphasizes the best qualities out of these varying leadership approaches that have developed historically. For women who fought so hard to have new views of leadership embraced, blending in these other styles can feel threatening, problematic, or like selling out. Yet, I believe the future is best served by a leadership approach that embraces women's perspective but combines it with the best of other approaches that have emerged and that aligns with current pressures in our environment. Women seeking out differing leadership perspectives and showing the ability to navigate among various approaches will be pivotal to the success of higher education in the future.

## NOTE

1. However, it is important to note that women have experienced significant discrimination even as their skills were strongly aligned with academic values (Wolverton et al., 2009).

## REFERENCES

Airini, Collings, S., Conner, L., McPherson, K., Midson, B., & Wilson, C. (2011). Learning to be leaders in higher education: What helps or hinders women's advancement as leaders in universities. *Educational Management Administration & Leadership, 39*(1), 44–62.

Allan, K., & Cherrey, C. (2000). *Systemic leadership: Enriching the meaning of our work*. Lanham, MD: University Press of America.

Astin, H. S., & Leland, C. (1991). *Women of influence, women of vision*. San Francisco, CA: Jossey-Bass.

Ayman, R., & Korabik, K. (2010). Leadership: Why gender and culture matter. *American Psychologist, 65*(3), 157–170.

Bensimon, E. M., & Neumann, A. (1993). Redesigning collegiate leadership: Teams and teamwork in higher education. Baltimore, MD: Johns Hopkins University Press.

Briskin, L. (2011). Union renewal, postheroic leadership, and women's organizing: Crossing discourses, reframing debates. *Labor Studies Journal, 36*(4), 508–537.

Brown, S., & Light, R. L. (2012). Women's sport leadership styles as the result of interaction between feminine and masculine approaches. *Asia-Pacific Journal of Health, Sport and Physical Education, 3*(3), 185–198.

Chandler, D. (2011). What women bring to the exercise of leadership. *Journal of Strategic Leadership, 3*(2), 1–12.

Collier, J., & Esteban, R. (1999). Governance in the participative organisation: freedom, creativity and ethics. *Journal of Business Ethics, 21*(2–3), 173–188.

Dahlvig, J. E., & Longman, K. A. (2010). Women's leadership development: A study of defining moments. *Christian Higher Education, 9*(3), 238–258.

Day, D. V. (2001). Assessment of leadership outcomes. In S. J. Zaccaro & R. J. Klimoski (Eds.), *The nature of organizational leadership* (pp. 384–410). San Francisco, CA: Jossey-Bass.

Delta Cost Project. (2013). *College spending in a turbulent decade*. Delta Cost Project.

Eagly, A. H., & Johannesen-Schmidt, M. C. (2001). The leadership styles of women and men. *Journal of Social Issues, 57*(4), 781–797.

Ferren, A., & Stanton, W. (2004). *Leadership through collaboration*. Westport, CT: Greenwood Press.

Fine, M. G. (2009). Women leaders' discursive constructions of leadership. *Women's Studies in Communication, 32*(2), 180–202.

Gerzema, J., & D'Antonio, M. (2013). *The Athena Doctrine: How women (and the men who think like them) will rule the future*. San Francisco, CA: Jossey-Bass.

Isaac, C., Griffin, L., & Carnes, M. (2010). A qualitative study of faculty members' views of women chairs. *Journal of Women's Health, 19*(3), 533–546.

Kezar, A., Carducci, R., & Contreras McGavin, M. (2006). *Rethinking the "L" word in higher education: The revolution on research in leadership.* San Francisco, CA: Jossey-Bass.

Kezar, A., Chambers, T., & Burkhardt, J. (Eds.). (2005). *Higher education for the public good: Emerging voices from a national movement.* San Francisco, CA: Jossey-Bass.

Kezar, A., & Sam. C. (2010). *Understanding the new majority: Contingent faculty in higher education* (Vol. 1, ASHE Higher Education Report Series). San Francisco, CA: Jossey-Bass.

Komives, S., Lucas, N., & McMahon, T. (1998). *Exploring leadership: For college students that want to make a difference.* San Francisco, CA: Jossey-Bass.

Korabik, K. (1990). Androgyny and leadership style. *Journal of Business Ethics: Perspectives on Women in Management Research, 9*(4/5), 283–292.

Lipman-Blumen, J. (1996). *Connective leadership.* New York, NY: Oxford University Press.

Melero, E. (2011). Are workplaces with many women in management run differently? *Journal of Business Research, 64*(4), 385–393.

Nielsen, S., & Huse, M. (2010). The contribution of women on boards of directors: Going beyond the surface. *Corporate Governance: An International Review, 18*(2) 136–148.

Northouse, P. (2013). *Leadership: Theory and practice.* Thousand Oaks, CA: SAGE.

Park, D. (1997). Androgynous leadership style: An integration rather than a polarization. *Leadership & Organization Development Journal, 18*(3), 166–171.

Pearce, C., & Conger, J. (2002). *Shared leadership: The hows and whys.* Thousand Oaks, CA: SAGE.

Penney, S., & Neilson, P. (2010). *Next generation leadership: Insights from emerging leaders.* New York, NY: Palgrave Macmillan.

Powell, G. N., & Butterfield, D. A. (1989). The "good manager" did androgyny fare better in the 1980s? *Group & Organization Management, 14*(2), 216–233.

Roseman, E. (1986). The androgynous blend: Recipe for a perfect supervisor?. *MLO: medical laboratory observer, 18*(8), 46–48.

Rost, J. (1993). *Leadership for the 21st century.* Westport, CT: Greenwood.

Safarik, L. (2003). Feminist transformation in higher education: Discipline, structure, and institution. *The Review of Higher Education, 26*(4), 419–445.

Sherry, P., & Neilson, P. (1999). *Next generation leadership: Insights from emerging leaders.* New York, NY: Palgrave McMillan.

Slaughter, S., & Rhoads, G. (2004). *Academic capitalism.* Baltimore, MD: Johns Hopkins University Press.

Spillane, J. P. (2012). *Distributed leadership* (Vol. 4). New York, NY: John Wiley & Sons.

Wolverton, M., Bower, B., & Hyer, P. (2009). *Women at the Top: What women university and college presidents say about effective leadership.* Sterling, VA: Stylus Press.

Zemsky, R. (2009). *Making reform work: The case for transforming American higher education.* New Brunswick, NJ: Rutgers University Press.

CHAPTER 8

# APPROACHES
# OF WOMEN LEADERS
# IN HIGHER EDUCATION

## Navigating Adversity, Barriers, and Obstacles

**Amy B. Diehl**

Given that much has been written about the challenges women face in leadership and the fact that the gender gap in higher education leadership persists (American Council on Education, 2012; Lennon, 2013), I wanted to find out how women who have attained senior leadership positions in higher education have handled personal adversity and professional barriers. This chapter summarizes relevant literature about what women bring to and encounter in leadership and then explores data gathered from interviews with 26 women presidents, provosts, and vice presidents. The research question guiding these interviews was: "How do women leaders in higher education make meaning of adversity?" The interviews examined whether participants had experienced adversity or professional barriers, what such experiences meant to their lives, and how they responded. The strategies employed by the women to navigate adversity will be outlined in this chapter, followed by a discussion of the factors that contributed to the ability to get through their difficult situations.

*Women and Leadership in Higher Education*, pp. 135–151
Copyright © 2014 by Information Age Publishing
All rights of reproduction in any form reserved.

In the course of my interviews, I met a former university president who invited me to her condominium in a retirement community. When I asked her to share her most significant life adversity, she matter-of-factly replied, "The death of my husband." Given that this former university president was now 79 years old, I assumed that she had recently lost her husband and was coming to grips with life without him. However, what she said next surprised me: "I was 42. He was 47."

Throughout my interviews, one observation that emerged was that everyone had a story, and it was usually not the story I expected to hear. This woman's husband had passed away four months after a diagnosis of a terminal illness; she was teaching at a university and had two young teenagers at the time. This former president recalled that the relationship she had enjoyed with her husband was a full partnership in which they did everything together. They had raised their children, planned their spending, shared household tasks, enjoyed vacations, and socialized with other couples. All of a sudden, however, her world had been turned upside down. Although she felt disempowered as a result of losing her husband at such a young age, she quickly realized that she had no other choice but to become self-reliant to survive. Starting over as a professor and single mother, this woman became a trailblazer as the first female provost and the first female president in her state system, surviving adversity and subsequently thriving. What factors contributed to her ability to overcome what she perceived to be the most significant adversity of her life, yet move on with confidence? The answer lies in the concepts of reframing, resilience, and self-efficacy.

## WHAT WOMEN BRING TO LEADERSHIP

Before considering the challenges women leaders face and how these challenges may be overcome, it is important to understand what women bring to leadership. Women bring different task and interpersonal styles into leadership, in part because of how they have been socialized. Women are typically socialized to work in groups, express empathy, be inclusive, and help others to succeed (Bornstein, 2007; Payne, 2001); they also tend to be selfless and concerned for others (Eagly, 2007; Eagly & Carli, 2007; Helgesen & Johnson, 2010), which helps them build relationships and establish trust (Bornstein, 2007). As Helgesen and Johnson (2010) stated, due to their socialization, women are accustomed to "monitoring emotional cues, anticipating what others might need, and making subtle adjustments in order to avoid potential conflicts" (p. 41).

Notably, the ways in which women typically differ from men in their leadership style are consistent with good management practices (Eagly & Chin, 2010). Good leadership has recently been defined as having a future-oriented focus in which leaders empower their followers to contribute to organizations (Eagly, 2007). Two meta-analyses of studies of leadership styles (Eagly, Johannesen-Schmidt, & Engen, 2003; van Engen & Willemsen, 2004) have concluded that women, when compared to men, tend to be more participative and democratic, characteristics viewed to be consistent with good leadership. Women also tend to be more transformational in leadership style, mentoring and developing followers, and they are somewhat more positive in their managerial approach, using rewards rather than reprimands (Eagly, 2007; Eagly et al., 2003).

Women's approach to leadership may also be more flexible and situational than that of men, allowing them to match their style to an institution's needs (Bornstein, 2007). In a study of 182 college and university presidents conducted in 2002, Bornstein (2007) found that 41% of women respondents but only 25% of male respondents indicated that they applied a style of leadership appropriate to a given situation. According to Eagly and Chin (2010), women in leadership are often expected to take charge in a fashion similar to their male colleagues but are also expected to be warm and friendly. Therefore, women leaders may adopt a more androgynous leadership style—incorporating both masculine and feminine components—to meet the demands of the situation (Eagly & Chin, 2010; Madsen, 2008).

Beyond the benefit of the leadership style and skills that women bring to the workplace, their influence extends broadly both within and beyond higher education. When women in top-level leadership positions serve as role models, mentors, and sponsors to younger women, they can influence and inspire women of this generation and generations to come (Sandberg, 2013; The White House Project, 2009). Additionally, increasing the numbers of women in higher education leadership will allow male students, staff, and faculty the opportunity to work with talented women, which is a valuable experience as the gender balance in the workforce changes (The White House Project, 2009).

## WHAT WOMEN ENCOUNTER IN LEADERSHIP

Although women leaders can positively influence organizations, many authors (Ely, Ibarra, & Kolb, 2011; Fletcher, 2001; Haveman & Beresford, 2012; Rhode & Kellerman, 2007; Williams, 2001) have documented that women who take on leadership roles encounter a special set of barriers simply because they are women. According to Acker (1992), the subordination and exclusion of women has been built into ordinary institutional functioning because historically men have developed and dominated institutions related to law, politics, religion, the academy, the state, and the economy. Although organizations have adopted policies prohibiting overt forms of sex discrimination, Ely et al. (2011) noted that impediments to women's advancement may be more subtle and elusive than deliberate discrimination. Researchers, including Ely et al., are now focusing on the concept of second generation forms of gender bias involving barriers arising "from cultural beliefs about gender as well as workplace structures, practices, and patterns of interaction that inadvertently favor men" (p. 475).

The barriers faced by women leaders as they strive to advance and succeed professionally can be termed gender-based leadership barriers (Diehl, 2013). These barriers operate at all levels of society—societal, organizational, and individual. At the societal level, cultural constraints on women's own choices (Haveman & Beresford, 2012; Rhode & Kellerman, 2007), the association of leadership perceptions with masculinity (Lucas & Baxter, 2012; Schein, 2001), and gender stereotyping (Hofstede, 2009; Pittinsky, Bacon, & Welle, 2007; Rhode & Kellerman, 2007) may prevent women from moving forward in leadership work. Barriers within organizations include tokenism (Broughton & Miller, 2009; Kanter, 1977; King, Hebl, George, & Matusik, 2010), exclusion from informal networks (Catalyst, 2004), lack of mentorship opportunities (Catalyst, 2004; McDonald & Westphal, 2013), lack of sponsorship (Hewlett, Peraino, Sherbin, & Sumberg, 2010; Ibarra, Carter, & Silva, 2010), the dynamic that women "get disappeared" (Fletcher, 2001, p. 3) in organizations when contributing relationally, salary inequalities (Compton & Palmer, 2009; Kulich, Trojanowski, Ryan, Alexander Haslam, & Renneboog, 2011), gender discrimination (Diehl, 2013; Eagly & Carli, 2007; Ely et al., 2011; Ibarra, Ely, & Kolb, 2013), and workplace harassment (Diehl, 2013). Barriers affecting women at an individual level include work-family conflict (Heilman & Okimoto, 2008; Poduval & Poduval, 2009; Williams, 2001) and communication style (Violanti & Jurczak, 2011). In sum, at least 13 distinct types of gender-based leadership barriers have been identified in the literature, any of which may hinder women's advancement and success in leadership. When these barriers accumulate, they can inhibit both women's ability to see themselves as leaders and the ability of others (men and women) to see them as leaders (Ely et al., 2011; Ibarra et al., 2013). As Ely et al. (2011) noted, the result is that the status quo is maintained: "women's underrepresentation in leader positions validates entrenched systems and beliefs that prompt and support men's bids for leadership" (p. 475).

## WOMEN LEADERS AND ADVERSITY

As summarized above, the approaches that women typically bring to leadership are effective; however, women continue to be underrepresented in higher education leadership, and they face many barriers. To find out how women in influential leadership positions in colleges and universities have faced and navigated through adversity, barriers, and obstacles, I conducted face-to-face, hour-long interviews with 26 women presidents, provosts, and vice presidents from a variety of institutions across the Mid-Atlantic states. One participant was retired; the rest were active in their positions. These women ranged in age from 39 to 79 and had worked in higher education administration anywhere from 1 year to 36 years, with an average of 20 years.

My research question was: "How do women leaders in higher education make meaning of adversity?" According to the *Oxford English Dictionary* ("Adversity," 2014), adversity is a condition of misfortune, distress, difficulty, or hardship. I invited participants to tell me about anything, major or minor, that had stood in their way personally or professionally. Realizing that women may face significant difficulty in the workplace but may not use the term "adversity" to describe their specific experiences, I included the words "barrier" and "obstacle" in my interview questions. The *Oxford English Dictionary* reflects that these words represent related concepts of anything immaterial that prevents progress or stops advancement. I used a semi-structured interview protocol that included questions focusing on the most significant episodes of personal and professional adversity the women had faced and any professional barriers and obstacles they had encountered. I recorded each interview and then personally transcribed the voice recordings.

The interview data were analyzed in several steps using Patton's (2002) content analysis methodology. First, I created a classification system by coding the interview transcripts with labels that corresponded to themes. I then performed a logical analysis across the themes to explore their interconnections, which allowed me to generate new insights to organize the data. Lastly, I performed an interpretative analysis to more fully understand the meanings in the data. To ensure accuracy and transparency throughout the process of data analysis, I sent transcripts and preliminary findings to participants for their feedback.

Every participant told me stories of significant adversity or challenge in their personal and professional lives. The types of adversity were wide-ranging, such as discrimination, personal relationship conflict, professional interpersonal conflict, serious health issues, childhood sexual abuse, death of a spouse, and work-family conflict. The women had also experienced professional barriers and obstacles that they perceived to be related to their gender, such as exclusion from informal networks, tokenism, lack of mentoring, workplace harassment, and salary inequalities.

Many of the women I interviewed struggled to make sense of the adversities they had experienced in their lives. They questioned both the cause and purpose, why the adversity had happened, and what it meant to their lives. They also reported having struggled with self-blame, despite evidence to the contrary, wondering what they may have done to cause their adversity. Some were able to find closure by settling on a meaning for their adversities or by concluding that since "bad things happen to people," no particular meaning could be attributed to the situation described. These participants reported that reaching closure allowed them to move forward with self-confidence and a sense of empowerment. However, those who were unable to find closure by making sense of their adversities described having lost confidence in themselves and feeling disempowered as a result of the event.

## Strategies to Navigate Adversity

Regardless of whether they were able to come to a sense of closure, all of the women in my study communicated that they learned strategies to navigate their adversities. These strategies typically fell into two categories: (1) empowering self and (2) reaching out to others. All of the participants described how they had empowered themselves through steps such as looking for alternatives, taking care of themselves, remaining patient, and refocusing their attention on other parts of their lives. They also described choosing strategies that involved reaching out to other people for support and encouragement. Of all the strategies that were described by the participants, reaching out to their support network was the most common. The women discussed their reliance on many people in their lives, including spouses, partners, family members, friends, internal and external colleagues, team members, supervisors, mentors, board members, household help, and administrative support staff. One provost described her process of developing this kind of community of supportive people "who don't necessarily have to be the people that are in your hallway."

To successfully navigate adversity, the women in my study noted that they had not relied simply on one single strategy. Adversity is a complex phenomenon in which "you don't have that much control," as one university president told me. Participants accordingly reported how they had used combinations of strategies and were willing to try strategies that were new to them. One vice president described how she learned to be open to "different approaches to challenging situations." The use of multiple strategies to get through adversity was illustrated in my interview with a chief technology officer who survived a terrible car accident in which her car was hit by a landscaping truck from behind. The collision propelled her car into the path of an oncoming freight truck, demolishing her vehicle. As a result of this accident, she suffered a closed head injury, herniated disks in her back and neck, and post-traumatic stress disorder. This chief technology officer not only survived but described how she had subsequently thrived by using four strategies to recover from her accident. First, she was *persistent* and patient during the slow healing process. For example, she initially suffered memory loss. On the advice of her neurologist, she delayed starting a graduate program to allow time for her brain to heal, which took a full year. Second, she participated in both physical and mental health *therapy* to recover her physical and emotional strength. Third, she attended workshops to learn to keep her emotions under control—a form of *preparation*. Fourth, applying the strategy of *perspective*, she used positive self-talk, telling herself, "I will get well." Although this chief technology officer has some lingering effects from the accident, she maintains a positive attitude and a sense of determination and fearlessness.

To navigate adversity, the women used many strategies to empower themselves and reach out to others, and they used these strategies in combination by selecting those which they thought would work. Table 8.1 summarizes the strategies for empowering self, while Table 8.2 summarizes the strategies for reaching out to others.

## Getting Through Adversity

Even though participants learned strategies to navigate their experiences with adversity, many reported that their experiences had negatively impacted their self-esteem and sense of power for months and even years. In fact, some participants were still struggling with feelings of insecurity and disempowerment when I interviewed them. Yet notably, many had found ways to succeed in getting through adversity despite these feelings. What factors enabled the women to do this? Three concepts emerged from the data: reframing, resilience, and self-efficacy.

**Reframing**. Reframing is the process used to change a negative perception into a positive or neutral one, making it less stressful (Seaward, 2009). The goal of reframing is to allow room for a change in perception (Seaward, 2009) by examining alternate views and explanations (Bolman & Gallos, 2011). To reframe a situation, the individual must *assume responsibility*, *face the reality* of the situation, and take steps to *resolve the issue* causing stress (Seaward, 2009).

Several of the women described how they had reframed negative perceptions of their experiences into positive or neutral perceptions.

**Table 8.1.  Strategies for Navigating Adversity: Empowering Self**

| Strategy | Definition | Example |
|---|---|---|
| Alternatives | Seek out options to work around or leave the adverse situation. | "If I can't go through the front door, I've got to go in the side door. I've got to find a different strategy, a different system, a different way of going." |
| Depersonalize | Don't take it personally. | "You have to be tough.... You can't be one of those people where your feelings get hurt really easy and you take it personally." |
| Faith | Seek out a higher power. | "A lot of it was the grace of God.... It was a lot of my faith getting me through that." |
| Family-friendly workplace | Advocate for workplace policy that supports combining family and career. | "I received a paid family medical leave [to have a child.] ... I think other ways these places have [been supportive] is recognizing you might be out with a sick child and allowing you to do that." |
| Persistence | Keep moving and have patience. | "I don't let stuff stop me. I'm like, 'Anything's possible. There's always roadblocks to everything but just keep going.' That's what I do; I just keep going." |
| Perspective | Be optimistic and consider what's really important in life. | "There's way more validity in having a positive attitude than it fluffily appears to be.... Imagining the success of it. Seeing it as just a problem to be overcome. Looking at it as a part of the journey.... Nothing is altogether that important, except your integrity and your love for your family." |
| Preparation | Anticipate and prepare for obstacles. | "I had to, at all times, realize that I had to be über-prepared because the environment didn't anticipate that I was up to the challenge." |
| Privacy | Keep adversity private. | "It's important for those people who are really in your corner ... to know. And other than that, I think a line of privacy where people don't go is important." |
| Refocus | Focus on other parts of life. | "I got through it because I had things I had to do. I had to think about [my children]. I had to give them support that everything was okay. Life was going to be okay. We were going to be okay. And I had my job." |
| Self-care | Make time for personal needs and interests such as sleep, exercise, and vacation. | "Exercising, staying physically fit [and] healthy because you can take on a whole lot more when you're healthy." |

**Table 8.1.    (Continued)**

| Strategy | Definition | Example |
|---|---|---|
| Self-reflection | Reflect on the situation and be open to change. | "[I] use some reflection to figure out what is it that is preventing me from getting there. Sometimes there's some truth to what is being said to you. You have to be willing and open to accept that." |
| Self-trust | Rely on gut instinct. | "The other thing that has gotten me through so many things is trusting my gut.... A couple of times I've allowed myself to be persuaded by others and gone against my gut; it's proven I was wrong." |
| Speak up | Voice concerns, ideas and opinions. | "I was the one who was brave enough to say …'We feel mistreated. We'll work as hard as you want us to, but you can't … mistreat people and expect them to perform at their optimal performance.'" |

Some types of adversity were more easily reframed than others. For example, those who experienced work-family conflict were able to retrospectively broaden their perspectives to focus on the positive, such as the ability to use their experiences to mentor and support others. While women who had experienced more traumatic adversity (e.g., loss of spouse, infertility, and health issues) were keenly aware of their losses, many described how they had reframed their adversities positively by focusing on subsequent new opportunities. For example, one president who was unable to have children channeled her energy into serving the young people at her university. Other participants reframed adversity into a more neutral perception by depersonalizing it, focusing on thoughts such as "this is not about me."

In some instances, participants reported that adversity was challenging to reframe. The women who lacked support from supervisors or institutional leadership and felt they had no other choice but to leave their jobs found it especially difficult to form positive or neutral perceptions of their situations. Lack of support from institutional leadership was also hard to depersonalize and in some cases the negative repercussions were considerable, such as significant financial losses.

The retired university president from the introduction to this chapter described how she had reframed her experience with adversity. When this woman lost her husband at a young age, she *assumed responsibility* for the situation. As the head of her household, she became responsible for raising two young children by herself. She *faced the reality* of the situation and

### Table 8.2.   Strategies for Navigating Adversity: Reaching Out to Others

| Strategy | Definition | Example |
|---|---|---|
| Build trust | Build trust and relationships with stakeholders. | "The first part of my career as a vice president was about reestablishing partnerships on campus, so that the faculty trust you when you say, 'We're spending money on this capital project versus this. It's for these reasons.' And they trust you because you've built some political capital and credibility." |
| Legal support | Get legal support. | "I went to a lawyer because I was afraid. [The lawyer] helped me draft a letter.... He said, 'If you don't address this, you're accepting every allegation that they're making. If you do address it, they don't need to respond to you, but you have in writing that you're countering everything.'" |
| Role models | Find individuals to emulate. | "I got to watch [a female president] do things and imagine myself doing it.... So I felt very comfortable being a female president and knowing I didn't have to follow a male model." |
| Support network | Build and use a personal support network. | "No one does it on their own. No one does. I think it's really important that you have a group of people that you can talk to, get advice from, believe in, understand, and who understand you." |
| Therapy | Talk to a counselor, psychologist, or psychiatrist. | "There's still a stigma on therapy. I'm a big believer that there's times you need it if nothing other than to be honest with yourself in a way you can't with anybody else in the world." |

became self-reliant. She pulled herself together, looked ahead, assessed her responsibilities to herself and other people, and developed a new life path which enabled her to survive. Finally, she took steps to *resolve the issue* causing stress by refocusing her attention. She focused on her children until they were in college, and then turned her attention to her profession, taking her first permanent position in higher education administration. Although this retired president told me that she had "no choice" but to "develop a life path that enabled [her] to survive," she retrospectively reframed her loss as an experience that led to opportunities she would not have had otherwise.

**Resilience.** In addition to reframing their experiences, many participants described how they had developed and strengthened a sense of resilience while navigating through adversities. According to Grotberg (2003), resilience is "the human capacity to deal with, overcome, learn from, and even be transformed" (p. 1) by adversity. To better explain what resilience is and how it works, Wagnild (2010) described five characteristics of resilience: *meaningful life, equanimity, self-reliance, existential aloneness,* and *perseverance.* The analysis of interview data clearly indicated that participants in my study exhibited these characteristics, as described below.

*Meaningful life* refers to having a sense of one's meaning or purpose in life. This sense of purpose helps individuals to move forward when difficulties are encountered (Wagnild, 2010). A majority of the women described their sense of purpose to be helping and supporting others. Some described their motivation to contribute to the growth of young people by serving in higher education administration. Others discussed using their experiences with adversity to help other people experiencing similar types of hardship.

Just as having a meaningful life contributes to resilience, a sense of *equanimity* also aids resilience. Equanimity is a balanced and flexible perception of life and experiences. Resilient individuals understand that life is not all good or all bad and are open to many possibilities. They remain optimistic, even when the situation seems doubtful, because they are willing to look for new opportunities (Wagnild, 2010). Many of the women I interviewed demonstrated how their experiences with adversity had helped to build their sense of equanimity. Several gained perspective in their lives, which included "not sweating the small stuff" and the ability to view trying situations as "a part of the journey." A few participants described how they had learned to appreciate the good sides of life, such as kindness in others and spending time away from work. Facing adversity set several of the women on paths that would have otherwise not been possible. These women took advantage of new opportunities, such as the chance to grow professionally through academic programs and more challenging work.

In addition to developing a sense of equanimity, many participants described how they had become more self-reliant through their struggles with adversity. *Self-reliance* is the ability to recognize and rely on personal capabilities as well as draw on past experiences to guide actions. Through the knowledge learned from success and failures, individuals refine, adapt, and strengthen skills throughout life (Wagnild, 2010). Some participants felt they had no choice but to become self-reliant to survive. Others used the knowledge gained from navigating adversity to successfully address subsequent challenges. According to a few participants, the experience of going through adversity had taught them to trust their "gut" when, upon retrospective, they realized their instincts about their adverse situation had been correct.

Beyond learning self-reliance, several participants shared how they also developed their sense of *existential aloneness* in dealing with adversity. Existential aloneness is the realization that each person is unique and that while some experiences can be shared, others must be faced alone. In fact, much of what one faces in life must be faced alone. Embracing existential aloneness involves getting to know oneself well, understanding one's own strengths and weaknesses, and recognizing one's own worth (Wagnild, 2010). In dealing with adversity, several participants described how they gave serious thought to their character, actions, and motives. Through this process of self-examination, they learned who they were and what they were made of. "[The adversity] made me strong," as one provost explained. They came to understand their strengths and weaknesses and to accept themselves, even when they could not change their situations.

*Perseverance* is the last characteristic of resilient people. Perseverance is the ability to remain involved in reconstructing one's life in the midst of adversity or discouragement. It includes setting realistic goals and attaining them, overcoming roadblocks in the process (Wagnild, 2010). To get through adversity, many women in my study recounted how they simply kept moving and remained patient, even when the process was long (sometimes months or years). Many set goals, such as finding new jobs and learning new skills, and attained them. For example, one vice president explained how she had persevered through a doctoral program while working full-time, going through a divorce, and raising three children. Several described feeling that they had no choice but to seek out alternatives; one president who was forced from her position told me: "You become the victim, and you may have to choose a different path." When circumstances or people stood in their way, these women persevered in the search for other options, despite regretting the need to do so.

**Self-Efficacy.** In addition to reframing their experiences and developing resilience, many participants described how their experiences of navigating adversity had increased their sense of self-efficacy. Self-efficacy is the ability to achieve desired results or outcomes (Colman, 2012). According to Bandura (1997), individuals perceive their level of self-efficacy related to particular courses of action. Perceived self-efficacy influences both choice of activities and how long one will persist in the face of obstacles. Consistent with Bandura's research, participants in this study described ways in which they had learned to be successful by tapping four factors that expand one's sense of self-efficacy: *enactive mastery experience, vicarious experience, verbal persuasion,* and *physiological states.*

First, *enactive mastery experience* is the most influential source of efficacy information because it is based on personal mastery of the activity in question (Bandura, 1997). Some participants reported ways in which their perceived self-efficacy had been expanded through their own accomplishments. This was especially true for those who looked for and found new jobs to escape adverse working environments. Those who learned to manage both a demanding career and a family also increased their perceived self-efficacy, discovering that they could "reach beyond" where they thought they could reach.

Second, *vicarious experience* also influences one's sense of self-efficacy. Seeing others succeed in an activity or course of action helps individuals to believe that through improved performance and persistence, they can also succeed (Bandura, 1997). Vicarious experiences of this type were reported by some participants as having increased their self-perceptions of self-efficacy. Many described having male and female mentors and role models from whom they learned and gained confidence. For example, some studied other women in leadership positions, such as previous supervisors and female presidents in higher education, to learn how they could be effective while leading in male-normed cultures.

Third, *verbal persuasion* is recognized as influencing one's behavior and sense of self-efficacy. According to Bandura (1997), individuals believe others when others persuade them that they can master an activity or cope successfully. Several of the women I interviewed described how verbal encouragement from others had played a significant role in building their sense of self-efficacy. The verbal persuasion of others was especially useful when the women's self-esteem was low. Words of encouragement such as "you can do it" from spouses, partners, friends, and colleagues contributed to these participants developing confidence to attempt new courses of action such as applying for and accepting new positions.

Last, according to Bandura's (1997) research, *physiological states* influence efficacy expectations. When individuals feel very anxious, they may consider themselves as less capable; conversely, when people feel calm, they may consider themselves as more able. The physiological state of individuals contributed to their sense of self-efficacy; for example, many of the women endured emotional stress, lack of sleep, and lack of appetite during adversity, leading them to question their self-efficacy. Learning to manage negative physical effects was described by some participants as being important to decreasing their perception of stress and better managing the adverse situation. Among the strategies mentioned was the recommendation of taking a deep breath to help calm nerves. The chief technology officer who was involved in the car accident described how she learned to slow her breathing and lower her heart rate when under stress.

**Illustration**. Even though some participants had come to a sense of closure over their adversities and some felt more empowered and more confident as a result, not all did. Yet even those who felt disempowered and less confident described how they had navigated one or more situations of adversity. The question remains: How did the women leaders get through adversity even when it had negatively impacted their self-esteem and power? The story of a college provost in my study provides an illustration. One day a new female faculty member came to this provost in tears, after a male vice president had verbally berated her over the quality of a document. The vice president had been at the college for more than 30 years and had a history of treating people poorly, but he was also very close to the college president. The provost confronted the vice president about his behavior and took the incident to the president. Although the provost attempted to stand up to the bullying behavior, she soon discovered that she was not supported. Feeling that she had no other choice, the provost resigned her position within six months of the bullying incident and began to rebuild her life. This woman reported having felt insecure, demoralized, and disempowered as a result of what had happened. In addition, the job loss devastated her family finances when she was forced to use credit cards to pay for living expenses. She was unable to reframe or make sense of what had happened. Even so, after 15 months of searching, she attained a new position as a provost. What made this woman successful? Put simply, she was *resilient*, and she increased her *self-efficacy*. She learned to believe in herself to achieve her goal.

Demonstrating her resilience and self-efficacy, this provost chose three strategies to empower herself and reach out to others. First, she recognized that even though she was a victim, she would have to find her own *alternatives* to build a new life in a new location. Second, she was *persistent*, and she did not give up. She applied for 132 positions across the country. From those 132 applications, she had 32 telephone interviews and 12 face-to-face interviews. At the end, she had two job offers for provost positions. This means that she has 130 rejections! Despite rejection after rejection, she chose to keep going, rebuilding her faith in herself, until she achieved her goal. Last, she used her *support network*. Even when she did not believe in herself, she reached out to others, including her husband and her mentor, who provided her with encouragement to keep going. At the time of our interview, which was after she had successfully obtained a new position, this provost had not yet made sense of what had happened and still felt insecure and disempowered. However, she did not let these feelings stop her from moving her life and career forward.

## CONCLUSION

It is clear that the road to leadership success for women is full of barriers and obstacles, including many that are gender-related and others that are not. The women leaders I interviewed survived adversity, barriers, and obstacles, and some even thrived due to their resilience, self-efficacy, and their ability to reframe adverse situations. In overcoming the challenges that had been placed in their path, these women chose to not let barriers stop them. Even when the future was unknown and their options seemed limited, they kept moving forward by taking steps to empower themselves and reach out to others. Because learning to navigate adversity is not easy, the results of this study of women leaders may be valuable for students of leadership development and for women who aspire to leadership positions or to further current careers in leadership.

## REFERENCES

Acker, J. (1992). From sex roles to gendered institutions. *Contemporary Sociology, 21*(5), 565–569. doi:10.2307/2075528

Adversity. (2014). *Oxford English dictionary.* Oxford, England: Oxford University Press.

American Council on Education. (2012). *The American college president: 2012.* Washington, DC: American Council on Education.

Bandura, A. (1997). *Self-efficacy: The exercise of control.* New York, NY: W.H. Freeman.

Bolman, L. G., & Gallos, J. V. (2011). *Reframing academic leadership.* San Francisco, CA: Jossey-Bass.

Bornstein, R. (2007). Why women make good college presidents. *Presidency, 10*(2), 20–23. Retrieved from http://www.acenet.edu/the-presidency

Broughton, A., & Miller, L. (2009). Women in senior management: Is the glass ceiling still intact? *ISGUC: The Journal of Industrial Relations & Human Resources, 11*(4), 7–23.

Catalyst. (2004). *Women and men in U.S. corporate leadership: Same workplace, different realities?* New York, NY: Author.

Colman, A. M. (2012). Self-efficacy. In J. Scott & G. Marshal (Ed.), *A dictionary of psychology* (3rd ed.). Retrieved from http://www.oxfordreference.com/views/ENTRY.html?subview=Main&entry=t88.e906

Compton, S., & Palmer, L. B. (2009). If you don't ask, you'll never earn what you deserve: Salary negotiation issues among female administrators in higher education. *NASPA Journal About Women in Higher Education, 2*(1), 167–187. doi:10.2202/1940-7890.1030

Diehl, A. B. (2013). *Making Meaning of Adversity: Experiences of Women Leadership in Higher Education* (Doctoral dissertation). Retrieved from ProQuest Dissertations & Theses Full Text database. (UMI No. 3589972)

Eagly, A. H. (2007). Female leadership advantage: Resolving the contradictions. *Psychology of Women Quarterly, 31*(1), 1–12. doi:10.1111/j.1471-6402.2007.00326.x

Eagly, A. H., & Carli, L. L. (2007). *Through the labyrinth: The truth about how women become leaders.* Boston, MA: Harvard Business School Press.

Eagly, A. H., & Chin, J. L. (2010). Diversity and leadership in a changing world. *American Psychologist, 65*(3), 216–224. doi:10.1037/a0018957

Eagly, A. H., Johannesen-Schmidt, M. C., & Engen, M. L. v. (2003). Transformational, transactional, and laissez-faire leadership styles: A meta-analysis comparing women and men. *Psychological Bulletin, 129*(4), 569–591. doi:10.1037/0033-2909.129.4.569

Ely, R. J., Ibarra, H., & Kolb, D. M. (2011). Taking gender into account: Theory and design for women's leadership development programs. *Academy of Management Learning & Education, 10*(3), 474–493. doi:10.5465/amle.2010.0046

Fletcher, J. K. (2001). *Disappearing acts: Gender, power, and relational practice at work.* Cambridge, MA: MIT Press.

Grotberg, E. H. (2003). *Resilience for today: Gaining strength from adversity.* Westport, CT: Praeger.

Haveman, H. A., & Beresford, L. S. (2012). If you're so smart, why aren't you the boss?: Explaining the persistent vertical gender gap in management. *The ANNALS of the American Academy of Political and Social Science, 639*(1), 114–130. doi: 10.1177/0002716211418443

Heilman, M. E., & Okimoto, T. G. (2008). Motherhood: A potential source of bias in employment decisions. *Journal of Applied Psychology, 93*(1), 189–198. doi:10.1037/0021-9010.93.1.189

Helgesen, S., & Johnson, J. (2010). *The female vision: Women's real power at work.* San Francisco, CA: Berrett-Koehler.

Hewlett, S. A., Peraino, K., Sherbin, L., & Sumberg, K. (2010). *The sponsor effect: Breaking through the last glass ceiling.* Boston, MA: Harvard Business Review.

Hofstede, G. (2009). Geert Hofstede™ cultural dimensions. Retrieved from http://www.geert-hofstede.com/hofstede_united_states.shtml

Ibarra, H., Carter, N. M., & Silva, C. (2010). Why men still get more promotions than women. *Harvard Business Review, 88*(9), 80–126. Retrieved from http://hbr.org/2010/09/why-men-still-get-more-promotions-than-women/ar/1

Ibarra, H., Ely, R., & Kolb, D. (2013). Women rising: The unseen barriers. *Harvard Business Review, 91*(9), 60–68. Retrieved from http://hbr.org/2013/09/women-rising-the-unseen-barriers/ar/1

Kanter, R. M. (1977). *Men and women of the corporation.* New York, NY: Basic Books.

King, E. B., Hebl, M. R., George, J. M., & Matusik, S. F. (2010). Understanding tokenism: Antecedents and consequences of a psychological climate of gender inequity. *Journal of Management, 36*(2), 482–510. doi:10.1177/0149206308328508

Kulich, C., Trojanowski, G., Ryan, M. K., Alexander Haslam, S., & Renneboog, L. D. R. (2011). Who gets the carrot and who gets the stick? Evidence of gender disparities in executive remuneration. *Strategic Management Journal, 32*(3), 301–321. doi:10.1002/smj.878

Lennon, T. (2013). *Benchmarking women's leadership in the United States, 2013*. Denver, CO: Colorado Women's College.

Lucas, J. W., & Baxter, A. R. (2012). Power, influence, and diversity in organizations. *The ANNALS of the American Academy of Political and Social Science, 639*(1), 49–70. doi:10.1177/0002716211420231

Madsen, S. R. (2008). *On becoming a woman leader: Learning from the experiences of university presidents*. San Francisco, CA: Jossey-Bass.

McDonald, M. L., & Westphal, J. D. (2013). Access denied: Low mentoring of women and minority first-time directors and its negative effects on appointments to additional boards. *Academy of Management Journal, 56*(4), 1169–1198. doi:10.5465/amj.2011.0230

Patton, M. Q. (2002). *Qualitative research and evaluation methods*. Thousand Oaks, CA: SAGE.

Payne, K. E. (2001). *Different but equal: Communication between the sexes*. Westport, CT: Praeger.

Pittinsky, T. L., Bacon, L. M., & Welle, B. (2007). The great women theory of leadership?: Perils of positive stereotypes and precarious pedestals. In B. Kellerman & D. L. Rhode (Eds.), *Women and leadership: The state of play and strategies for change* (pp. 93–125). San Francisco, CA: Jossey-Bass.

Poduval, J., & Poduval, M. (2009). Working mothers: How much working, how much mothers, and where is the womanhood? *Mens Sana Monographs, 7*(1), 63–79. doi: 10.4103/0973-1229.41799

Rhode, D. L., & Kellerman, B. (2007). Women and leadership: The state of play. In B. Kellerman & D. L. Rhode (Eds.), *Women and leadership: The state of play and strategies for change*. San Francisco, CA: Jossey-Bass.

Sandberg, S. (2013). *Lean in: Women, work, and the will to lead*. New York, NY: Alfred A. Knopf.

Schein, V. E. (2001). A global look at psychological barriers to women's progress in management. *Journal of Social Issues, 57*(4), 675–688. doi:10.1111/0022-4537.00235

Seaward, B. L. (2009). *Managing stress: Principles and strategies for health and well-being*. Sudbury, MA: Jones and Bartlett.

van Engen, M. L., & Willemsen, T. M. (2004). Sex and leadership styles: A meta-analysis of research published in the 1990s. *Psychological Reports, 94*(1), 3–18. doi: 10.2466/pr0.94.1.3-18

Violanti, M. T., & Jurczak, L. P. (2011). The effect of sex and gender on perceptions of leaders: Does situation make a difference? *Advancing Women in Leadership, 31*(1), 45-56. Retrieved from http://advancingwomen.com/awl/awl_wordpress/

Wagnild, G. M. (2010). Discovering your resilience core. Retrieved from The Resilience Scale website: http://www.resiliencescale.com/papers/pdfs/Discovering_Your_Resilience_Core.pdf

The White House Project. (2009). The White House Project report: Benchmarking women's leadership. Retrieved from http://thewhitehouseproject.org/documents/Report.pdf

Williams, J. (2001). *Unbending gender: Why family and work conflict and what to do about it*. Oxford, England: Oxford University Press.

CHAPTER 9

# WOMEN LEADERS, AUTHENTICITY, AND HIGHER EDUCATION

## Convictions and Contradictions

**Rita A. Gardiner**

This chapter considers the interconnections among authenticity, women's leadership, and an ethic of care. In addition to drawing upon relevant literature, key findings from a phenomenological inquiry conducted with 10 senior women leaders in higher education are examined and discussed. The material presented in this chapter is divided into three sections. In the first section, several dominant themes within the authentic leadership literature are examined, including the observation that there are some conceptual gaps in current research. In the second section, an argument is made that considering an ethic of care may deepen our understanding about the significance of relational ways of leading, thus suggesting the importance of thinking about authentic leadership from a more comprehensive perspective. In the third section, the research methodology and key findings from the aforementioned study are discussed. In concluding the chapter, the argument is made that by attending to women's experiences of leading, insights can be gained about the connections among gender, authenticity, and leadership within the context of higher education.

*Women and Leadership in Higher Education*, pp. 153–168
Copyright © 2014 by Information Age Publishing

## AUTHENTIC LEADERSHIP

The concept of authentic leadership gained popularity with the publication of George's (2004) book *Authentic Leadership: Rediscovering the Secrets to Creating Lasting Value*. Partly in response to the escalation of leadership malpractices, George argued for the importance of developing a new ethical leadership theory and practice that would challenge leaders to act in a more genuine manner. In short, authentic leadership was proposed as an alternative leadership theory that would address the ongoing ethical and organizational challenges of the 21st century and contribute to restoring public trust.

At approximately the time that George's (2004) business bestseller was published, the topic of authentic leadership was generating increasing interest within the academic community. The dominant scholarly perspective on authentic leadership was the developmental viewpoint advanced by Avolio and colleagues, who built upon earlier work related to transformational leadership (Avolio, Gardner, Walumba, Luthans, & May, 2004). Transformational leadership refers to the ways in which charismatic leaders are able to effect organizational change in part through the positive influence of their powerful personalities (Bass & Steidlmeier, 1999). Recently Avolio (2013) noted that the authentic leadership construct emerged from a revisioning of transformational and charismatic leadership. According to Avolio and Gardner (2005), authentic leadership is comprised of four distinctive aspects: *self-awareness*, *balanced information processing*, *relational transparency*, and *internalized moral perspective*. The first aspect of authentic leadership, *self-awareness*, enables leaders to understand their strengths and weaknesses, and to be mindful of the effect they have on others. The second aspect of authentic leadership, *balanced information processing*, involves the ability of leaders to analyze information objectively and, as a result, to improve their decision-making. *Relational transparency*, the third aspect of authentic leadership, represents a leadership characteristic of being trustworthy and demonstrating appropriate emotional responses in relating to others. Finally, *internalized moral perspective* is reflected in an authentic leader being guided by internal values rather than societal pressures.

One way for leaders to avoid societal pressures and remain true to their values is through greater self-knowledge (Avolio et al., 2004; Shamir & Eilam, 2005). Through this heightened sense of self-awareness, Avolio et al. (2004) argued that authentic leaders are better equipped to build strong organizations and foster trust. In their description of authentic leadership, scholars sometimes refer to existential phenomenologists, such as Heidegger (1927/1962), to bolster their claims that authentic leaders must be resolute in their determination to succeed. However, Heidegger also argued that care is foundational to authenticity, something rarely noted in the current leadership literature (Ciulla, 2009).

Recently, the question of whether a leader can (or should) be fully authentic has been debated from a variety of perspectives. For example, Alvesson and Sveningsson (2013) argued that it is impossible to verify whether a leader is authentic or not, since it is not possible to fully ascertain another person's intentions. Because leadership is a relational phenomenon, Ladkin and Spiller (2013) maintained, it cannot be fully understood by focusing primarily on the leader. An overemphasis on a leader's individual characteristics may serve to diminish the importance of relationships, potentially undermining the benefits of a more holistic approach to leadership. Notably, Bornstein (2009) has suggested that it is inappropriate for leaders to consider authenticity to be the *sine qua non* of leadership, given that the leadership role carries with it certain expectations that leaders must embody. Bornstein has focused on the array of ethical dilemmas faced by leaders, advising that leaders should constantly question whether a particular action is in line with the best interests of an organization, as well as their personal values (Bornstein, 2009). Given that people hold differing opinions regarding what constitutes ethical behavior, Bornstein maintained that each act must be considered within its particular situation.

This attention to context is also pertinent to Eagly's (2005) approach to the topic of authentic leadership. Eagly adopted the term "relational authenticity" to describe how leaders can promote social values that followers are willing to embrace, thereby strengthening their organizations. Although some leadership scholars had previously assumed that followers are persuaded by a leader's words, Eagly has argued that, in many communities, "values are contested ground" (p. 461). Hence, followers need to have confidence not just that the leader has a particular set of values, but that those values will benefit the organization as a whole. It is this sense of synergy between a leader's values and an organization's willingness to accept those values that is critical. In all cases, context matters. However, an appreciation for the influence of context is often missing from authentic leadership discussions.

According to Eagly (2005), other omissions in current discussions of authentic leadership must also be addressed, such as how a leader's identity influenced that individual's ability to succeed. In particular, Eagly noted the tensions that can occur when a female leader displays a lack of stereotypical feminine behavior (e.g., by being aggressive); yet a similar action from a male leader may go unnoticed. In understanding leadership, therefore, gender must be taken into account. Yet Sinclair (2013) asserted that few scholars interested in the topic of authentic leadership have addressed issues of gender. Considering authentic leadership through a gendered lens is important, because gender norms shape both how leaders view themselves and the relationships between leaders and their employees.

In considering the merits of a relational approach to authentic leadership, an exploration of an ethic of care may enrich our understanding, adding an important new perspective. In the section that follows, an ethic of care is presented and discussed as being foundational to developing an ethical practice in leaders that is responsive to others. The argument is made that attending to care, alongside responsibility, can enrich a relational approach to authentic leadership.

## An Ethic of Care

An ethic of care is concerned with the "affective, embodied, and connected notions of morality" (Hamington, 2004, p. 32). Although care is often regarded as a feminine virtue, Gilligan (2011) contended that it is best understood as "a relational ethic, grounded in a premise of interdependence" (p. 23). A caring ethical practice has a dual function; it is concerned with the "well-being of those in the relation and the well-being of the relation itself" (Held, 2006, p. 12). In short, an ethic of care offers a complementary approach to questions of justice and morality that is grounded in human relationships (Gilligan, 2011).

An ethic of care can offer insights into why a focus on relational authenticity is so important to leaders. For example, when characterized by an ethic of care, a relational approach to leadership reveals a fundamental responsiveness among people (Ciulla, 2009). A caring approach to leadership, according to Ciulla, requires leaders to act in a manner that takes into account both duty and emotion. Combining aspects of duty and emotion ensures that leaders carry out their duties effectively and empathetically. Thus, caring and responsibility are fundamental components of ethical leadership. Moreover, to act responsibly means that leaders refrain from treating employees in an exploitative fashion. A central component of what it means to lead caringly, therefore, is to resist treating others in an instrumental way. If leaders are to act justly, they need to demonstrate care for others.

Adopting a caring approach has merit because caring for others is a fundamental aspect of the human condition (Arendt, 1958). Leading with attentiveness to an ethic of care may enrich our understanding of leading in an ethical way because it respects the essential connections among human beings. Thus leaders, irrespective of gender, may benefit from considering how an ethic of care complements current thinking about authentic leadership because of its emphasis on relationships.

## RESEARCH STUDY

The study that is foundational to this chapter is part of a broader theoretical investigation into the interconnections among gender, authenticity, and leadership. The purpose of this qualitative study was to ascertain how senior women leaders described their experiences of authenticity, or lack thereof, within a higher education context. Before turning to a discussion of key findings, information is provided regarding the study participants and research methodology.

### Participants

Ten senior leaders in universities or women's colleges in Canada, the Philippines, and the United States were the participants for this research study. Five participants were, or had been, presidents of higher education institutions. The other five interviewees were either university vice presidents or had held major responsibility for research institutes. During the course of conducting the research, three participants self-identified as women of color and two others self-identified as coming from working-class backgrounds. This diversity of cultural, racial, ethnic, and class backgrounds provided a conceptual richness to the study.

The interviews focused primarily on participants' experiences of leading in an administrative role in one or more higher education settings. Because of financial restrictions, the semistructured interviews were conducted by telephone, with each interview lasting between 45 and 90 minutes. Each participant was sent a copy of the interview transcript to ensure that the conversation was represented accurately for purposes of data analysis. All follow-up conversations between the researcher and participants were conducted via e-mail. Table 9.1 contains brief information about each participant. In the interest of participant confidentiality, pseudonyms have been assigned to the participants.

### Research Methodology

The qualitative research methodology adopted for this study was phenomenology. A phenomenological investigation requires the researcher to listen attentively to how research participants describe the phenomenon in question (Van Manen, 1997). Even though the scholar will have developed a working knowledge of a particular topic, it is through hearing from others how they made meaning out of a shared experience that the researcher gains deeper insight. A fundamental characteristic of this methodology is

**Table 9.1.   Research Participants**

| Name | Job Title | Country of Origin |
|---|---|---|
| Kate | President | Canada |
| Dianne | Vice President | America |
| Jane | Associate Vice Provost | America |
| Laura | International Project Leader/Vice President | Jamaica |
| Alison | Director, Leadership Institute | America |
| Jennifer | Former Director, Diaspora Centre | Trinidad |
| Olive | Former President | America |
| Claire | President (recently retired) | America |
| Teresa | President | Philippines |
| Jill | President | America |

to bring to light hidden dimensions of a particular phenomenon. Although the researcher eventually identifies common themes in the data during the analysis phase, it is also appropriate that research participants offer contrasting ways of thinking about a phenomenon, given that individuals understand the phenomenon differently as a result of their unique life experiences. As such, in phenomenological inquiry both thematic patterns, as well as outlying exemplars, are pertinent to the task of obtaining a fuller understanding of the phenomenon being researched.

When conducting a phenomenological study, Thomas and Pollio (2002) maintain that there are two important criteria in relation to eligibility. First, the participant must have some experience of the particular phenomenon being studied and, second, the participant must be willing to talk about that phenomenon. Although some researchers have argued for multiple interviews, Thomas and Pollio contended this is unnecessary provided that the interviewer has conducted preliminary interviews to test the interview protocol. In the case of this study, preliminary interviews were conducted, following which the interview protocol was refined and retested over a period of several months.

Three major themes emerged from this study, each shedding light on the experiences of women leaders in relation to questions of authenticity in the context of higher education leadership. A theoretical triangulation of narrative data exposed the ways in which these female leaders' experiences echoed existing literature on the value of care and relationships, the effects of gender socialization, and the difficulty of negotiating one's personal convictions within institutional frameworks. The fact that participants described similar experiences—despite differences in age, race, background, and location—highlights important commonalities that would beneficially be addressed in forthcoming literature on authentic leadership.

## RESEARCH FINDINGS

To recap, the primary purpose of this qualitative study was to obtain insight into how senior women leaders described their experiences of authenticity, or lack thereof, within the context of a higher education environment. The study is part of a broader philosophical investigation into the intersection among gender, authenticity, and leadership. In the broader investigation, it is argued that Arendt's reworking of Heidegger's concept of authenticity offers critical insights into leadership (Gardiner, 2013). In this qualitative study, three main themes arose from the data analysis of interviews with the 10 female leaders in higher education. The first theme related to care and relationships. The effects of gender socialization constituted the second theme. The third theme concerned the conflicts that arose in the minds of the participants when institutional expectations were perceived to be incongruent with the leader's personal convictions. These themes highlighted some of the complexities and contradictions of women's experiences of leadership in academia in relation to authenticity.

## Care and Relationships

For these women leaders, a strong connection existed between trying to lead in a caring way and a commitment to social justice. Many of those interviewed described how they initially chose to pursue higher levels of leadership because they were committed to creating a more just environment within their respective institutional settings. One participant (Olive), for example, described the reasons why she agreed to take on a presidential role:

> I wasn't interested in just being a college president to be a president. I had no ambitions for that at all, but when [the institution] asked me to think about it, I mainly did it because I cared a lot about advancing the cause of women's liberation and progress in the world.

From Olive's perspective, the motivation to lead was informed by her desire to bring about gender justice and social change. Other participants also articulated a connection between their motivations to lead and a concern for gender and social justice.

The leaders in this study also described how the building of strong relationships was fundamental to their understanding of what it meant to lead in an authentic manner. However, significant disagreement was evident among study participants regarding the usefulness of authenticity as a way of thinking about leading ethically. Although the majority regarded authenticity as being fundamental to their ideas of leading, others did not find it a helpful descriptor, preferring terms such as integrity or genuineness to describe their leadership.

Most participants identified as a goal of their leadership the creation of an environment where people could express themselves without fear of reprisal. Specifically, they emphasized the critical importance of leaders gaining others' trust. Several of the participants also discussed the importance of being candid in order to promote trust, especially in communicating why particular decisions are being made. As Jill explained:

> It is vital for a leader to lay out the choices, and then identify shared values, and then prioritize in a way that reflects those values. This is crucial for authentic leadership because, if people don't understand why the leader is making these decisions, there's suspicion and mistrust and it creates a toxic culture. However, if a leader makes decisions while keeping people informed, this creates collegiality and collaboration in the face of adversity.

For effective leaders who are committed to authenticity and an ethic of care, even sharing difficult news was viewed as preferable to withholding information. Several research participants maintained that authenticity in leadership related to an openness in the sharing of information, good and bad. By listening to voices of dissent, these leaders described how they learned from different perspectives, becoming more thoughtfully engaged with a problem and better able to find a solution.

Research participants also emphasized the importance of developing mutual respect through meaningful relationships. For Alison, leadership was "all about being in relation to others." Authentic leadership, in her view, meant "being genuine with one another and creating clear expectations through talking with one another about the relationship." Although a relational approach to leadership was viewed as desirable, leaders also described how important it was to be prepared to face conflict. In reflecting back on how she had coped with a challenging situation, Claire stated:

> I had to learn how to deal with not being loved and to stay focused on the long-term good. That wasn't easy. I learned to deal with people's anger—a very important lesson. People often respond in anger when changes seem threatening to them. So I had to learn more about what the roots of their anger were and find ways to diminish their sense of threat.

Over time, Claire reported she had developed effective strategies for dealing with anger, so as not to take the animosity personally. Although these women aspired to lead in a relational way, they also expressed awareness of the need to act independently and from conviction when necessary.

The necessity to remain in control of emotions was a dimension of their leadership role that many participants discussed. On numerous occasions, leaders described how important it was for them to show courage, even when they felt anxious. Leaders, as Bornstein (2009) has noted, not only have a duty to themselves but also a duty to others. As such, it is not always possible to lead in a manner that is congruent with one's inner feelings. For the female leaders interviewed in this study, acting in contradiction to their inner emotions was not perceived as inauthentic, but rather as a requirement of the leadership role. For example, Kate, as incoming president, described how nervous she felt giving her first speech to faculty and staff at an institution where employee morale was low. Rather than letting her anxiety show, it was critical for Kate to appear confident. In her words:

> I needed to build the case for change…. It was about refocusing the whole institution. I said this is the plan we are going to follow; here's how you can get involved. I joked with the audience that many years before I had my thyroid out, and I said to them, "The night before I had my throat cut I wasn't as nervous as I am standing here in front of you today." Part of those nerves was that I truly believed that if we worked together we could turn the place around. I felt like I had an hour and a half to at least get some of the sense of excitement about where we could go, what we could do, and how we could all be in this together.

Although Kate felt anxious, she displayed courage because that was what the situation required of her. Other participants agreed that leaders must sometimes mask their genuine feelings in order to get the job done. Such scenarios brought to light the difference between the exhibition of genuine feelings and the performative demands of a leadership role. From the perspective of the leaders interviewed for this study, this "inauthenticity" was an integral part of performing the requisite leadership role.

## Gender Socialization

In analyzing the data from the 10 female leaders in this study, it was clear that gender socialization had a definite effect on the leadership experiences of most study participants. For example, some participants described how their physical appearance seemed to carry undue importance. Several women discussed how their wardrobe played a part in how they were perceived as leaders, a finding consistent with Sinclair's (2013) observation that female leaders can be undermined by stereotypical assumptions regarding their appearance. In considering the additional burden in terms of trying to conform to what an ideal woman leader is supposed to look like, Jill observed:

> All of these expectations about what it is to be an effective woman leader... men never have to think about including wardrobe issues. And so it's a challenge to have to think about all of these things. That people will judge me based on whether I have my nails done, whether my hair's done, whether I wear a particular dress, my weight, all of these things....

Other leaders expressed frustration that a disproportionate focus on their appearance detracted from the efficacy of their actions. Kate offered a striking description of this type of gender stereotyping:

> I have done presentations to rooms where because of the grace of the audience they've jumped up to their feet, and it's been wonderful and spontaneous and amazing, and I've come off the stage and I've had a man say to me: "That was fantastic, that's wonderful, but where did you get your suit? I'd like to buy one similar for my wife."

Although this individual's comments may have been well-meant, Kate perceived his superficial evaluation as undermining her performance, not least because his comments were made in a loud voice. His response served to reinforce gender bias by discounting the merit of Kate's presentation in favor of her appearance. This account, which was not atypical across the experiences of participants, served to illustrate that a female leader's attire can be a defining factor in how she is perceived by others, thus detracting from her actions.

Research participants also described how stereotypical ways of thinking about gender can create an inner dissonance between learned behavior and some women's perceptions of their abilities. Several participants described how their lack of confidence as young women had negatively affected their view of themselves as leaders. In Jane's words:

> I spent a lot of time in my younger years trying to be the way that I was supposed to be, thinking this is how a professor is, this is how a graduate student is, rather than thinking about "Who am I?" and "What do I bring to this?"

Other participants reiterated Jane's assertion that gender socialization had negatively affected their belief in what they could accomplish. Many of these leaders discussed how hard they had worked on themselves to overcome self-doubt. Clearly, the data from this research indicated the extent to which gender socialization is costly, impeding not only a woman's ability to succeed but also her perception of herself as having the requisite leadership abilities.

## Convictions and Contradictions

In the interviews, women leaders discussed the contradictions that influenced their ability to act in line with their convictions. For example, some participants described how the desire to act in a genuine manner is complicated by the fact that leaders are sometimes required to uphold institutional standards that may differ from their own. Several identified the challenge of attempting to conform to organizational expectations regarding a particular style of leading that seemed counterproductive. For example, Kate explained: "Sometimes people try to be the leader that they think the organization wants or expects, and they get trapped into feeling they have to lead in a particular way. I think, in the long run, it destroys your soul." Summing up her response to this tension, Kate argued for the importance of feeling "comfortable in your own skin doing something that you love. And doing it the best way you know how.... I think that how we do things matters as much as what we do." Similar comments about the importance of leading in a manner that felt right to the individual emerged during several of the interviews.

Research participants described how the desire to lead in a manner that feels right depends in part upon the leader's fit with an institution. During the interviews, women leaders described how other sources of identity, such as race or class, had influenced them in their leadership roles. For example, Jennifer illustrated how being perceived as an outsider, as a result of her race and gender, had made leading more challenging for her:

> The difficulty I experienced was leading from a position as the outsider. And that creates its own problems, not of your making, but it leads to either some people accepting you and overlooking your difference, your diversity, and others will not. Regardless of what you do, as a leader you cannot please everyone. I just had to keep on my path.

Jennifer recognized that, despite her best efforts, she could not alter the negative perceptions that some people had of her leadership. Rather than letting their racist or sexist attitudes negatively affect her, Jennifer indicated that she simply tried to stay focused. Other participants reiterated a similar perspective. Marlene, for example, described the importance of not compromising on core values:

> What I've learned as an authentic woman leader is you do not compromise on those core values that you have. If I see a wrong, I will redress it. If you don't want me to speak about a wrong that I see, don't engage me because I will not compromise on things that are wrong. There are many things that are wrong. I see it all the time, you know, successful women getting passed over, racism, sexism, so that you have to have that core value.

Marlene's account emphasizes how important it is to resist compromising on what matters most. In this study, class prejudices also affected some women's experience of leading. As a first-generation college student from a working-class background, Jill described how others could make her feel as if she was an imposter, and as if she did not deserve her place in the academy. She described how alumnae had, on occasions, brought their friends to visit her so that they could see for themselves how articulate Jill was in person. From these accounts, it became evident that gender alone is not sufficient for understanding the challenges some leaders face. Rather, it is important to consider how issues of racism and classism have a bearing on the abilities of individuals to lead successfully despite encountering prejudice.

Throughout the interview process, the participants frequently discussed the challenge of articulating their commitment to remain steadfast to their values in the face of perceived organizational expectations. Some leaders described how they had chosen to leave a previous institution rather than compromise in areas that mattered deeply to them. Jill described one such situation:

> I started an initiative to make SATs optional because I believed that they are discriminatory. There were gender biases and class biases inherent in the standardized test that we used to get into the university, and into certain schools, and so that was the case where I had some true supporters, but there were many people who were opposed. I failed ultimately in my objective. It was frustrating, and so I left the institution. I didn't want to work in an institution that didn't share the values that I shared.

Jill's frustration at the institution's decision not to change its policies contributed to her decision to leave the place where she had been employed for over two decades, rather than compromise her values. Similarly, other women leaders described how they gave up the fight for institutional change, choosing to seek new career opportunities, rather than remain in an environment they viewed to be incongruent with their personal values.

Other women leaders described how they had encountered gender bias within the structures of their institutions. This bias was perceived to be a detrimental factor when trying to effect positive change. Claire reflected on the difficulties she had faced in the early years of her administrative career:

> When I became an academic dean, and later a vice president for academic affairs in the early 1970s, I quickly discovered that I was one of a few women present among a sea of men in dark suits at committee meetings and conferences. It was really challenging since men were not used to having women in leadership positions.... It was challenging to be what can only be described as an "outsider" on formerly all-male terrain. It was much more difficult to help create educational access and equity for women, girls, and students of color when I, myself, had to work to be accepted by my male colleagues.

In her account of her earlier leadership experiences, Claire described how challenging it was for her as a woman in leadership to gain support for institutional change. Over time, however, her outsider status merely strengthened Claire's resolve to succeed in her goal of improving access to education for all students.

The experiences of individuals can influence their perceptions of themselves and their leadership for years, or even decades. In Claire's case, one example from over four decades earlier was used to illustrate the ongoing challenges of those who have historically been marginalized in academic settings. Kate's similar example, drawn from several years earlier, revealed how gender discrimination continues to influence women's leadership.

> I had a very humbling moment when I was negotiating my contract. I told the chair of the board what I expected and he said, "That's a lot of money for a young girl like you." (I was 40.) I was tempted to say, "And if I were a man, would you ever have thought of making that comment?"

Kate's recounting of this personal experience reflects how some women in higher education leadership have faced discrimination in relation to equal pay, a finding recently confirmed by Lennon (2013).

## DISCUSSION

The key findings of this study serve to expand our understanding of the phenomenon of authentic leadership. In particular, these women leaders' narratives emphasized the extent to which they perceived leadership to be a relational enterprise that must be grounded in mutual respect. Viewing authentic leadership through a relational lens revealed previously hidden aspects that speak to the experiences of women in senior-level higher education leadership. As such, the study reaffirmed previous assertions made by Eagly (2005) that gender has an effect on how authentic leadership is (and should be) embraced by women leaders.

These research findings are also a response to Sinclair's (2013) call for additional research in higher education that is attentive to how gender norms have an effect on whether leaders are perceived as authentic. In self-reported descriptions of their leadership experiences, most of the participants in this study commented that their gender had negatively influenced their ability to navigate institutional barriers and to act in a manner that they considered to be true to their values.

Although qualitative research findings are not generalizable, the narratives reflect some of the ongoing challenges that women leaders face. In addition to gender, these findings indicate that it is important to consider how other identity factors affect leadership. For those women leaders who also experienced racism or classism, these additional dimensions of prejudice were, at times, a further obstacle in obtaining community acceptance of their leadership. Thus, the goal of leading authentically can be an even greater challenge for those who potentially face multiple forms of prejudice. Despite these challenges, the female leaders in this study stressed the value of building strong relationships through caring leadership and the importance of remaining focused on the greater good.

Based on these key findings, the argument is made that incorporating an ethic of care into leadership theory could advance our understanding of leadership effectiveness. Clearly there is some caution in arguing for caring leadership, given how women have historically been stereotyped. Nevertheless, it is important to recognize that an ethic of care is not about women's leadership per se but also about the kind of society we wish to envisage. Although arguing for a leadership praxis that takes into account care and relationships may appear somewhat naïve given the constant demands for greater efficiency and growth in higher education, an emphasis on relational authenticity could add value to the organizational culture of colleges and universities. It is often argued that leaders need to be both ethical and efficient. Based on this research and a review of the literature, the argument is made that accomplishing this goal would involve being more attentive to an ethic of care.

In conclusion, attending to women's experiences of leading within the context of higher education affords insights into the connections among gender, authenticity, and leadership. Specifically, the argument is made that authenticity cannot be contained within a conceptual framework of leadership that ignores gender. What leaders can do, as these women have demonstrated, is commit themselves to intentionally developing authentic and ethical practices that take into account responsibility and care. This relational practice requires leaders to make decisions in a manner that balances personal desires with a genuine respect for others. In short, it is time for leaders to place care at the heart of leadership.

## REFERENCES

Alvesson, M., & Sveningsson, S. (2013). Essay: Authentic leadership critically reviewed. In D. Ladkin & Spiller, C. (Eds.), *Authentic leadership: clashes, convergences, and coalescences* (pp. 79–100). Northampton, MA: Edward Elgar.

Arendt, H. (1958). *The human condition.* Chicago, IL: Chicago University Press.

Avolio, B. (2013). Preface. In D. Ladkin & Spiller, C. (Eds.), *Authentic leadership: clashes, convergences, and coalescences* (pp. xxii–xxvi). Northampton, MA: Edward Elgar.

Avolio, B. J., & Gardner, W. L. (2005). Authentic leadership development: Getting to the roots of positive forms of leadership. *The Leadership Quarterly, 16*(3), 315–338. doi:10.1016j.leaqua.2005.03.001

Avolio, B. J., Gardner, W. L., Walumbwa, F. O., Luthans, F., & May, D. R. (2004). Unlocking the mask: A look at the process by which authentic leaders impact follower attitudes and behavior. *The Leadership Quarterly, 15*(6), 801–823. doi:10.1016/j.leaqua.2004.09.003

Bass, B., & Steidlmeier, P. (1999). Ethics, character, and authentic transformational leadership behavior. *The Leadership Quarterly, 10*(2), 181–217.

Bornstein, R. (2009). Ethics and leadership: A former president reflects on the pivotal role of character in the college presidency. *Journal of College & Character, X*(3), 1–6.

Ciulla, J. (2009). Leadership and the ethic of care. *Journal of Business Ethics, 88*(1), 3–4. doi:10.1007/sl0551-009-0105-1

Eagly, A. (2005). Achieving relational authenticity in leadership: Does gender matter? *The Leadership Quarterly, 16*(3), 459–474. doi:10.1016/j.leaqua.2005.03.007

Gardiner, R. (2013). Cameo: a powerful antidote: Hannah Arendt's concept of uniqueness and the discourse of authentic leadership. In D. Ladkin & C. Spiller (Eds.), *Authentic leadership: Clashes, convergences, and coalescences* (pp. 65–69). Northampton, MA: Edward Elgar.

George, B. (2004). *Authentic leadership: Rediscovering the secrets to creating lasting value.* San Francisco, CA: Jossey-Bass.

Gilligan, C. (2011). *Joining the resistance.* Cambridge, England: Polity Press.

Hamington, M. (2004). *Embodied care: Jane Addams, Maurice Merleau-Ponty, and feminist ethics.* Urbana, IL: University of Illinois Press.

Heidegger, M. (1962). *Being and time.* (J. Robinson & E. Macquarrie, Trans.). Oxford: Blackwell. (Original work published 1927).

Held, V. (2006). *The ethic of care: Personal, political and global.* Oxford, England: Oxford University Press.

Ladkin, D., & Spiller, C. (Eds.). (2013). Introduction: Authentic leadership: Clashes, convergences and coalescences. In *Authentic leadership: clashes, convergences and coalescences* (pp. 1–18). Northampton, MA: Edward Elgar.

Lennon, T. (2013). *Benchmarking women's leadership in the United States*. Retrieved from www.womenscollege.du.edu/benchmarking-womens-leadership/

Shamir, B., & Eilam, G. (2005). What's your story? A life-stories approach to authentic leadership development. *The Leadership Quarterly, 16*(3), 395–417. doi:10.1016/j.leaqua.2005.03.005

Sinclair, A. (2013). Essay: Can I really be me? The challenges for women leaders constructing authenticity. In D. Ladkin & C. Spiller (Eds.), *Authentic leadership: Clashes, convergences and coalescences* (pp. 239–252). Northampton, MA: Edward Elgar.

Thomas, S. P., & Pollio, H. R. (2002). *Listening to patients: A phenomenological approach to nursing research and practice*. New York, NY: Springer.

Van Manen, M. (1997). *Researching lived experiences: Human science for an action sensitive pedagogy*. London, England: The Althouse Press.

CHAPTER 10

# MADAME PRESIDENT

## Gender's Impact in the Presidential Suite

**Mary L. Bucklin**

The United States is in the midst of a cultural shift that has allowed women to move into some of the previously all-male leadership domains. The number of women presidents in higher education is trending upward, rising from the "token" status of 13.8% in 2006 (American Council on Education [ACE], 2007) to "minority" status of 26% in 2011 (American Council on Education, 2012a). Female presidents now lead several major doctoral-granting universities; however, men continue to hold the majority of presidential positions in higher education (ACE, 2012a). Although some view the presence of women in the presidential role in various high-profile universities as a major step toward equality, little research has been conducted to understand the lived experiences of the women leading within that context (Madsen, 2008). Before equality can be claimed, it seems appropriate to examine the experiences of these women once they have obtained the position, including the potential influences of sexism on their effectiveness in carrying out their presidential duties.

This study sought to understand the dynamics faced by women holding one of the most powerful and influential positions in education today—the presidency of a doctoral-granting university—by asking the questions: What effect, if any, does gender have on the presidents or their ability to

*Women and Leadership in Higher Education*, pp. 169–185

do their jobs, and what can we learn from these women's experiences? The research explored the experiences of female university presidents, with particular attention devoted to areas described by the presidents as related to gender and perceptions of presidential effectiveness.

## LITERATURE REVIEW

When addressing the topic of women in the workplace, one of the first issues, if not *the* first issue, that often comes to mind is gender inequity. Research has identified that patterns of inequity in women's employment are common across many sectors of society, including higher education. As summarized in the foundational chapters of this volume and elsewhere, those patterns continue to be evident in the female-to-male earning gap, differentiations between traditional career paths based on gender, and other gender-related societal expectations (Hesse-Biber & Carter, 2005; Sandberg, 2013).

Gender-role socialization creates assumptions that (a) the work experience of men is the norm, thus complicating the potential advancement of women in a variety of ways; (b) women historically have tended to choose professions that align with their perceived *natural* qualities of being nurturing and being concerned with relationships (e.g., nursing, teaching, social work, and library work); and (c) women have traditionally been expected to follow nature and have a family, thus investing less into themselves and their career and more into their children and husbands (Catalyst, 2005). These assumptions contributed to perceptions of gendered ways of being that become deeply ingrained values in the workplace. According to Hesse-Biber and Carter (2005), "This 'preconscious level' of culture can be compared to a paradigm, or a way of thinking. A paradigm provides a conceptual window through which individual members of an organization can understand their social reality" (p. 211). The traditional paradigm that the woman's place is at home taking care of the family and the man's place is at work providing for the family has influenced decisions about hiring, promotions, and policies in the workplace (Hesse-Biber & Carter, 2005).

A report by Catalyst (2005) on women's career advancement described how gender stereotyping in the business sector influences the work experiences of both men and women. These stereotypes contribute to the gender gap in leadership by perpetuating the misconceptions that women are innately different from male leaders and do not possess the requisite leadership qualities. For example, Catalyst reported differences in "the extent to which women and men engage in democratic decision-making" (p. 9). The report also noted the stereotypical assumptions that "women take care, men take charge" (p. 9) as influencing perceptions of women's ability to lead.

Another influence of stereotypes on the experiences of female leaders is the perceived incongruity between expectations of women's behavior and expectations of leaders. Eagly (1987) has noted: "Many of these expectations are normative in the sense that they describe qualities or behavior tendencies believed to be desirable for each sex" (p. 13). When the behavior expected of a leader does not match the desired behavior of the gender role, the incongruity becomes problematic. For example, if a newspaper runs a picture of a female president sporting a pair of pom-poms before an important basketball game, the image fulfills a gender expectation of the woman being a cheerleader and supporter of the men; however, the image does not appear to be "presidential" and thus may lead to questions about her judgment or leadership abilities. Nidiffer (2001) explained: "Individuals who, by virtue of their gender … appear unlikely to possess leadership traits, must overtly demonstrate their competence and 'prove themselves' to be good leaders" (p. 104).

Explanations of the underrepresentation of women in the highest levels of administration in business, politics, and education have been the focus of studies for more than 30 years. One early prominent report, titled *Good for Business: Making Full Use of the Nation's Human Capital*, was issued by the Federal Glass Ceiling Commission (1995). The glass ceiling was frequently used to describe the ability of women to see top-level positions but not attain them; more recently, the metaphor has shifted to a labyrinth (Eagly & Carli, 2007) or a jungle gym (Sandberg, 2013).

Eagly and Carli (2007), who popularized the metaphor of the labyrinth in recent years, provided a context for the image:

> A small number of women have successfully negotiated the labyrinth that impedes most women's progress on the path toward … [positions as] CEOs of large corporations, presidents of universities and foundations, senators, members of presidential cabinet, and governors of states. (p. 27)

The metaphor of the labyrinth illustrates the slow pace of women's progress toward top leadership positions and discouragers on that journey, including the subtle and perhaps unconscious prejudice against women leaders that allows only a few to reach such positions and often at a high price.

Negotiation of the labyrinth relates in part to the incongruity between stereotypical expectations of women's behavior and expectations of leaders, which historically have been aligned with male norms (Eagly & Carli, 2007; Sandberg, 2013). Once the labyrinth has been successfully navigated, the effects of the incongruity do not cease and may, in fact, increase. This incongruity between the gender roles of women and the expectations of leaders is significant to this study.

Role congruity theory (RCT), originally proposed by Eagly and Karau (2002), offers an explanation of how gender roles (and gender stereotypes) contribute to the complexities facing women who aspire to leadership. In brief, traditionally masculine characteristics such as decisiveness are typically aligned with the characteristics of a "leader," thus legitimating men's (and limiting women's) access to and use of power (Eagly, 2007; Heilman, 2001; Heilman, Wallen, Fuchs, & Tamkins, 2004). Basically, RCT proposes that when women and men are actors in the world, their actions should be congruent with the behavioral expectations prescribed by their gender. Diekman and Goodfriend (2006) have summarized the influence of RCT: "This theory predicts that rewards accrue when the presumed characteristics of group members align with the demands of relevant social roles. In contrast, devaluation results when characteristics misalign with role demands" (p. 370). This devaluation for violating prescriptive stereotypes "can result in social and economic reprisals" (Rudman & Fairchild, 2004, p. 156). Eagly (2007) has described the detrimental implications of RCT for women: "This incompatibility not only restricts women's access to such leadership roles but also can compromise their effectiveness" (p. 6). Even when female leaders are effective, scholars who have studied the influence of gender stereotypes on women in managerial positions have found them to be viewed as less socially skilled or less personable (Heilman et al., 2004).

These conflicting and contradictory expectations, creating a structure of prejudice in which female leaders work, can require them to expend valuable energy (emotional, psychological, and physical) in order to function well. Furthermore, the additional effort required to work through these biases often requires that women subjugate their other interests and responsibilities (e.g., as daughters, wives, mothers, and community members) to the pressures of their leadership role, causing a possible second failing that people may choose to use against them.

## RESEARCH METHODS

This qualitative study used open-ended, semistructured interviews that focused on the leadership experiences of eight women serving as current or former presidents of public, doctoral-granting universities. Because the number of women who fit the research criteria is so small, maintaining these women's anonymity was of the utmost importance. Accessing the presidents' university web pages, professional vita, speeches, professional journals, books, newspaper articles, state records, and videos provided background information about each participant's education, experiences, and current position so that interview time was used more efficiently and interview questions could lead to specific issues or experiences that were relevant to this study.

The interviews conducted with the presidents allowed them to discuss their leadership experiences, particularly in relationship to their gender. The interviews lasted from 48–100 minutes and were held in the office the presidents. Interview questions included:

- What identities (e.g., mother, feminist, sports fan) did you claim publicly in your inauguration speech? Why?
- Have you chosen to hide any identities while on the job? Why?
- What kinds of words do people use to describe you and your performance?
- Are you aware of someone labeling you in order to criticize you? If so, were those labels gendered?

The interview protocol allowed the presidents the freedom to expand on any topic that arose, and in every case, stimulated discussion of a variety of topics and stories that the presidents shared. After each session, the interview was transcribed by a professional transcriptionist and then returned to the president for review. The participants were then allowed to correct, explain more clearly, or delete anything said, including the opportunity to remove the entire interview from the research project.

## RESULTS AND DISCUSSION

Data analysis of the interview transcriptions indicated that the influence of gender on these leaders extended into the presidential suites of these doctoral-granting universities. Notably, the participants reported that they did not allow gender-related challenges to deter them, nor did they think that identifying an attack or accusation as being gendered would be wise or helpful to them or their institution. This unwillingness to be deterred may be one of the reasons these women reached positions at the top of their field. Additionally, the data analysis made clear that these women had largely ignored the glass ceiling and "play[ed] by male rules and allow[ed] themselves to be judged by male standards" so as not to be marginalized (Wilson, 2007, p. 2). These women's paths to the presidency were similar in that all had advanced in academia as "the first" woman in many, if not all, of the positions they had previously held (e.g., department chair, assistant dean, dean, assistant and associate vice president, vice president/provost, and president). One president commented on the influence of this phenomenon on her leadership:

> I think it's a big deal because you never got described as anything besides *the first woman president*.... I also think it adds pressure because ... there are more things that are criticized about women than about men, such as clothing, such as hair style, such as attitude, treatment, virtually everything gets put into a box and that is *female*, which is really interesting; it doesn't happen with men.

This participant and the others in this study felt that they were never viewed simply as a president. Rather, gender was perceived to be coloring everything, including her successes and failures. Summing up that conviction, the president commented: "I think whatever you do is viewed through a gender lens rather than simply the act."

The pressure to lead effectively that was felt by these female presidents was influenced by the concern that the whole group known as *women* would be judged as incompetent if this individual woman was not successful. This expressed concern was reiterated in a round-table discussion involving women who served as presidents of Ivy League institutions (Radcliff Institute for Advanced Study, 2007). Ironically, although many men have not succeeded as university presidents, their failures have not affected other men's opportunities or hampered all men in the same way as one woman's failure could potentially impact other women's opportunities.

## Gender and Making It to the Presidency

Not surprisingly, these presidents experienced the same types of challenges that are often characteristic of other women a variety of fields. Perhaps the most basic struggle articulated by participants was a concern related to attempts to combine the mother/wife's role in a home with the role of a professional woman in academe. Female leaders who have children are often considered to be the primary care provider, thus the parenting role can still be more detrimental to women's careers than to men's. One of the participants remarked:

> If you're looking at personal costs, I think you will find women at different stages in their lives better able to balance professional and family needs. When you have really young children, it can be tougher than it is when they're more grown and ... pretty much on their own.

In fact, most of the women in this study had entered their first presidency relatively late in life (in their 50s). Not only does having children affect women's advancement, but desiring to advance can contribute to women delaying or restricting having children (Eagly & Carli, 2007; Hesse-Biber & Carter, 2005). In fact, the American Council on Education's report on "The American College President 2012" indicated that women presidents are "more likely to have altered their careers to raise children or care for their spouses" (p. 14). One of the participants in this study reflected: "I think the greatest sacrifice for me has been in my personal life, in my marriage, children; I *never* imagined that I would parent an only child." Her comment was supplemented with an acknowledgement that the decision to advance into academic leadership rarely impacts a man's personal life in the same way.

Professional advancement for women can also be constrained by being bound to a certain location due to familial constraints (Eagly & Carli, 2007). One president described how this dynamic had limited her professional options: "In that stage of my career where, once I got the doctorate ... I didn't leave because I was a place-bound female academic and chose to stay where my husband was employed." She added the perception that gender had similarly prevented many in her generation from even envisioning administrative leadership early in their professional careers:

> I didn't start out knowing this is where I'm going to go and this is how I'm going to get there. I would have divorced sooner if I'd figured that out sooner because that was one of the constraints in my career.... The later generations are much more [aware of the need to plan ahead]. I believe they're much more comfortable with setting a direction and then making their personal life sort of work toward that, so all those things slowed me down. And I probably lost a decade that men tended ... to not have lost.

For this president, being raised in a generation prior to the women's movement and the fight for equality had influenced her professional choices.

Another president also described familial constraints; however, she and her second husband were able to work out those similar issues in a constructive manner.

> I was married and following my husband a little bit, [and then] we took turns; one move for me and one move for him. We had to balance that, and we balanced it in that way so that I didn't just traipse around the county following him.... It's a second marriage for both of us so I think we were both much more helpful to each other. He's older than I am, so the first years I was carrying his briefcase, and we had to wait for my career to get legs.

In summary, most of the women in this study indicated that the gender role expectations in the home affected their career path to the presidency.

## In the Presidential Suite

Not only were the career paths of these eight female presidents somewhat similar, many also described their ideas concerning the duties associated with the presidency. Notably, all of the participants commented that a woman president must be able to demonstrate, first and foremost, that she understands athletics and finance. The participants also identified diversity as an important issue for higher education meriting the president's attention, that effective communication is critically important, that team-building is a common if not preferred style of leadership, and that their gender had influenced their role in the presidency—how people saw them, how people reacted to them, and what people expected from them. In fact, all but one of the participants articulated clearly that gender had not only played a role in their struggle to secure the presidency but also their presidential roles. Interestingly, the single participant who initially disagreed with that assessment later offered some stories that suggested gendered influences on various situations.

Interview responses indicated that the presidents were very aware of gender on the dynamics of their work and that navigating those dynamics was important to their effectiveness. One of these female leaders commented:

> There were some real concerns after I got here ... because I hired a woman provost.... Some of the old guard were *growling* about how the women were taking over, and a bunch of man-haters in office.... So there may still be a level below the surface.... If there is something that is different and you don't like what's different, it's because there's a woman in office.

This example, as well as the comments about seemingly small issues such as "panty-hose days" (more formal occasions) or wearing too much or not enough of the school's colors, illustrated some of the less critical ways in which the influence of gender was played out in relation to the presidential role. Additionally, the presidents described situations in which gender influenced their thinking regarding how to get things done or to influence accessibility and communication. For example, one president described addressing the gender balance in her office:

> I learned ... that some of the male faculty used to have ... trouble talking with women ... and so I always made sure I had a *man* in my office. They wouldn't come and ask me or tell *me*, but they would tell him and then he

would tell me, so, that's an important [thing] for women to understand, and I'm not sure it works in the reverse.

However, this president also described how both men and women sought out communication with her:

> I have a senior associate from the faculty ... and a lot [of issues] get funneled his way. But oftentimes men have come to me to unload their problems as have women, women more frequently. In fact, what I find are women who in the past have felt that they had no voice were more than happy to come up to the first woman whatever and share with her their angst, and I listen— sometimes I'm sympathetic; sometimes I'm less so.

The women presidents reported that they found themselves embracing and sometimes rejecting the nurturing role expected of women in general. One of these leaders described her more pragmatic perspective on leadership, stating:

> You just continue to work with people. This is really functionally a people business, and you develop a network where people at least trust who you are and what you say. They may not like how you dress or who you are, but they can trust what you say and your motive for saying it.

From the perspective of this president, trustworthiness and consensus building were of paramount importance, particularly in light of certain constituencies having gendered expectations of them.

## Gender Role Expectations

Considerable research has focused on the "double bind" (Catalyst, 2007) that creates added challenges for women in leadership. In short, while people expect women to embrace certain gender-related norms (e.g., being empathetic and caring), if a female leader acts *too* feminine, she risks losing their respect. Yet women in leadership who adopt socially expected male behaviors also face criticism. One of the female presidents described the challenge of this balancing act:

> I think the problem that women have is that everyone wants you to be sweetness and light, and if you are sweetness and light then you're too soft to make tough decisions. On the other hand, if you're tough, really strong people understand you need to be tough. But there's that whole group of people that really don't want you to be tough. They don't like it, and they tell you about it, but then you just have to let it go.

The solution to the dilemma articulated by this president was the choice not to take such criticisms personally. The other presidents interviewed also commented on facing issues related to the double bind (Catalyst, 2007). One of the participants described these dynamics as an ever-present tension:

> So the question is whether people get to know you.... You have to sort of *earn* your way into the community.... For me, there were lots of points where you could get angry at something and be upset about the way you are introduced, how you're dealt with. Ultimately you just have to sort of continue to work through it, [to] be comfortable.

From the perspective of most of these university leaders, the way of addressing the challenges of gender bias in leadership is to analyze the context and find a way to work within that context as constructively as possible.

In contrast to the majority, one of the eight presidents reported that she did not worry about gender incongruity at all. She stated: "I don't think I make any compromises in my femininity even for other women who might have [an opinion] of my behavior or attire or style that they think is too *feminine*, for lack of a better word." For this president, being herself was the most effective way to face gender biases, and being apologetic for who she was or how she dressed, spoke, or acted was not her style.

In addition to simply being aware of gender in their presidential roles on a regular basis, these leaders identified one issue for which gender-appropriate behavior simply did not work for women leaders. Stereotypically, men are expected to be tough-minded and decisive, whereas women are expected to be empathetic and collaborative. One president summarized the challenge of addressing these stereotypes:

> Frequently you are a woman and you argue forcefully for something in a room with a set of men. They will see it as kind of over the top or emotional or passionate when really, if you were a guy, they would say, "They have a good strong opinion." ... They're not intentionally discriminating, but you can see the coloring that gender roles bring to what's seen as appropriate or inappropriate.

The appropriateness of being decisive and taking action, along with the gender-related complexities faced by female leaders, was evident in the interviews of all of these female leaders. Despite the challenges, being tough enough to do the job well was something the participants described as being true of themselves. In fact, some wore their toughness as a badge of honor:

- "When I'm being presidential, I'm *really presidential.* I don't do it all the time, but I'm quite capable of it."
- "One dean called me an iron fist in a velvet glove."
- "I'm not going to sit here and take it.... If that's being a bitch, fine. I know... that I have the power to intimidate."
- "I am who I am as a person, as a woman, and I'm going to lead in that way. Can I be tough? Sure as shootin' I can be tough. The police officers here call me 'Steel Magnolia'."
- "You know, I think women are very tough. I think, I don't see weak women, and I don't see women in these positions that cave."
- "I probably go after people.... [I've] become more of a street fighter."
- "Sometimes I get too ... I'll use the word *emotional* or *forceful*, more than I would have wanted to. Sometimes I am too strong."
- "In a man's world, if they want to call me *tough* and they think it's a kick-ass kind of thing that could happen to them; okay, look out!"

Future research might beneficially explore the extent to which female leaders intentionally find ways to show that they are "man enough" and the extent to which such a response is required of women in top-level leadership roles.

Another aspect of a presidency that was explored during this research is the power of the position. The gendered stereotype of power is that men want to gain and maintain power; in contrast, women prefer to disperse power, preferring a collaborative style and valuing healthy relationships (Helgesen & Johnson, 2010; Sandberg, 2013). When asked whether these presidents liked having access to the power that accompanied her position, all responded affirmatively. One president responded: "I think you wouldn't survive in these positions, it would be pretty disingenuous to say 'No' to that. But, power is a very complex construct, right? I'm obviously more comfortable with the notion of *impact* than of *ambition*." The data analysis from this research suggested that these women had attained their positions in part by crossing over into territory that is often considered to be male-normed, using some of the requisite skills to lead effectively.

## Public Conflicts

All of the presidents described public experiences during their years in office that they viewed as having been influenced by gender. They indicated an initial tendency to be reticent to talk about the personal impact of these interactions in order to avoid the perception that they were complaining. For example, when asked if gender influenced her presidential role, one participant responded, "I try not to add gender as a complicating factor because I don't think it helps you. I don't think playing the gender card is at all useful in the public domain." Another president summarized emphatically that gender influences everything:

> This is going to sound like an odd thing and I'm sure no one else in your interview protocols has said this, but I don't think *anything* is *not* gendered.... I don't even know how to ... answer that because *absolutely* it's gendered! Now, does that mean it's intentionally discriminatory? No, most of the time not. Does it mean it's only thrown at women? No! But, yeah, it's got to be gendered; I mean we are who we are.

Another president illustrated the role of gender in a public setting through a story about the dynamics of a meeting in which she was the only woman. A decision was not going the way some of the men wanted it to go, and their level of frustration was mounting. She recounted:

> So one of them asked for adjournment and then they [could] all go to the restroom and make the decision. And I said, just before they left, "If you guys go in there and make that decision without me, I'm coming right in after you!" So, yes, you know, it does matter how they will talk to each other and *where* they will talk with each other ... but I *knew* where they were going to discuss it, so I couldn't be a part of it. It was the only place they could go, which was the men's room.

In summary, although the presidents are clearly aware of the role that gender played in their leadership experiences, they seemed to be hesitant to describe situations that showed its impact on them in contrast to communicating their excitement about various aspects of their leadership journeys into the presidency. Interestingly, several of the participants chose to communicate concerns about the gender dynamics of being in top-level leadership by sharing stories of situations other women presidents had faced. Perhaps this tendency was consistent with the desire of these women to project their hard-earned toughness. However, usually toward the latter stages of the interview, after a level of comfort had developed, more personal stories made their way into the conversation. This dynamic emerged particularly in the stories of presidential experiences in the public domain that dealt with sports.

### Sports

Six of the eight participants described at least one incident during their presidential tenure in which they had faced problems related to athletics at their institutions; all indicated that the situation had escalated into public, personal attacks on the president. Even the two who did not provide such an example seemed to understand the importance of athletics and spoke about other female presidents facing controversies in this area. One of these leaders observed that a public conflict over athletics could "take down a woman president a lot faster than [they] will take down a man. Ask Betsy Hoffman [former Chancellor of the Colorado system]. You know, she may tell you it was other things, but it was football that took her down." Another commented, "Yes, sports, particularly football, can be a nightmare to deal with." In fact, in a personal conversation with the wife of a former male president she empathized with the women presidents of NCAA Division I institutions, commenting: "If you are the most fortunate of presidents, you don't have a football team."

All of the participants commented that Division I sports made the job of the university president more difficult and more public; when the president was female, the attacks were not only personal but gendered. When asked if individuals had criticized her leadership for reasons related to gender, one president responded: "Oh, yeah. They attack ... one [of my attackers] is a rather vicious sports columnist and then there were public opinion commentators on television, you know they *love* a controversy." When asked how to respond to such public challenges, one president who had been through an extended, personal attack explained:

> Again there was a lot of back and forth and name calling and sports radio.... The things they call you hurt, but you just obviously [pause].... If it's in the newspaper I read it, but I don't listen to talk radio. It can be absolutely insane. Fortunately there were enough like-minded people on the other side, who didn't come to my defense so much as they said, "Hang in there, this will pass.... We are with you, you've made the right decision."

It was clearly important to this president that others were on her side or agreed with her action even if they would not publicly identify themselves as supporting her position. After further reflection, she described the lessons she learned from the experience:

> The one thing you know is that you have to communicate much more than you ever thought you should have to and then that you're going to be misunderstood.... You do need to know enough about why they are passionate about [sports] and what the issues are, to hang in there ... knowing what they are about and knowing what you're about and trying to hang in there and frankly deciding if the cost is worth it and not taking on every battle.

This participant underscored the importance of choosing battles: "and there are battles. All of the battles ... consume [time] and the emotional energy and preparing for the next meeting where you know this may be an issue. [After] every speech ... there is going to be a question about this." Certainly, the event took its toll.

Another president recognized the importance of having strength and tenacity in order to see herself through a difficult public conflict. She described with confidence how she led with that kind of strength:

> You know, I think women are very tough. I think, I don't see weak women and I don't see women in these positions that cave.... You make decisions and you think, "Oh my God, should I back down from this?" And I thought about that a lot ... and I would say to the cabinet, .... "Should we back down?" and they would say to me, "No! No! It's going and you can't back down, you've got to stick with it."

Despite knowing that "It would have been a whole lot easier to say, 'you know, just let it go,'" this president held firm, her supporters reinforcing her commitment. However, she also commented on her awareness that they weren't the ones "getting the crap!"

A third president also recognized the requirement for leaders to have a "very thick skin" in order to continue in a high profile leadership role. Commenting that "If you don't, you don't do these jobs," her advice to others was direct:

> Do the best you can, and you have to just ignore times when people decide to take potshots or attack, whatever it might be. Just ignore it and get on with the work and hope that ultimately you're judged by the actions and the results that flow from this. Not everyone can do that. [Some say that] men develop some kind of thick skin. I think we have different coping mechanisms because what it is, really, is developing the coping mechanisms of being able to ignore.

Another of the participants reinforced the importance of resilience and supportive colleagues, commenting: "In spite of the fact that I really got maligned for [making the changes I did], there were an awful lot of people that really appreciated it as well. I got a *lot* of support." Yet another president described her disappointment at not being able to obtain public support from the politicians or her board: "The Regents, with the governor, were supportive, but they weren't verbal, they weren't out front supportive." Therefore, developing a thick skin and having a group of supporters—not necessarily individuals who will show their support in public—were the keys to the success of the presidents in weathering these storms and getting the job done.

Although addressing public issues cost the presidents and their institutions time and energy, two of the participants described positive outcomes from their handling of such controversies. One president commented:

I think there are sort of two answers to [how public, personal attacks impact a president's ability to do her job] from my perspective. One is, it *does* hamper your ability to get a lot of other things done. I mean there's just a reality to that. Not just because it saps your own energy, but because other people are spending their time doing it and there's uproar and…. I think the other thing is that to the extent that you can build on it for some of the things you do care about, … there was some positive element of being able to use it as an example of how hard it is for universities, *even* universities, to handle diversity and diverse perspectives…. But, yeah, there's no question that those kinds of high-profile issues can sap an awful lot of institutional time and energy, and the president feels that.

When asked whether she had lost social capital over a particular disagreement with some public detractors, another president said, "In an uncanny way, [we] could not have gotten more publicity about what matters most to this institution than by making such an iconic decision."

Interestingly, when asked whether the public attacks that related to athletic conflicts were more painful than the other conflicts, one president responded: "You know, that's kind of interesting. I actually find almost the opposite. When it's out there openly that way, … you don't have to spend your time trying to convince people that that was gendered. It's pretty obvious, really." Another suggested, "You've always got to rise above the fray. Just remember, this is not about you." Relatedly, a third participant commented, "You have to decide very early on what your values are; you need to stay true to those values, and you have to be willing to give up your job for them."

Because athletics is a dimension of university life that generates passions, it is one area in which the conflicts and attacks that occur can and do become personal and gendered. Across the eight presidents in this study, clearly a great deal of time and energy was expended in dealing with such issues. One president expressed a certain determination regarding how she faced these types of conflicts:

Well, you just deal with it. There's no good answer to that. You simply don't show that it hurts. It always does, I mean, I think anybody is lying that says, "I just let it roll off, it's no big deal." It always hurts and anything personal to you, … when you're trying your best to do a really good job and you trust other people and you get torpedoed [pause]…. It's part of the job, you understand it, and even though you understand it, it doesn't make it feel any better, and you just have to let it go, you just don't have any choice, and you just move on.

Moving on seemed to be a consistent theme of these female presidents, one of whom summarized her perspective: "Some of these criticisms *sting*, and then I have to talk myself out of them. I can say, 'Well, it's really not....' [pause] The fact they're grieving me doesn't mean I've done any-thing bad, it means they're making a *point.*" The simplest, and yet most instructive, response regarding what these presidents had learned about dealing with conflicts and attacks was, "You have to handle it with class."

## CONCLUSION

The female presidents interviewed all understood that being president of a university is a difficult job, one that could at times be complicated by gender. However, these women described themselves as being dedicated to working for the good of the university, choosing to invest their efforts there rather than emphasizing issues related to gender.

As is true for the findings of all qualitative research, it is important to note that these women's experiences do not represent the experiences of all women. The experiences of these women are theirs alone, yet the col-lection of these women's perceptions of the experiences allows for critical analysis and painting a portrait that more accurately represents the dynamics faced by women in top-level leadership of some of the most prestigious universities in the United States. Additionally, understanding their experiences and explanations may guide future research related to women and leadership in higher education.

Finally, the commitment to protect the anonymity of these eight presi-dents required that the details of specific examples and stories could not be revealed; doing so might have allowed future generations of leaders to better understand subtle dimensions of the situations discussed. Hope-fully, when these "first women presidents" retire, they will be able to openly share their stories and help the public to know more fully what impact gender had on their top-level leadership experiences.

## REFERENCES

American Council on Education. (2007). *The American college president 2007.* Wash-ington, DC: American Council on Education.

American Council on Education. (2012a). *The American college president 2012.* Washington, DC: American Council on Education.

American Council on Education. (2012b). ACE convenes discussion on women in higher education leadership. Retrieved from http://www.acenet.edu/news-room/Pages/Discussion-Women-Leadership.aspx

Catalyst. (2005). *Women "take care," men "take charge": Stereotyping of U.S. business leaders exposed.* New York, NY: Author.

Catalyst. (2007). *The double-bind dilemma for women in leadership: Damned if you do, doomed if you don't.* New York, NY: Author.

Diekman, A. B., & Goodfriend, W. (2006). Rolling with the changes: A role congruity perspective on gender norms. *Psychology of Women Quarterly, 30*(4), 369–383.

Eagly, A. H. (1987). *Sex differences in social behavior: A social-role interpretation.* Hillsdale, NJ: Erlbaum.

Eagly, A. H. (2007). Female leadership advantage and disadvantage: Resolving the contradictions. *Psychology of Women Quarterly, 31*(1), 1–12.

Eagly, A. H., & Carli, L. L. (2007). *Through the labyrinth: The truth about how women become leaders.* Boston, MA: Harvard Business School Press.

Eagly, A. H., & Karau, S. J. (2002). Role congruity theory of prejudice toward female leaders. *Psychological Review, 109,* 573–597. doi:10.1037/0033-295X.109.3.573

Federal Glass Ceiling Commission. (1995). *Good for business: Making full use of the nation's human capital.* Washington, DC: U.S. Department of Labor.

Heilman, M., Wallen, A. S., Fuchs, D., & Tamkins, M. M. (2004). Penalties for success: Reactions to women who succeed at male gender-typed tasks. *Journal of Applied Psychology, 89*(3), 416–427.

Heilman, M. E. (2001). Description and prescription: How gender stereotypes prevent women's ascent up the organizational ladder. *Journal of Social Issues, 57*(4), 657–674.

Helgesen, S., & Johnson, J. (2010). *The female vision: Women's real power at work.* San Francisco, CA: Berrett-Koehler.

Hesse-Biber, S. N., & Carter, G. L. (2005). *Working women in America: Split dreams* (2nd ed.). New York, NY: Oxford University Press.

Madsen, S. (2008). *On becoming a woman leader: Learning from the experiences of university presidents.* San Francisco, CA: Jossey-Bass.

Nidiffer, J. (2001). New leadership for a new century: Women's contribution to leadership in higher education. In J. Nidiffer & C. T. Bashaw (Eds.), *Women administrators in higher education: Historical and contemporary perspectives* (pp. 101–131). Albany, NY: State University of New York Press.

Radcliff Institute for Advanced Study. (2007). Women at the top: The changing face of the Ivies, *2006–2007 Voices of public intellectuals.* Cambridge, MA: Author.

Rudman, L. A., & Fairchild, K. (2004). Reactions to counterstereotypical behavior: The role of backlash in cultural stereotype maintenance. *Journal of Personality and Social Psychology, 87*(2), 157–176.

Sandberg, S. (2013). *Lean in: Women, work, and the will to lead.* New York, NY: Alfred A. Knoph.

Wilson, M. C. (2007). *Closing the leadership gap: Add women, change everything.* New York, NY: Penguin Books.

# PART IV

**LESSONS FROM THE TRENCHES:
PERSPECTIVES FROM FEMALE PRESIDENTS**

CHAPTER 11

# LEADERSHIP LEGITIMACY, MANAGED AUTHENTICITY, AND EMOTIONAL STABILITY

## Keys to a Successful Presidency

**Rita Bornstein**

After 14 years as president of Rollins College and the subsequent years of consulting, speaking, and publishing on issues of leadership, governance, fund raising, and women in the presidency, I find myself returning to several themes that I consider key to a successful presidency. These themes are (1) the quest for legitimacy, (2) managed authenticity, and (3) emotional intelligence. Those presidents who lose their jobs are generally unsuccessful in leading effectively for reasons related to one or more of these three areas.

These themes may appear to be influenced primarily by style and personality rather than competence. I would argue that the ability to fulfill competently the many challenges of the presidency (including financial management; fund raising; student success; and relationships with the board, faculty, and community) is directly related to management style and personality. Presidents establish their legitimacy based in large part on the competent handling of their responsibilities and the demonstration of appreciation for the institutional culture. Each of the themes I

*Women and Leadership in Higher Education*, pp. 189–195
Copyright © 2014 by Information Age Publishing
All rights of reproduction in any form reserved.

discuss reflects lessons that I have learned from experience, observation, conversation, and research. As I elaborate on each of these themes in the pages that follow, I will also discuss the ways in which they interact with the experiences of women presidents.

## SECURING LEGITIMACY

Presidents need to be accepted as legitimate before they can successfully promote change. Legitimacy is accorded presidents when constituents view them as effective leaders and a good fit with the institution's culture (Hollander & Julian, 1978). New presidents often feel pressure from constituents, especially the board of trustees, to act quickly and decisively to make changes in senior staff, strategic direction, or institutional ranking. One president in a Midwest institution ignored the central role of a much-admired provost in the life of the institution and removed him. This president took a number of unpopular actions early in his tenure without any faculty consultation. He never achieved legitimacy and a few years later, after a faculty no-confidence vote, was removed from office by the trustees.

Newly appointed presidents are most frequently asked, "What is your vision for us?" Unless an institution is in crisis, it is dangerous for a new president to move too quickly to present a vision or make big changes. Before acting, new presidents should first understand the history and culture of the institution and the hopes and frustrations of constituents, especially the faculty, alumni, and trustees. At the same time, while moving cautiously on major changes in personnel and institutional vision, new presidents should insist on the kind of systemic changes that make things work better. Examples of such changes include improving access to human resources, ensuring timeliness of grant and contract proposals and reports, clarifying the guidelines for tenure and promotion decisions, and creating a more easily navigable class registration for students.

Both women and men who become presidents feel obligated to display decisiveness and authoritativeness. They tend to emulate the top-down leadership style that is familiar to them. However, the trend today is for leaders to be collaborative, innovative, entrepreneurial, and flexible. Because of women's life experiences, they typically bring these attributes to the presidency. However, the influence of women's leadership styles is emerging slowly, in part because women still represent only about one quarter of all presidents (King & Gomez, 2008).

Every new president struggles to be accepted in a new environment. Even when the president comes from within the institution, the view from the presidency makes things look different; similarly, the president looks different to former colleagues. These *new* relationships must be renegotiated. Gaining legitimacy, however, does not mean this status is permanent. Legitimacy is fragile. A president's acceptance by constituents as a good leader and a good fit with the culture is often shredded by divisive clashes and crises. Presidents must keep working at maintaining legitimacy. By the time a faculty votes no confidence in the president, or board members are seeking feedback on the president's performance from constituents, the situation is probably not salvageable.

## MANAGING AUTHENTICITY

Authentic leadership is often touted as a worthy goal. It is important for presidents to be themselves and to let people know who they are. I have learned, however, that although constituents may say they would like to know the person within the role of president they are, in fact, more interested in effective role performance. And, presidents performing their roles cannot and should not always express their personal opinions and preferences. A certain degree of role distance and formality is appropriate. When former Harvard president Lawrence Summers gave voice to his belief that women have less aptitude for science than do men, he was speaking authentically but disregarding the customary role of a president. Summers was forced to resign amidst a national firestorm about his remarks. Presidents must learn to filter their speech, recognizing that they are always presumed to be speaking officially on behalf of their institutions.

Presidents quickly learn that their every utterance is transmitted quickly over the informal networks lurking in all institutions. Although new presidents are eager to demonstrate their openness and transparency, they need to filter their discourse knowing that every comment will be scrutinized for hints about possible changes in institutional direction. Experienced presidents learn when to be discreet and when to speak frankly.

Setting boundaries between the role of president and the person within that role should not diminish the incumbent's ability to express and act upon her or his values and ethical principles. Constituents must perceive their president as trustworthy and interested in their welfare. Presidents should be circumspect about sharing controversial personal beliefs. They must be cautious about supporting candidates for political office. And, they obviously cannot share all the information they have with every constituency. While openness and transparency can contribute to trust building, it is not necessary or helpful for the president to discuss controversial opinions that are unrelated to the educational mission.

The presidency brings with it a bully pulpit that, if well used, can enhance the reputation of the institution. Although they cannot be unguarded about political topics or controversial social issues, presidents can and should speak out on education concerns, helping to educate internal and external constituents. They can also provide a platform for complex issues to be debated by others.

Institutions depend on the goodwill and support of people in both political parties who hold very different views of the world. Trustees and donors reflect similar differences in perspective. There are frequent stories about alumni and other donors who withhold financial support when the president takes an action or speaks out on something with which they disagree. Presidents should take note of such responses and communicate with those who may be disaffected, but should not allow such reactions to drive their decisions.

Both men and women need to manage the degree of authenticity they display, although for many the lack of complete forthrightness may seem dishonest. However, this view is naïve. A woman president, with whom I worked, complained frequently to her staff about her trustees. Such negative public comments about volunteers, personnel, or students are completely inappropriate and have a long shelf life.

Effective leaders know that there are times when it is prudent to be circumspect and that there are topics and beliefs that should not be raised. The challenge is to know when it is beneficial to be completely authentic and when it is necessary to exercise restraint. As Goffee and Jones (2005) noted, "Managers who assume that their authenticity stems from an uncontrolled expression of their inner selves will never become authentic leaders. Great leaders understand that their reputation for authenticity needs to be painstakingly earned and carefully managed" (p. 8).

There are circumstances that, with the passage of time, allow presidents to be more authentic. One such scenario is likely to emerge from the trend away from the hierarchical model of leadership to one characterized by inclusion and consultation. Leaders who are more egalitarian than authoritarian may find it necessary to be authentic and transparent most of the time. Another circumstance that can facilitate more authentic relations occurs with longevity and familiarity. Even so, presidents must always be cautious about what they say and to whom. I believe that presidents can be circumspect with constituents without compromising their authentic core.

## EMOTIONAL INTELLIGENCE

Presidents are often terminated after exhibiting a pattern of inappropriate behavior. Such presidents may be described as hot tempered, uncommunicative, condescending, adversarial, or arrogant. I believe that presidents who exhibit such behavior can be characterized as lacking emotional intelligence. According to Goleman (2011), there are four parts to emotional intelligence: self-awareness, managing our emotions, empathy, and social skill. Women's experiences as caregivers and peacemakers may give them an advantage in this arena. Additionally, men are often taught to suppress their emotions, which may make them less sensitive to others. Goleman reported that women have an edge over men in this area, although he cited research that found no gender differences among top performers. Greenstein (2000), in his study of U.S. presidents, suggested that emotional intelligence is one of the characteristics that distinguishes presidential effectiveness. He noted that a president must "manage his emotions and turn them to constructive purposes, rather then being dominated by them and allowing them to diminish his leadership" (p. 6). Although Greenstein was discussing executive leadership at the national level, presidential search committees in higher education should take his advice: "Beware the presidential contender who lacks emotional intelligence. In its absence all else may turn to ashes" (p. 200).

Presidential search committees should attempt to determine the strength of a candidate's emotional intelligence. Committee members can approach this by questioning candidates about past behavior in specific situations. The information is useful since we know that past behavior is a good predictor of future behavior. Candidate behavior during the search process can also provide clues about emotional intelligence. Is the candidate a good listener? Does the candidate mix well in social situations? Does the candidate perform well in stressful situations? Reference checking should also include queries about the candidate's behavior in a variety of circumstances. It is vital that committees agree in advance not to settle for someone who may be emotionally unstable, unable to filter her or his discourse, or unlikely to gain legitimacy. If no appropriate candidate emerges, the committee should be reconstituted and the search begun anew.

The evidence is strong that a presidency will be short-lived when the selected individual cannot handle her or his emotions. Emotional intelligence is vital in the everyday lives of presidents as they respond to challenging personnel issues and handle unpredictable situations. It becomes especially important when facing a hostile faculty, an irate student body, critical neighbors, or personal attacks.

## OVERCOMING DEFICITS

Serving as a college or university president is a great honor. The role absorbs most of an incumbent's time and energy. It presents major challenges that call on all the experience and knowledge a president embodies. While most presidents have a successful tenure in office, the failures garner wide media scrutiny and have a negative effect on an institution's reputation and a president's career. Given the consequences of poor performance, it would be helpful for aspiring presidents to study and reflect on the issues I have raised and to work at overcoming obstacles to success. They should seek out mentors, training programs, and opportunities to gain knowledge and experience with elements of the presidency that may be unfamiliar (e.g., fundraising, budgeting, public speaking, working with a board).

To assure a new generation of successful presidents, higher education institutions and associations need to take responsibility for preparing potential leaders for the job. Sitting presidents and other senior administrators can be helpful by mentoring potential presidential candidates. Mentors should provide information about the history and organization of higher education and the responsibilities of the presidency. They can also help those interested in a presidency to assess their own behavior in various situations and learn to control their emotions as well as their speech.

We need many more aspiring presidents in the pipeline. A survey by the American Council on Education found that almost half of college presidents were aged 61 or older (King & Gomez, 2008). With a great wave of retirements coming, we do not have a rich source of candidates available. According to the survey, 40% of presidents came from the position of chief academic officer. However, many provosts and chief academic officers surveyed, both men and women, indicated that they were simply not interested in a presidency.

Similarly, many women and minorities, who are underrepresented in administration generally, report having limited aspiration to such a demanding and difficult position. Nationally, African Americans represent just 4.5% of the faculty and 7.6% of senior academic affairs officers. People of color comprise 82% of chief diversity officers and these specialized leaders represent a pool of talent that could be intentionally developed and mentored to assume broader institutional roles (King & Gomez, 2008). Institutions could also do a lot more to assist female students and professors by providing child care, easing the tenure process, and offering support in times of stress. Finally, institutions can provide encouragement and programs for those with presidential potential.

Women who successfully clear the hurdles of a presidential search have a special challenge. From the outset they have to fight against stereotypes about women in leadership. If women are accommodating and consultative, they may be perceived as too soft. If they are decisive and strong, they may be called dragon ladies. They are under constant scrutiny regarding what they wear, what they say, how they say it, and how they react to negative publicity. In addition, they are scrutinized for how they supervise their senior staff and how they work with their boards. Achieving legitimacy, moderating the impulse to be completely authentic, and remaining emotionally controlled are challenging for all new presidents, but gender-based expectations continue to create unique obstacles to the success of women in leadership.

No matter how experienced new presidents are, they are likely to be more successful if the board and others have put together a transition plan. Under a good plan, the president is introduced to key constituents, to the history and culture of the institution, and primed on the institution's key issues. After an appointment to a presidency, an executive coach can be helpful in restraining a president's exuberance for making immediate major changes, reacting intemperately to conflict, or misreading the institutional culture. Any one of these behaviors can torpedo a presidency within months.

Once new presidents have achieved legitimacy and been accepted into the culture, they are positioned to enhance the reputation of their institutions. They can attract positive attention in a variety of ways: becoming active in local and national organizations and boards, writing for publication in local and national media outlets, and speaking on education topics. And, to avoid common missteps, presidents should absorb the three lessons I have described. First, gain legitimacy by making thoughtful decisions, demonstrating competence, and connecting with the institutional culture. Second, be authentic but understand the responsibilities of the role as well as the appropriate limitations of completely authentic behavior. Finally, learn emotional control and reflect before responding in difficult situations. With some work and guidance, the next generation of successful presidents will be ready.

## REFERENCES

Goleman, D. (2011, April 29). Are women more emotionally intelligent than men? *Psychology Today*, [Web log post]. Retrieved from http:// www.psychologytoday.com/blog/the-brain-and-emotional-intelligence/ 201104/are-women-more-emotionally-intelligent-men

Goffee, R., & Jones, G. (2005, December). *Managing authenticity: The paradox of great leadership*. Boston, MA: Harvard Business Review OnPoint. Retrieved from http://hbr.org/2005/12/managing-authenticity-the-paradox-of-great-leadership/ar/1

Greenstein, F. I. (2000). *The presidential difference: Leadership style from FDR to Clinton*. Princeton, NJ: Princeton University Press.

Hollander, E. P., & Julian, J. W. (1978). Studies in leader legitimacy, influence and innovation. In L. Berkowitz (Ed.), *Group processes* (pp. 115–151). New York, NY: Academic Press.

King, J. E., & Gomez, G. G. (2008, January). *On the pathway to the presidency: Characteristics of higher education's senior leadership*. Washington, DC: American Council on Education.

CHAPTER 12

# DOCS, JOCKS, AND OTHER WILDLIFE

## The Challenges and Potential for Women Leaders in the 21st Century Public Research University

### Ann Weaver Hart

The modest increase in the proportion of college and university presidencies held by women over the past several decades is notable and widely known, reaching 26.4% in 2011 (American Council on Education, 2012). This growth has occurred gradually, beginning with community and traditional liberal arts colleges, spreading to include state universities, and eventually moving to major research universities both private and public. Each sector has its unique challenges, many of which have special importance for women moving into leadership positions where they are the first woman to fill the role or are seriously underrepresented in the sector. When four features of complex universities are combined—major research achievements, land-grant roles, big-time sports, and academic medicine—they compound the traditional gender dynamics faced by women presidents and chancellors.[1] For the few of us who lead one of the 12 super land-grant universities in the U.S. with all of these components, their dynamics present opportunities and challenges quite different from any other setting.[2]

*Women and Leadership in Higher Education*, pp. 197–204
Copyright © 2014 by Information Age Publishing

## MAJOR RESEARCH UNIVERSITIES IN THE 21ST CENTURY

Special challenges face major research universities in the 21st century. A primary driver of the U.S. economy, these institutions have had decades of growth interrupted only occasionally by short-lived recessions. However, the economic model that sustained this growth collapsed in 2007–08. While all publicly supported universities faced dramatic declines in state funding (on the order of 35–40% for many, including those in Arizona),[3] research universities also faced reduced funding for core research activities from traditional federal sources.

After 30 years of moderate but steady growth, funding for major research has been flat or declining in all federal agencies except the National Institutes of Health [NIH] (American Association for the Advancement of Science, 2013). Even at the NIH, which had its research budget nearly tripled from 1995 to 2005, funding has leveled off (NIH, 2013).

In the past, ground-breaking basic research at universities across the United States has been converted into innovations that positively influence our lives. However, discovery and its application in major innovations have been highly decoupled, and entrepreneurs who invent new ways of using knowledge were commonly removed from those who discover that knowledge. As the decline in federal resources implies, these models for funding research and the mechanisms for applying it that have dominated the academy over the past decades are not feasible in the economic and political context that we face today.

Consequently, academic leaders will need to focus more on financial modeling, strictly applied standards that tie financial decisions to ambitious academic aspirations and specific plans, and deliberate structures and integrated partnerships with industry and business. Combining these strategies allow research universities to compress development timelines and integrate the people involved in innovation, outcomes that hold the key to the future. None of these trends draws on the traditional areas of academic focus women have pursued in the past, creating one significant challenge for aspiring women leaders (Hill, Corbett, & St. Rose, 2010).

In addition to the painfully slow progress women have made in achieving top leadership roles in business in the United States, where women "continue to hold only about 14% of executive officer positions, 17% of board seats, and constitute 18% of our elected congressional officials" (Sandberg, 2013, p. 5), a brief scan of doctorate recipients by field over the past 30 years confirms that women have not traditionally chosen disciplines that receive the most external funding in grants and contracts; they are far less likely than their male counterparts to select these funded disciplines in which to specialize. According to the National Science Foundation's report *Doctorate Recipients from U.S. Universities: 2012*, women earned only 28.6% of doctorates in the life sciences in 1982—the single-most-funded area of research based on data published by the National Center for Science and Engineering Statistics. Twenty years later, in 2012, that percentage of earned doctorates had risen to 55.7%, a remarkable change, yet other areas of research have not experienced nearly the same levels of growth for women earning doctorates and entering the profession (National Science Foundation, 2013). As Curtis (2011) pointed out in "Persistent Inequity: Gender and Academic Employment," the number of women in the higher education student body does not equate to more women in the profession, particularly in leadership roles or as full professors. What a double whammy!

In the competition for leadership opportunities in major research universities, this gender-related discipline imbalance is a simple issue of numbers. While my own career has been so unusual that one must be cautious not to generalize from my experience, I was immediately confronted with accusations that my own PhD field made me unsuited for my new leadership role when I was appointed as dean of the graduate school. I was told that "I have a problem," because my doctorate is in educational administration.

I have spoken to other women leaders who have found that questions arise about their ability to understand the critical variables and standards of rigor that are central to funded big science if they are not themselves funded scientists. This prejudice assumes one must have personal experience in every aspect of every component of an organization in order to be a leader. Thus, fewer women with this experience often means fewer women will be selected for the pool of seriously considered applicants in presidential and chancellor searches. While noteworthy examples such as Mary Sue Coleman, Mary Ann Fox, Shirley Tilghman, and others are becoming more common, and women from the social sciences such as political science and economics are having a major impact, these dynamics continue to negatively impact the number of leadership opportunities for women.

Disciplinary differences are compounded by remarkable shifts in funding patterns from federal agencies in the recent past, particularly the change in funding from the NIH, which increased from just over $11 billion in FY 1998 to $27 billion in FY 2003 and has since leveled off around $30 billion annually (NIH, 2000, 2013). While not the only source of funding for medical science research, this increase has had a large impact on the kind of research that is performed, with the medical sciences comprising nearly a third of total higher education research and development (R&D) expenditures in FY 2012 (Britt, 2013). This change in the amounts and sources of traditional funding and the need to diversify funding for the research mission of our great research universities raises new challenges for women who aspire to lead. Women have made progress in business, economics, finance, and nanotechnology within research-extensive colleges of business, but the confluence of big science, dramatic changes in financial models, academic medicine, big sports, and politics has an impact that cannot be overemphasized.

In recent years, political trends have also placed women leaders in the epicenter of change, especially since the beginning of the great recession. While funding from states for the great public research universities has been declining gradually as other funding entitlements such as Medicaid, prisons, and various other social programs have captured state budget priorities, the dramatic declines in state support that occurred over the past six years (as much as 40% in some states) created a situation unprecedented in post-World War II decades. University presidents and chancellors, better schooled in the skills of academic success than in the hurly-burly world of political negotiations, will need to acquire and successfully apply skills and knowledge rarely required for university leadership roles in the past. Women in these leadership roles will face the additional challenge of confronting traditional gender expectations that can negatively impact the way they are perceived by counterparts during intense negotiations.

These trends will place significant requirements on women aspiring to leadership in major research universities. Women will need to become versed in the standards of rigor and disciplinary contexts of all areas of study, regardless of their own academic backgrounds. They will need to seek and successfully fulfill roles that require political engagement, as well as facility dealing with major donors, boosters, and alumni. They will be called upon to be innovative, entrepreneurial, and open to completely new models of financing their institutions, even as they shore up the missions and protect the core values of their institutions. This mix of responsibilities will require women to seek career experiences that provide them with the knowledge and skills that will dominate the work of university leaders in the coming century, even though these skills have been uncommon in the same roles in the previous (and very successful) decades of American higher education.

## BIG TIME SPORTS IN MAJOR RESEARCH UNIVERSITIES

I believe that the community-building (both within a university and with its supporters), entertainment, and reputational contributions made by successful competition in highly visible big-time college athletics are a tremendous addition to college life. At the same time, failure to succeed and the concomitant gaps between cost and funding undoubtedly place huge burdens on the operating budgets of colleges and universities. My experience at universities in conferences such as America East, The Colonial Athletic Association, the Atlantic-10, Hockey East, The Mid-America Conference, and the Pac-12, with sports programs at both the football championship series level and the football bowl series level, and with a variety of levels of success and intensity in men's and women's basketball, has made me sensitive to the broad variation in the financial, cultural, and political roles big-time sports play in modern U.S. universities.

Social bonding plays an important role in sports, especially in communities where the university is the center of social and cultural life. Athletics is front and center in these settings, and there is more than a little truth in the old saying among university presidents that either the docs or the jocks will get you every time (more on the docs later). Additionally, governing boards, politicians, National Collegiate Athletic Association (NCAA) regulatory requirements, and other pressures create sometimes unrealistic expectations and an often hypercritical environment.

Gender dynamics clearly have affected the changes in college sports over the past several decades and critics abound. In *Who Calls the Shots?*, Estler and Nelson (2005) described the rise of intercollegiate athletics as, in part, a response to the challenge to male dominance posed by the suffrage movement in the post-Civil War era: "Victorian expectations of masculinity conflicted with a perception that an intellectual life was more feminine in nature ... when the presidents of the new universities (or old ones in new incarnations) needed students and funds" (p. 59). Thus, they continue, college sports linked academics to masculinity and provided a public spectacle (often through football) to create support for intellectual endeavors that generally attracted suspicion.

While Title IX has had a positive impact on the gender balance both in funding and the leadership of athletics programs, this cultural history still has an impact on the norms associated with intercollegiate sports (Estler & Nelson, 2005). Because athletics are inextricably tied to the growing entrepreneurialism of many research universities, the fundraising, public relations, and partnership-building components of a university president's role can be complicated by the sometimes still male-dominant sports culture.

## ACADEMIC MEDICINE: BIG OPPORTUNITIES AND BIG RISKS

The 12 super land-grant universities in the United States confront every one of the high risk or gender influenced issues in university leadership I have discussed thus far—Association of American Universities research status, land-grant designation, and big-time sports. These universities also have the complexity and the benefits of academic medicine in the mix. Women who aspire to leadership in these universities need to be persistent and focused on securing opportunities to gain the knowledge and experience necessary to ensure their success.

The challenges facing our great public universities with medical schools are widely discussed, with issues ranging from funding, to accreditation, to the quality of training.[4] The financial model that has sustained U.S. allopathic medical education for decades relies on operating margins generated by their affiliated clinical academic medical centers to fund the educational and research missions integral to the high quality of the biomedical advances of post-World War II healthcare. The future of these funds is uncertain and under great pressure in the current volatile healthcare environment. Our safety net hospitals are squeezed by huge increases in the number of uninsured patients caused by the great recession and increases in Medicaid insured patients under the Affordable Care Act. Medicaid patients' coverage has never met the actual costs of treatment (for example, at the University of Arizona Health Network, reimbursement for Medicaid patients generally covers 65% of the cost of care provided), and the fact that no increases are being contemplated in the total federal funding means that the gap must be addressed in other ways. Because these hospitals are often also our academic medical centers where highly specialized and cutting-edge care is provided, the challenge is one that university presidents will have to confront directly.

This confluence of pressures is the reality facing leaders in super land-grant universities, even as funding for the traditional educational mission has fallen dramatically. Various combinations of these factors will face each university well into the future. In many ways, our very best public universities are caught in the proverbial trap between the frying pan and the fire (or the devil and the deep blue sea), and creative, dramatic changes shaped by these future leaders will make all the difference in the success of higher education and healthcare in the U.S. What better challenge could aspiring women leaders face?

## BUILDING A LIFE IN THE MAJOR RESEARCH AND MAJOR SPORTS LEADERSHIP SETTING

In summary, I encourage young women to aspire to leadership in these very difficult and challenging times. I promise that they will not be bored. At the same time, as Sandberg (2013) points out, not every woman will want to make the commitments and compromises necessary to lead incredibly complex universities in challenging circumstances. An article in *Forbes* magazine recently argued that being a university president or chancellor is possibly the most challenging leadership role in the United States (Ashgar, 2013). I do not disagree; however, it is also extremely rewarding as the quality of our future is at stake. I encourage young women in academic careers to think about leadership roles for themselves and to become informed about the knowledge and experiences necessary for their success.

## NOTES

1. By "big-time sports" I am referring to NCAA Division I schools that have football programs and that are in conferences with automatic bids for the NCAA Men's and Women's Division I Basketball Championship.
2. The schools I refer to alongside the University of Arizona are: Michigan State, Ohio State, Penn State, Rutgers, Texas A&M, UCLA, the University of Florida, the University of Illinois at Urbana-Champaign, the University of Minnesota—Twin Cities, the University of Missouri—Columbia, and the University of Wisconsin-Madison.
3. The University of Arizona's ABOR peers had an average decline of 20.1% from FY 2008–9 to FY 2011–12, with extremes of a loss of 39% at UCLA and a gain in funding of 4.6% at the University of Maryland-College Park. In-state, the UA, Arizona State University, and Northern Arizona University had an average decline of 33.6% (U.S. Department of Education, 2014).
4. See, for instance, "Med Schools Are a Target for Universities Seeking Prestige and New Revenues" by Kevin Kiley (2012), John K. Iglehart's (2011) "The Uncertain Future of Medicare and Graduate Medical Education," and Kim VanPelt's (2012) "Graduate Medical Education in Arizona: Growing the Physician Pipeline."

## REFERENCES

American Association for the Advancement of Science. (2013). *Guide to R&D funding data—historical data*. Retrieved from http://www.aaas.org/page/guide-rd-funding-data-%E2%80%93-historical-data

American Council on Education. (2012). *The American college president 2012*. Washington, DC: American Council on Education.

Asghar, R. (2013, November 15). The toughest leadership job of all (it's not what you think). *Forbes*. Retrieved from http://www.forbes.com/sites/robasghar/2013/11/15/the-toughest-leadership-job-of-all-its-not-what-you-think/

Britt, R. (2013, November). Higher education R&D expenditures remain flat in FY 2012. National Science Foundation, National Center for Science and Engineering Statistics. Retrieved from www.nsf.gov/statistics/inbrief/nsf14303

Curtis, J. W. (2011). *Persistent inequity: Gender and academic development.* Address presented at AAUP New Voices in Pay Equity, An Event for Equal Pay Day,

April 11, 2011. Retrieved from http://www.aaup.org/issues/women-academic-profession.

Estler, S. E., & Nelson, L. J. (2005). *Who calls the shots? Sports and university leadership, culture and decision making.* San Francisco, CA: Wiley Subscription Services.

Hill, C., Corbett, C., & St. Rose, A. (2010). *Why so few? Women in science, technology, engineering, and mathematics.* Washington, DC: AAUW. Retrieved from www.aauw.org

Iglehart, J. K. (2011). The uncertain future of Medicare and graduate medical education. *The New England Journal of Medicine, 365(14),* 1340–1345. doi:10.1056/NEJMhpr1107519

Kiley, K. (2012, September 20). Get me a med school! Stat! *Inside Higher Ed.* Retrieved from insidehighered.com/news

National Science Foundation, Science and Engineering Doctorates. (2013). Doctorate recipients, by sex and broad field of study: Selected years, 1982–2012. *Doctorate recipients from U.S. universities: 2012.* Retrieved from nsf.gov/statistics/sed/ 2012/pdf/tab14.pdf

National Institutes of Health, Office of Budget. (2000). History of congressional appropriations, 1990-1999. Retrieved from officeofbudget.od.nih.gov/approp_hist.html

National Institutes of Health, Office of Budget. (2013). History of congressional appropriations, fiscal years 2000–2012. Retrieved from officeofbudget.od.nih.gov/approp_hist.html.

Sandberg, S. (2013). *Lean in.* New York, NY: Knopf.

U.S. Department of Education, National Center for Education Statistics. (2014). *Integrated Postsecondary Education Data System:* 2012 data [State Appropriations Data Set]. Retrieved from http://nces.ed.gov/ipeds

Van Pelt, K. (2012, March). Graduate medical education in Arizona: Growing the physician pipeline. *Arizona Health Futures.* St. Luke's Health System. Retrieved from slhi.org

CHAPTER 13

# TWENTY-FIRST CENTURY PRESIDENTS MUST WORK WITH MULTIPLE STAKEHOLDERS AND BE AGENTS OF CHANGE

**Sherry H. Penney**

As a former university president, I am pleased to share my passion for the position of president and to write about some of the lessons learned. I hope to encourage women, whether at the beginning or at a later juncture in their careers, to focus their professional goal on becoming a university president. In my years of asking girls and young women what they wanted to be when they made a career choice, I heard astronaut, doctor, lawyer, writer, professor, and other such careers, yet I never heard "college president." This needs to change, because a college president is one of the most important and rewarding (yet sometimes frustrating) positions for a woman to undertake in the 21st century. But, are we ready for it? Yes, of course!

It is my hope that there will be many more women who will be assuming presidential leadership roles in the next few years. In fact, our aim should be for a reasonable balance between male and female presidents. Given that more than 50% of the undergraduate students are women, we need, as a start, at least 50% female presidents and 50% female trustees.

*Women and Leadership in Higher Education*, pp. 205–211
Copyright © 2014 by Information Age Publishing
All rights of reproduction in any form reserved.

Unfortunately, women remain underrepresented in the presidency at 24.6% (Cook, 2012). What does it take to get there, what kind of skills and experiences are needed, how does one deal with the many constituencies that are involved, and how does one serve as a successful change agent? These are the topics to be addressed in this chapter.

Unlike many other professions, there is no one path to the presidency. If individuals want to be a doctor, they go to medical school. Similarly, to be a lawyer, people go to law school, or to be a minister, they enroll in divinity school. Yet, the route to a college presidency is less concrete. There are several strategies in addition to that of following the traditional academic path that typically means a doctorate, publications, and conference presentations. Some presidents have come to the position having been a provost or dean, but others served as chief financial officer or chief development officer, with a few from the business or legal world. No matter which path women decide to take, it is important that they establish their academic credentials. Interestingly, Eagly and Carli's (2007) work described women's routes to top positions by using the metaphor of a labyrinth, often involving a series of starts and stops, trying one path, and if that does not work, trying another. I like this analogy because women should not be discouraged if their career does not go in a straight line up the traditional ladder. A career progression, which includes taking lateral positions and special assignments along the way, offers the individual a rich breadth of experiences as she prepares to enter the senior-most leadership role.

The traditional path was not my experience. After a short stint on the faculty teaching U.S. history at a liberal arts college, I obtained a program evaluation administrative position working for a state board of higher education. This role opened my eyes to the major differences between how faculty and administrators spend their time, and it helped me realize that individuals in significant administrative positions can wield substantial power for change.

Women can begin their quest for a leadership position by assessing the broader skills required for effective administrative work, and then find ways to develop them. Volunteering for task forces, for example, can increase one's overall understanding of postsecondary education issues. Learning how to raise money and obtain grants, and serving on budget committees in order to understand every facet of university finance, are also valuable experiences. Women should be willing to lead a successful change initiative. They can attend one or more of the excellent programs available to advance women's leadership skills; for example, Higher Education Resource Services (HERS), the American Council on Education (ACE), and other organizations offer leadership institutes, as do many universities. Women should take every opportunity to develop and expand their networks, including political and business contacts as well as leaders in education. Women who plan to become presidents need to attend national education conferences, present papers, and accept speaking engagements whenever possible. Their resumes should speak to these skills as well as their academic backgrounds. Also, women should let it be known that they want to move into roles of increasing responsibility. Women cannot expect to automatically be offered the opportunity to interview for a presidency after handling a job well in another area; rather, they must be proactive.

I also add gaining a familiarity with athletics to the list for those who plan to lead four-year institutions. In my opinion, women who want to become presidents need to know sports, love sports, and speak sports. The majority of trustees are men, and sports "talk" is a language that is familiar to them. When women show an interest in sports, it will help trustees be more at ease with women who are pursuing leadership roles. When I was appointed interim president of the University of Massachusetts system in 1995, one of the first tasks that the trustees asked of me was to go to the University of Massachusetts Amherst and meet the basketball coach, John Calapari. I was told that I needed to reassure him of my continued support. I did so, and we made the "final four" that year. Successful sports teams are important to trustees and alumni.

When a woman becomes a president, she soon discovers how different the role is from that of a faculty member. Presidents have myriad responsibilities and rarely have all the knowledge they need as they examine a particular issue. It is often not simply a question of making a good choice versus a bad one; presidents must often make the least objectionable choice of many unpleasant alternatives. They need to decide on the course of action that is best for their campus. Presidents continually switch gears, smile, and then quickly move on to the next challenge.

Presidents manage and lead very complex organizations with their own security/police force, health service, housing and food services, child-care centers, transportation networks, libraries, a museum or two, theaters, and the list goes on. These functions are in addition to the academic areas that involve teaching, research, and service. All the various sectors of the institution need to work seamlessly and effectively so that the academic mission can be fulfilled.

As presidents master the complexity of this kind of leadership, they must keep in mind the large number of direct constituents they will need to deal with on a daily basis: trustees, faculty, students, staff, alumni, political and business leaders, union representatives, funders, neighbors, and community leaders. Each group will want something different; for example, students want lower fees and tuition while faculty want raises, better offices, and more convenient parking. Alumni want winning sports teams, and trustees want all of these and more, especially the president's undivided attention!

One of the president's major tasks involves spending a significant amount of time communicating, sometimes over and over, to the same groups or individuals who are striving for clarity about the various issues on campus. Presidents need to provide their constituents opportunities to ask questions and hear directly from the president. Recognizing that not every decision will be popular, presidents hope that individuals will recognize the complexities and the challenges of making decisions in the best interest of the institution. Thus, it is essential that all the groups are kept informed and that the message is consistent. A president cannot give one message to the students and another to the faculty or alumni. Messages can be tailored to address each group's concerns, but mixed signals are not acceptable. Communication should include several modes—e-mail, memoranda, tweets, and letters will work, but they are not enough. The various constituencies also need face-to-face time with the president on a regular basis, and the president should always be available when a problem arises. Presidents must be clear, candid, and honest. If the answer is not immediately available, it is sometimes dangerous when those in leadership pretend to have one. It is preferable to explain what is known and indicate that more data are needed before providing an answer or possible solution. Presidents need to help staff balance the concerns of these constituencies while also determining the priorities of the calendar and who can be seen immediately in an emergency.

When potentially controversial decisions must be made (e.g., setting tuition and fees, construction projects, admission standards, faculty workloads), each of the individuals or groups involved should be consulted initially and along the way. Presidents may need to focus on each of these entities in a single day, either in person, phone, or via other means to answer their questions. Presidents must also have a clear strategy for working with the media and decide who communicates with the press and who does not. The president's role with the press and how contacts are handled in a timely way is crucial.

As presidents interact with the various constituencies, they should be reminded that 21st century presidents must also be agents of change. The global economy and new technological advances mean that change is the new constant. This century is one characterized by ambiguity, constant change, and even chaos, so presidents will need to lead change efforts. I often say that we are in permanent whitewater; the image of what we face is an environment constantly changing in unanticipated ways.

In public discourse, leaders in education are often criticized for being slow to change and for making only minor changes, such as reducing administrative expenses and cutting travel and equipment purchases, rather than initiating overall change. Presidents are viewed as reluctant to seek new models that would make teaching and research more relevant and responsive to society. That message of reluctance to foster significant change has not been lost on our trustees, legislative bodies, and the public in general.

The list is long in terms of what must change in higher education: newer financial models, use of big data, the role of online and/or hybrid courses, revised academic programs, more responsive governance structures, flexible staffing patterns, and the continuous use of facilities. Not all campuses should make the same changes, but most will need to change more quickly and deliberately than they have in the past. New technologies and competency-based criteria for evaluation need to be considered as student learning outcomes are reviewed. Some faculty members resist moving courses online, but they will support a blended learning approach that combines online with some face-to-face instruction. Presidents will need to encourage instructional staff to discuss new options as part of their role in determining how best to improve and assess student learning in a changing world.

Campus governance must change too; faculty senates sometimes take too much time in repeated discussions, and student senates are often stuck in arguments about tuition and fees. Presidents also should work with campus groups and set clear guidelines on what role governance should play, who does what, and at what speed. Both faculty and students occasionally have difficulty facing the reality of higher education as a changing enterprise. Presidents must help the various constituencies see the big picture and the need for innovative approaches. For example, advanced technologies can be useful in learning, as well as in consolidating administrative functions.

Discussions involving challenges to tenure and the use of adjuncts and part-time "professors of the practice of" are becoming more and more frequent on campuses. Many institutions and some states are already experimenting with relaxing and/or altering tenure rules. But will this work on all campuses? Do campuses need revisions in policy and practice? I believe that we cannot continue to have so many adjunct faculty, who often are overworked, underpaid, and undervalued, in addition to being marginalized from the planning and governance decisions. Many non-instructional staff individuals are qualified to assist in various instructional areas. New models are needed in how we allocate and reward the academic work we do.

Presidents today must always look at physical plants to consider their utilization throughout the entire year and for more than eight to 10 hours a day. They should also explore other uses that might be possible for their campuses. For example, why can't campuses be available 24 hours a day and 12 months a year for expanded educational and community needs? An open campus of this type serves its own and the larger community in ways that benefit both.

New demands for assessment and accountability and how to evaluate changes to document whether they are working are also essential components of the change effort. In the last decade most institutions have worked on five- and 10-year plans. In today's climate of ambiguity, this will no longer suffice. Campus leaders must plan, yes, but they must also be ready to adjust plans and reassess on a regular basis.

So how can women in a leadership role on campus become successful change agents? Recognize that one of the most difficult things about change is the fear, sense of loss, and the uncertainty that accompanies it. Yet many prefer to avoid change and just muddle through. So a president needs to get the attention of those on campus and build trust, establish open lines of communication, and create a sense of urgency about why change is needed. For overviews on the change process, review Heifetz (1994), Kotter (1996, 2005), Heath and Heath (2011), Kanter (2003), Kanter and Stein (1992), and Kegan and Lahey (2009). In my leadership, John Kotter's (1996) eight-step change model has been particularly helpful.

Presidents should not make change a top-down effort. It must be a collaborative initiative that involves the major stakeholders. A coalition of supporters, extensive collaboration, and widespread inclusion are essential. A president never knows where the best ideas reside, and all possible ideas should be considered. With a team in place, a president can help the campus community understand the need for the change and what the future will look like when the change is in place (i.e., the vision of the future). There will be setbacks, of course, but the team can help the president decide next steps to move forward. Presidents must also identify the major obstacles to a change effort and confront them. They should watch for those who are merely paying lip service to the change efforts, and listen to the naysayers to know where and who the opposition is, thus avoiding surprises. Continual and extensive communication is a major part of any successful change effort and is a test of a president's role as a leader.

Also presidents must monitor the change. Changes that work well are reviewed and re-tuned regularly. As I outline these steps, I may make it sound easy, but it is not! Look for and celebrate the change efforts that are successful. Take the time to acknowledge, along the way, the incremental achievements and those involved. At the University of Massachusetts Boston, we had a successful change effort that moved the institution to doctoral status. It took seven years and involved the efforts of many; it was a collaborative effort, a team effort, deserving and receiving wide celebration.

College and university presidents must pay attention to their many constituents, guide their campuses through ambiguity, and help their institutions change in the ways that will make them relevant and excellent 21st century institutions; these are institutions that prepare students, faculty, staff, and alumni for future success. Presidents are fortunate because they have a voice that will be heard, and they occupy a leadership role that enables them to create the new 21st century educational models that are essential.

## REFERENCES

Cook, S. (2012). Women presidents: Now 24.6% but still underrepresented. Retrieved from www.wihe.com/displayNews.jsp?id=36400

Eagly, A., & Carli, L. (2007). Women and the labyrinth of leadership. *Harvard Business Review, 85*(9), 62–71.

Heath, C., & Heath, D. (2011). *Switch*. New York, NY: Random House.

Heifetz, R. (1994). *Leadership without easy answers*. Cambridge, MA: Harvard Business School Press.

Kanter, R. (2003). Leadership and the psychology of turnarounds. *Harvard Business Review, 81*(6), 58–67.

Kanter, R., & Stein, B. (1992). *The challenge of organizational change*. New York, NY: Free Press.

Kegan, R., & Lahey, L. (2009). *Immunity to change*. Cambridge, MA: Harvard Business Press.

Kotter, J. (1996). *Leading change*. Cambridge, MA: Harvard Business School Press.

Kotter, J. (2005). *Our iceberg is melting*. New York, NY: St. Martin's Press.

Sandberg, S. (2013). *Lean in*. New York, NY: Alfred A. Knopf.

CHAPTER 14

# NO TE DEJES

## Giving Voice to Issues That Choose You

### Juliet Garcia

When my father was about 8 years old, his family fled their home country to escape the turmoil and danger of the Mexican Revolution. When they crossed the border into the United States, their passport contained one photo of all six members of the family. I remember seeing the photo many years later and remembering how sad and exiled they all looked.

My mother was born in the United States, a member of a pioneer family in deep South Texas. Her father owned a mercantile store in downtown Harlingen but her family had to live on the "Mexican" side of town. Mexican families who lived in the small town could only swim in the public pool one day a year; the next day they cleaned out the pool.

My parents came of age during the Great Depression, a time when a college education was out of reach for most. And although both of them had excelled while in high school, neither was able to attend college. Their unfulfilled dreams for a college education fueled their desire to make sure that my brothers and I got ours. Every month, my parents placed $5 into individual savings accounts designated for one purpose and one purpose only—to fund our college education.

My brothers and I did graduate from college, as did most of the children of my uncles and aunts. In just one generation, education transformed a family that now includes lawyers, physicians, engineers,

*Women and Leadership in Higher Education*, pp. 213–218
Copyright © 2014 by Information Age Publishing
All rights of reproduction in any form reserved.

teachers, and me, the first female Mexican American appointed president of a college or university in the United States. My family's story represents the power of college education.

If in a democracy, the public—not the rich, not the elite, but the public—does not have access to high quality public higher education, there will be no sustained democracy. But if there is, we fling open the doors of a college education to produce a new generation of voters, of Americans, of people proud of their destiny here in the United States. And if we do that really well, they will be vested in our country, they will nurture it, they will protect it, and they will sustain it. I cannot image any more important work to be involved in than sustaining the democracy of this wonderful country.

For more than 20 years I have had the great privilege of leading the expansion of higher education opportunities in the border region that welcomed my father's family. The University of Texas (UT) at Brownsville sits one block from the Rio Grande River, the politically imposed border between the United States and Mexico that empties into the Gulf of Mexico just 30 miles south of the university campus at South Padre Island. Residing on the border had always been an advantage for those of us living and working in the binational and cross-border region, with a vibrant and dynamic flow of goods and services, relatives living on both sides of the Rio Grande River, and the rich tapestry woven by the interface of two languages and cultures. The region is a place that more closely resembled a Mediterranean port city than a city in Texas. With more than 30,000 degrees awarded during those two decades, UT Brownsville changed the lives of not just our graduates, but the lives of their families, as well as the community that now benefits from the contributions of the credentialed teachers, scientists, health care professionals, and business leaders.

It was with great astonishment, then, that in the fall of 2007 I found myself being sued by the United States government; the same government I thought I was sustaining by vesting new generations of students in the American dream. The tragic events of September 11, 2001 transformed our region dramatically. Post-9-11, like in other U.S. cities, passengers boarding planes in Brownsville had to go through new security measures and were subjected to intense questioning by officials from the Department of Homeland Security (DHS). But in cities located on the southern border of the United States, unlike elsewhere in the United States, we were also asked for proof of citizenship. And, what for us had previously been a routine trip from Brownsville to our Mexican sister city of Matamoros, or vice versa, to shop, conduct business, or just have dinner, was now discouraged by the new constraints of additional security procedures that at times slowed traffic almost to a halt.

One of the most intrusive outcomes of the new security initiatives was a law enacted in 2006 called the Secure Fence Act that required the U.S. government to build an 18-foot-high wall across 700 miles of the Texas-Mexico border by the end of 2008. When President Bush signed the Secure Fence Act he said, "Ours is a nation of immigrants. We're also a nation of law" (Stout, 2006). But then, the same President who called us a nation of law used that as the foundational argument to support the building of a fence, in the process approving the waiver of 27 federal laws so that the border wall could be built virtually without community input and without consideration for important historic, economic, environmental, and personal property rights.

In the fall of 2007, a letter came to the office of one of our vice presidents asking our university to allow the DHS to build a portion of this fence on the campus of our university. Doing so would essentially divide our campus and place more than 120 acres of our property on the south side of the border wall. Our Executive Council quickly gathered to assess this request and what it would mean for our students, our university, and our community. Every one of us realized the serious repercussions of the proposed fence to our safety, historical sites, environmental corridors, and stewardship of the resources that had been entrusted to us. The construction of a physical barrier to separate us from a friendly border nation ran counter to our university mission, which reads, in part, the university "convenes the cultures of its community, fosters an appreciation of the unique heritage of the Lower Rio Grande Valley and encourages the development and application of bilingual abilities in its students. It provides academic leadership to the intellectual, cultural, social and economic life of the binational urban region it serves" (University of Texas, 2014).

It was difficult for me to make sense of the fact that we were being sued by *our own government*. It was difficult to reconcile why our own government was attempting to forcefully seize our land and waive laws that had been enacted to protect our rights and our habitat. All for a fence, that most understand to be no substitution for good immigration policy. One member of our team reminded us of Benjamin Franklin's words, "Those who would give up essential liberty to purchase a little temporary safety deserve neither liberty nor safety" (Independence Hall Association, 1999-2014).

I realized that it was my responsibility to refuse to authorize the DHS request. We really had no choice, as I saw it. Unlike many others under similar attack by the DHS, we had resources with which to fight back. Many people were depending on us to give voice and advocacy for the fundamental freedom to be heard, to protect our property and those within it, and to honor the mission of our university. I thought back to what advice my parents might have offered, and I recalled words that I heard often as a child. *No te dejes vencer* is a phrase in Spanish to encourage someone not to be defeated by life or a difficult circumstance of life. The words are meant to encourage and to strengthen. It is a powerful phrase used among friends, by mothers to their daughters, and often by daughters to their mothers.

Strengthened by this, we began to strategically organize a strong coalition that included the campus community (some of whom risked losing their own family's historic lands due to the fence), the governing bodies for the university at both the local and state levels, and the community at large. Many local attorneys offered their services pro bono; the media was kept abreast through a dedicated university webpage; and our elected officials lent their support, with our senator, Kay Bailey Hutchinson, drafting a critical amendment to the Fence Act that required the federal government to seek local input. While the risk for any one of the members of the coalition was great, the critical mass it represented kept the entire group more insulated from various pressures that would surface.

The case quickly caught the attention of national and international news media and plunged the university and all of us associated with it into unwelcomed fame. Interestingly, whenever I would travel, people would take me aside and beg me to let them know if there was going to be an act of civil disobedience so that they could travel to join us. There is a wonderful novel named *Gilead* about fathers and sons and the spiritual battles that still rage in America's heart. One line from that novel seemed particularly relevant: "My grandfather had nowhere to spend his courage, no way to feel it in himself" (Robinson, 2006, p. 54). For many, the moment in which to spend our courage had arrived. We felt the responsibility to demand more of ourselves and of those we have entrusted to govern us. We were determined not to let this moment pass us by.

The resulting two-year legal dispute required me to appear in federal court three times. The first time we went before the federal judge, we were sued by the DHS for not allowing them right of entry to our campus. The second, because we sought relief from the court when those representing DHS refused to abide by the court order that asked us to jointly study alternative solutions to a physical barrier. The third time, we returned to the federal judge to present an agreement reached because persistence and reason prevailed; everyone finally sat down across from each other and, in good faith, devised an alternative solution.

The Friday before we were scheduled to go to federal court for the last time to hear the verdict, I asked to meet with the Faculty Senate on our campus. I wanted to prepare them for the possibility of a public loss. I wanted them to understand that, win or lose, we had stood our ground; we had taken a difficult position for all the right reasons. I wanted to remind them of the principles that were the foundation for all we did. We had raised our voice because we felt that the Secure Fence Act violated our principles and endangered our campus community.

On July 31, 2008, Federal Judge Andrew S. Hanen ruled that the federal government would not be allowed to build the 18-foot-high fence on university property. The solution seems so simple in hindsight, and yet it took returning to court three times and the efforts of countless individuals to come to an understanding. We agreed that we would standardize our current property line fencing and reinforce it in a way that would satisfy DHS requirements, while still retaining all rights and jurisdiction over our own property.

A few weeks later I addressed the faculty and staff at fall convocation. I asked them to turn their thoughts to trying to make sense of the many hours of hard work the negotiating team spent trying to come up with alternatives, trying to collaborate while being stonewalled, and trying to maintain support from the many authorities that we needed to continue the fight. I asked them to help us attempt to understand how to take this experience and use it to strengthen our university.

I am still not certain of how we will accomplish this end, but I am certain that we surfaced a place to use our courage. It was clear that we must similarly, somehow, teach our students to become advocates, to lead a principled life, to lead even when the odds of success are slim. It is events such as these that change a person and that change a society. We have a responsibility to help surface students' potential to transform not only themselves, but also the environment around them.

When I confer degrees each commencement, I say, "I now confer on you all of the rights and privileges and *responsibilities* thereto appertain." The rights of a degree are easy to accept, as are the privileges. It may be the right to apply for a better job or the privilege of a higher salary. But we cannot accept either the rights or the privileges without also accepting the responsibilities. This is what we must teach at our universities. We must teach our students to become engaged citizens, that their voices matter, and that they should become the next generation leaders on social justice issues.

Much has been written about the lack of modern-day university presidents who will speak on behalf of important issues. Presidents have been duly criticized for their lack of courage to use the bully pulpit for higher education. Father Theodore Hesburgh, longtime president of the University of Notre Dame, wrote in an essay in 2001 that appeared in *The Chronicle of Higher Education*, "Today's college presidents appear to have taken Voltaire's advice to cultivate their own gardens—and ...they are doing very well. We cannot urge students to have the courage to speak out unless we are willing to do so ourselves" (Hesburgh, 2001).

The years we spent in federal court were two of the most difficult years of my presidency. But in retrospect, I would do it all over again. I would do it because it demonstrates most vividly that in the same way that we tell our students that they have responsibilities that come with the privileges of having earned their degrees, we also have responsibilities that come with the privileges of our presidencies. If we hope to inspire our students to be courageous, we must first demonstrate our own courage.

## ACKNOWLEDGMENT

I would like to thank my assistant, Angela Kaberline Mccauley, for her valuable assistance with writing, editing, and refining this chapter. I consider her a coauthor of this chapter.

## REFERENCES

Hesburgh, T. M. (2001, February). Where are college presidents' voices on important public issues? *The Chronicle of Higher Education*. Retrieved from http://chronicle.com/article/Where-Are-College-Presidents/24966/

Independence Hall Association. (1999–2014). The electric Ben Franklin: The quotable Franklin. Retrieved from http://www.ushistory.org/franklin/quotable/quote04.htm

Stout, D. (2006). Bush, signing bill for border fence, urges wider overhaul. *The New York Times*. Retrieved from http://www.nytimes.com/2006/10/27/us/27bush.html?ref=us&_r=1&

University of Texas. (2014). Overview: The mission. Retrieved from http://www.utb.edu/vpaa/graduate/Pages/CATOVERVIEW.aspx

Robinson, M. (2006). *Gilead*. New York: NY: Farrar, Straus and Giroux.

# CHAPTER 15

# GROUNDED

**Karen Holbrook**

As I look back over 40-plus years in higher education to search for a thread that has been present throughout my career—a career that has spanned six research universities, one liberal arts college, and a range of different positions each with increasing levels of responsibility and leadership—I realize that I am looking for a constant or a theme that has kept me excited about higher education no matter what role I am serving. Each position has brought new opportunities, expectations, and challenges, with new successes and occasional disappointments, and over these many years the students and the trends in higher education have changed. Each position has also added new networks of people, some of whom belonged to entirely new categories of individuals than those who have been among the groups of the past. The transitions are invigorating and exciting. They provide an opportunity to refresh, to experience the joy of discovery, to grow and to add new tools, and to gain a broader perspective and enhanced capacity to do the job. Transitions can also be filled with uncertainty and are, therefore, frightening.

Transitions do not necessarily require giving up one role to assume another. Some things will be given up because they no longer "fit" into the repertoire of new activities, but there are "staples" which continue to underpin how one conducts daily responsibilities. Experience is accumulated and expanded upon with each transition and, if the move is to a new environment, there is a learning process that relies upon the support of others, draws upon previous experience, and demands personal *grounding*.

The thread or constant I mentioned at the beginning of this chapter *is* this grounding, and it is essential for stability across the transitions.

As I thought about what grounding means to me, it became apparent that being grounded is not always a positive—especially if one is a child who has been naughty and is "grounded" for a certain period of time, or if a pilot is "grounded" by bad weather or a mechanical error and confronted with many unhappy travelers. To others, being grounded can have a spiritual or emotional dimension of consciousness related to the current state of activity in which one releases personal energy and power; it can mean being in control or the awareness of living in the present state of reality. According to Pavlina (n.d.), "Being grounded means you have the stability, security, and control over your life. It means being ready to handle life's challenges instead of burying your head in the sand and pretending they aren't there."

Grounding, for me, has some of the same attributes as spiritual grounding. It provides a source of strength, a base or focus for many of my actions, and is an attribute that has given me identity, no matter what position I hold. It is a strong accompaniment to my values. So what *is* this thread, this constant—this grounding? To answer this question, I need to go back many years and describe what was *exciting* and *fun* about college and graduate school for me. I do not mean the parties, sporting events, extracurricular activities, and new relationships. I mean what was fun and exciting about the academic life, because it is those same elements that underpin every role I have taken throughout my life. It is those actions that have guided me in various leadership roles, sustained my interest and excitement in higher education, opened doors, and prevented any job from becoming routine.

As a college student, every semester brought the opportunity to sample new fields that were opened up to me by dedicated instructors who were anxious for their students to become as enamored with the subject matter as they were—and some of them were successful. The entrée to the subject by an expert was stimulating, but the real fun was the opportunity, and in most cases the necessity, to explore a topic more deeply on my own. It was the opportunity to spend time in the library, checking out armloads of books and journals, and photocopying articles (the Internet and Google did not exist) to synthesize information into a story that initially would have gaps and holes. I would then dig deeper to find information that would plug the deficits and produce something of value that I was pleased with. I love information and data, digging for both and using it to tell a story.

The same kind of synthesis occurred as I studied for final exams. I would purchase a poster-sized piece of drawing paper and proceed to lay out the material from an entire semester's course as a way of synthesizing the information and creating a story, concept, or picture as I refreshed what I had learned. By putting the pieces together in reviewing for the exam or writing a paper, this process helped me see how things fit together and, when they did not, I could understand why they did not. Thus it was an opportunity to explore how a correction could be made so that there was a fit. This may also explain my passion for working jigsaw puzzles!

The opportunity to build these kinds of knowledge-based pictures is the essence of graduate work; however, at this stage the material to be synthesized must, in part, be new. It must be the product of one's own research, underpinned with existing knowledge in the field contributed by others, with the privilege of having this work critiqued by colleagues. There are great highs when a gap that is missing knowledge is then filled through discovery. It may even be a breakthrough that opens up the next set of questions. This effort also paves the way for developing skills of precision writing, speaking, preparing presentations, seeking financial support, building networks, and serving others. All of these are active, mentally stimulating, and totally engaging processes. But this is not the point of the story.

So how do these personal experiences fit into a series of vignettes on leadership? Let me explain. Most of us started an academic career as I did, searching for a field that would sustain a lifetime of fulfillment, of making contributions to knowledge, and especially of learning through discovery. And, for most of us, there have been many turns in the pathway that take us into different fields or roles and perhaps even different careers. However, what has always been there for me is the grounding I gained from a research career: the fun of discovery, testing my creativity, learning or building something new, synthesizing information into a coherent statement or plan, committing to decisions, creating a team that partners in the process, executing the work, and creating a communication plan to disseminate the results. The process of research and discovery is my grounding, and I have used it throughout several leadership positions either as an approach to solving problems or as a way to engage myself creatively in enhancing university activities.

What I have described is a very hands-on series of activities, and it is these activities and personal investment—immersion in a project—that build one's reputation in a field and develop professional identity. People recognize individuals for these attributes and they are confronted with leadership opportunities—first related to one's academic field and then for higher level positions. But, quickly it becomes apparent that hands-on activities need to be handed off to others for implementation.

As one takes on increasingly senior-level leadership roles, it may seem like a separation from the teaching and research life of a faculty member.

In fact, it is the lessons learned in these very roles that ground how one functions as a leader. Research is carried out to find solutions to problems; leadership positions place an individual in a role to also find solutions to problems, and even though the problems in leadership positions are different from those that are investigated as a researcher, the process is the same. The facts are analyzed, input is sought from others, and a solution is proposed, evaluated, and presented. I have found through the years that many of these research skills carry over into leadership roles.

Problem solving in a leadership position can relate to situations in real time, as well as to forward-looking planning and development opportunities. I will cite a few examples from different institutions where insight was necessary to relieve misunderstandings or to probe a future possibility. A common problem at most universities is an inadequate amount of funding to support the research enterprise. The physical resources (e.g., space, equipment) are never enough, support for investigators and graduate students is limited, and incentive funds to initiate new programs or to commit a financial match for a grant are often inadequate or nonexistent. Faculty members do not understand why the facilities and administrative (F&A) money (i.e., indirect cost dollars returned to the institution for externally funded research) are not given back to them to reinvest in further research. To help faculty understand institutional use of F&A, I began a document at the University of Georgia entitled "The High Cost of Success in Research," using real data from institutional research support. This document was also the basis for an American Association for the Advancement of Science presentation when I was at Ohio State. It was then revised at the University of South Florida where it became the centerpiece of a bound, extended document developed to provide transparency to the budget of the Office of Research and Innovation (OR&I); it was used to explain why F&A was not returned *in toto* to funded investigators and to support, with five years of data, the productivity and accountability of the several divisions of OR&I (Holbrook & Sanberg, 2013).

Exploring new topics became a source of relaxation and recreation during my presidency at Ohio State University, taking me back to engage in research that I enjoyed as a faculty member. Most of my time was highly structured, but occasionally a topic arose that allowed some new "investigation" that I would take upon myself. Should the university accept funds from tobacco companies? Should the university develop a policy, establish a principle, and/or a practice? These questions led to a deep study of the tobacco companies that were offering the research funds and data on the effects of tobacco, smoking, and secondary smoke, as well as the practices of other universities and the constraints they placed on studies if they elected to take such funds. The document I created simply served to better inform discussion.

A second and more extensive study I took on followed an invitation to the university to become a partner with a for-profit company in India that had the goal of developing a land grant-type of comprehensive research university. It would open with a liberal arts and agriculture emphasis and then grow to include the professional schools. This seemed to fit the Ohio State profile and had the potential to be an exciting possibility. Ohio State would be the intellectual partner for the new university, and the company would be the venture partner. In order to even begin considering the possibility, I launched a personal research effort to learn as much about higher education in India as possible. I spent free time and weekends delving into the literature, the press, and government documents. The result was a 200-page document that I could present to the Ohio State Trustees to provide them with the background necessary to deliberate such a partnership. The relationship never came to pass, for many reasons, but the opportunity to learn about something that might benefit my institution and to delve into an area that was entirely different and intellectual was an opportunity to return to my love of exploring new situations.

A final example I will share harkens back to the practice I adopted during college days to establish a "plan," and this one did result in direct benefit to the university. The University of South Florida, like most universities today, was intent upon being a Global Research University with all of its ramifications in the institution's education, research, and outreach and engagement missions. The Office of International Affairs needed to refresh and to expand its vision, and thus "USF World" was established, but in name only, and it still needed to be developed into reality. Several USF Global Task Force Initiative Committees prepared white papers on topics across the university that should be incorporated into USF World. I became the leader of USF World, first under the auspices of the Office of Research, Innovation, and Global Affairs, and then, in order to focus fully on USF World, as the Senior VP for Global Affairs and International Research.

The first task was to design USF World. So, out came the large piece of paper, which I had packed in a suitcase in anticipation of a long cruise when I knew there would be time and peace to think creatively about this opportunity. The result was a visual model of how the component pieces of USF World fit together and engaged both university partners and community partners. The very complex diagram was subsequently critiqued by colleagues, a video was made to show how each component built upon the others, and the plan was revealed at a campus-wide retreat of administrative and faculty leaders.

A 400-page document titled "The University of South Florida—A Global Research University: A Vision for USF World" (Holbrook, 2012) describes the goals and aspirations for USF World, and provides background information about how and why U.S. universities have globalized. The point of the plan was to draft a roadmap that would guide the beginning of USF World so it could then be added to and/or revised by others who are engaged in this endeavor. The document was recently revised (Holbrook, 2014). Globalization is a topic that can be updated on an almost daily basis. The joy for me has been to see that this kind of research—a far cry from the biomedical research of my faculty career—is rewarded. USF World was the recipient of a Senator Paul Simon Award from the Association of International Educators (also known as NAFSA) for globalizing the university and an Andrew Heiskell Honorable Mention from the Institute of International Education. I have since retired from USF, and am using the document as the basis for a book on globalizing the university. It keeps me abreast of globalization and engaged in meaningful research.

Every leader will find his/her own grounding. It may not be immediately obvious, but it can be easily surfaced by asking yourself what kind of work you immerse yourself in versus the work you complete primarily because it is necessary. What gives you satisfaction and expands your horizons and, most importantly, what aspect(s) of your career will continue when you leave your position?

Earlier in this essay, I mentioned the goal of selecting a field that would lead to a "lifetime of fulfillment," a lifetime that hopefully extends well beyond a structured career. Leaving a position of leadership, with its intense schedule and responsibilities, removes many of the roles that filled the days (and evenings) and can require adjustment to having unstructured time. Like any transition, leaving a career of many years is filled with uncertainty, is somewhat frightening, and relies upon the carryover of experience and the aspects that were most exciting, meaningful, and provided a sense of accomplishment. The "thread" that provided grounding throughout career transitions will continue to offer you grounding during the process of moving into the next "career" of a very different nature. For me, the research I so enjoy continues as I serve as a higher education consultant to universities in the United States and abroad. What could be more exciting than learning about the culture, educational norms, and people of a country in the Middle East where I plan to spend considerable time over the next few years? Or using the experience and insight to help leaders of our universities acclimate to consolidation, build a research enterprise, streamline finances, and adopt new measures of accountability or deliberate online versus traditional pedagogy? Recognizing your grounding, whether it is professional, personal, or spiritual will continue to fulfill you as a leader of many and captain of your own peace of mind.

# REFERENCES

Holbrook, K. A., & Sanberg, P. R. (2013). Understanding the high cost of success in university research. *Technology and Innovation, 15*(3), 269–280.

Holbrook, K. A. (2012). The University of South Florida—A global research university: A vision for USF World. Retrieved from http://global.usf.edu/downloads/USF%20World%20Expanded%20Vision%20Document_10-18-12.pdf

Pavlina, E. (n.d.). 5 good ways to ground yourself. Retrieved from http://www.erinpavlina.com/blog/2009/07/5-good-ways-to-ground-yourself/

# ABOUT THE CONTRIBUTORS

## ABOUT THE COEDITORS

**Karen A. Longman** is professor and program director of the doctoral higher education programs at Azusa Pacific University, currently serving 100+ students from across North America and around the world. She previously spent six years as vice president for academic affairs and dean of the faculty at Greenville College (IL) and 19 years as vice president for professional development and research at the Washington, DC-based Council for Christian Colleges & Universities. Karen has directed a series of Women's Leadership Development Institutes and Women's Advanced Leadership Institutes since 1998. She is a coeditor of *Christian Higher Education: An International Journal of Research, Theory, and Practice* and edited a 2012 book titled *Thriving in Leadership: Strategies for Making a Difference in Christian Higher Education.* She is currently coediting the new International Leadership Association/Information Age Publishing "Women and Leadership" book series. Karen earned her PhD from the University of Michigan's Center for the Study of Higher Education.

**Susan R. Madsen** is the *Orin R. Woodbury Professor of Leadership and Ethics* in the Woodbury School of Business at Utah Valley University. She has also been heavily involved for the last decade in researching the lifetime development of prominent women leaders. She has personally interviewed a host of women university presidents, U.S. governors, and international leaders, and has two books published on her results. Susan has conducted related research in the United States, the six Arab Gulf countries, China, and recently in Eastern Europe. She has published over 60 articles in scholarly journals and presents often in local, national, and international settings. Susan is the founder of the International Leadership Association's Women and Leadership Affinity Group and has received numerous awards for her teaching, research, and service. She is coediting the new International Leadership Association/Information Age Publishing book series titled "Women and Leadership." She received her doctorate from the University of Minnesota in human resource development.

## ABOUT THE CHAPTER AUTHORS

**Kim Bobby** became the director of the Inclusive Excellence Group at the American Council on Education in July 2012. The Inclusive Excellence Group is focused on advancing women and people of color into senior leadership roles in higher education and ultimately into the college presidency. Before joining the American Council on Education, Kim was chief diversity officer and associate professor in the School of Education at the University of Puget Sound (WA). During her career, Kim has served in higher education and K–12 leadership roles contributing to educational reform for the New York City public schools. She has worked as a consultant to the College Board, the Bill & Melinda Gates Foundation, and the College Success Foundation. Born in Los Angeles, Kim received her doctorate in educational leadership and policy studies from the University of Washington, Seattle; master's in educational leadership from California State University, Sacramento; and bachelor's in business administration management from California State University, Fresno.

**Rita Bornstein** served as president of Rollins College from 1990-2004 and currently holds the Cornell Chair in Philanthropy and Leadership Development. Before coming to Rollins, she served as vice president at the University of Miami. She serves on the boards of the Association of Governing Boards of Universities and Colleges and the Dr. P. Philips Center for the Performing Arts. Rita has received numerous awards and three honorary doctorates. She consults, speaks, and writes on issues related to leadership, governance, and fund raising, and is frequently quoted in articles on higher education governance and leadership. Her books include *Legitimacy in the Academic Presidency: From Entrance to Exit* and *Fundraising Advice for College and University Presidents: An Insider's Guide*. Rita received her PhD from the University of Miami.

**Mary Bucklin** teaches and is codirector of the Women's and Gender Studies program at Northern Kentucky University. She works as an advocate for progressive, nonviolent social change in her teaching, her involvement in community groups, and the feminist choir (MUSE, Cincinnati's Women's Choir), for which she sings low alto. Mary believes in collaborative, active learning and works to meld classroom/community work with online learning as a means to democratize higher education. Her current interests focus on eco-feminism and experiential learning to encourage spiritual and intellectual growth and leadership development. She received her doctorate from the University of Cincinnati in urban educational leadership.

**Amy B. Diehl** is currently the director of systems and applications at Shippensburg University of Pennsylvania, where she has overseen various aspects of information technology for the past 19 years. She completed her PhD in administration and leadership at Indiana University of Pennsylvania, where she conducted qualitative research on the meaning of adversity for senior women leaders in higher education. Focusing her research on women and leadership, Amy has made numerous presentations on what women experience in leadership and strategies to overcome barriers they face. In 2013, she was selected for and participated in the Higher Education Resource Services Institute for Women in Higher Education Administration at the University of Denver. In May 2014, her participation in the Advancing Theories of Women and Leadership Colloquium at Utah Valley University allowed for focused attention on developing theory related to women's leadership.

**Lynn M. Gangone** is dean of Colorado Women's College and associate clinical professor, higher education, Morgridge College of Education, University of Denver. She previously served as visiting professor in George Washington University's Graduate School of Education and Human Development; vice president, Maryland Independent College and University Association; executive director, National Association for Women in Education; and vice president in development, and in student affairs, at Centenary College. Lynn is a national speaker and writer on gender equality, as well as leadership development and career advancement for women in higher education. She authored the lead article in *Journal About Women in Higher Education* (2008) and a chapter on women's leadership development in *Rethinking Leadership in a Complex, Multicultural, and Global Environment: New Concepts and Models for Higher Education* (2009). Lynn earned her doctorate from Columbia University, Teachers College in higher and postsecondary education with a concentration in organizations and leadership.

**Juliet V. García** has devoted her life's work to public service and has become a national thought leader in higher education innovation. In 1986 she was named the first female Mexican-American president of a U.S. college or university, as president of Texas Southmost College, before joining The University of Texas System as president of UT Brownsville in 1991. Juliet is a convener of important conversations. She has served on the transition teams of two U.S. Presidential administrations, was a member of The White House Initiative on Educational Excellence for Hispanic Americans, and chaired the Advisory Committee to Congress on Student Financial Assistance and the American Council on Education, the nation's largest higher education association. Among the many recognitions she has received for her work are the American Council on Education Lifetime Achievement Award, the Mexican consulate's Ohtli Award, and recognition by *Time* magazine as one of the Top 10 College Presidents in the U.S.

**Rita A. Gardiner** teaches women's studies and sociology at The University of Western Ontario and King's University College in London, Ontario, Canada. Her research looks at the intersections among gender, authenticity, and leadership. In addition to publications on gender and leadership, Rita has published several articles on Hannah Arendt and Simone de Beauvoir. She is currently working on a monograph on gender, authenticity, and leadership to be published by Palgrave MacMillan in 2015. Rita received her doctorate in 2014 from The University of Western Ontario in women's studies and feminist theory.

**Ann Weaver Hart** is the 21st president of the University of Arizona. Previously she served as president of Temple University from July 2006 until July 2012, when she assumed the presidency of the University of Arizona. Prior to her leadership of Temple University, Dr. Hart served as president of the University of New Hampshire, and as provost and vice president for academic affairs at Claremont Graduate University, in Claremont, California. At the University of Utah, she served as professor of educational leadership, dean of the Graduate School, and special assistant to the president. Ann holds three degrees from the University of Utah: a bachelor of science, master of arts in history, and a doctorate in educational administration. She is the author of *Principal Succession: Establishing Leadership in Schools* (1993), and coauthor of *Designing and Conducting Research: Education and Social Science* with C. Drew and M. Hardman (1996) and *The Principalship: Toward Professional Learning and Practice* with P. V. Bredeson (1996).

**Karen A. Holbrook** is currently a higher education consultant and senior advisor to the president at the University of South Florida. She recently served as the senior vice president for research and innovation, and as the senior vice president for global affairs and international research at University of South Florida. She has held positions as president of The Ohio State University, provost at the University of Georgia, vice president of research/graduate school dean at the University of Florida, and associate dean for research and professor of biological structure and medicine at the University of Washington School of Medicine (UWSOM). She has served on numerous boards of higher education organizations, corporate boards, is a trustee of international and national universities, and has served on advisory panels/councils for the National Institutes of Health, including the advisory committee to the past director of the NIH. Karen was a biomedical researcher and National Institutes of Health Merit Award investigator. She earned BS and MS degrees in zoology at the University of Wisconsin and a PhD in biological structure at the University of Washington School of Medicine.

**Barbara Kellerman** is James MacGregor Burns Lecturer in Public Leadership at the Harvard Kennedy School and, currently, visiting professor of business administration at Tuck School of Business at Dartmouth. Barbara was cofounder of the International Leadership Association, and is author and editor of many books including most recently *Bad Leadership*; *Followership*; *Women and Leadership* (coedited with Deborah Rhode); *Leadership: Essential Selections;* and *The End of Leadership*, which was named by *Choice* an "Outstanding Academic Title for 2013." She was ranked by Forbes.com among "Top 50 Business Thinkers" (2009) and by *Leadership Excellence* in the top 15 "thought leaders in management and leadership" (2008-2009 and 2010-2011). In 2010 she received the McFeeley award from the National Management Association for pioneering work on leadership. And in 2014 she was ranked 13th by Global Gurus in "World's Top 30 Management Professionals." Her next book, *Hard Times: Leadership in America,* will be published by Stanford University Press in September 2014.

**Nan Keohane** is president emerita of both Wellesley College and Duke University. She has taught political philosophy at Swarthmore College, Stanford University, and Princeton Universities, as well as Wellesley and Duke. Her publications include *Thinking About Leadership* (Princeton University Press, 2010), *Higher Ground: Ethics and Leadership in the Modern University* (Duke University Press, 2006), *Philosophy and the State in France: The Renaissance to the Enlightenment* (Princeton University Press, 1980), and *Feminist Theory: A Critique of Ideology* (coedited with Barbara Gelpi, University of Chicago Press, 1982). Nan is a member of the Harvard Corporation, the board of directors of the American Academy of Arts and Sciences, and the board of trustees of the Doris Duke Charitable Foundation. She received her BA from Wellesley College, her MA from St. Anne's College, and her PhD in political science on a Sterling Fellowship from Yale University; she was also a Marshall Scholar at Oxford.

**Adrianna Kezar** is professor for higher education at the University of Southern California and codirector of the Pullias Center for Higher Education. She is a national expert of change, governance, and leadership in higher education, and her research agenda explores the change process in higher education institutions and the role of leadership in creating change. Adrianna is well published with 14 books, over 75 journal articles, and more than 100 book chapters and reports. Her books include: *Enhancing Campus Capacity for Leadership* (Stanford University Press, 2011), *Organizing for Collaboration* (Jossey-Bass, 2009), *Rethinking Leadership Practices in a Complex, Multicultural, and Global World* (Stylus Press, 2009), *Rethinking the "L" Word in Higher Education: The Revolution of Research on Leadership* (Jossey-Bass, 2006), and *Higher Education for the Public Good* (Jossey-Bass, 2005).

**Tiffani Lennon** chairs the Law and Society and Community-Based Research programs at the University of Denver–Colorado Women's College. Before her academic career, Tiffani helped to frame strategic litigation to systematically address rights violations; she has authored several policy reports with national implications. Her research areas include comparative political economics. Additionally, Tiffani has been engaged as a visiting lecturer around the world, teaching within the legal and economic development spaces. She has received numerous public and private grants to conduct research and policy analysis on marginalized communities. Tiffani's latest work is a national study on women's leadership across 14 sectors in the United States. Her book, *Recognizing Women's Leadership: Strategies and Best Practices for Employing Excellence*, was released in August 2014. Tiffani earned a juris doctor degree and received an LLM degree from the University of London, Birkbeck College of Law. Her dissertation focused on feminist political economics in southern Africa.

**Sherry Penney** served as the chancellor of the University of Massachusetts Boston from 1988–2000, as interim president of the University of Massachusetts system in 1995, and interim president of SUNY Plattsburgh from 1986–1987. From 1982-1988 she was the vice chancellor for academic programs, policy, and planning in the State University of New York (SUNY) system. Sherry previously was associate provost at Yale University from 1976-1982. After retiring as chancellor, Sherry was appointed the "Sherry H. Penney Professor of Leadership" in the College of Management at UMass Boston, serving from 2000-2012. She was also the founder of the Center for Collaborative Leadership at UMass Boston. Some 500 young professionals completed that executive leadership program during 2002-2012. She has coauthored two books and authored another, in addition to writing numerous articles for professional journals. Her research interests focus on leadership, higher education, and advancing women. She has taught at Union College, Yale University, SUNY Albany, and UMass Boston.

**Deborah L. Rhode** is the Ernest W. McFarland Professor of Law and the director of the Center on the Legal Profession at Stanford University. She is the former president of the Association of American Law Schools, the former chair of the American Bar Association's Commission on Women in the Profession, and the former director of Stanford's Institute for Research on Women and Gender. She writes primarily in the area of legal ethics and gender equity and is the author or editor of 20 books and some 250 articles. She writes a column for the *National Law Journal* and has published in the *New York Times*, The *Washington Post*, the *Boston Globe*, *Slate*, and *Ms*. Her books on gender include *The Beauty Bias* (2010); *Women and Leadership: The State of Play and Strategies for Reform* (with Barbara Kellerman, 2009); *The Difference "Difference" Makes: Women and Leadership* (2003), and *Speaking of Sex* (1997).

**Lorri Sulpizio** is the coordinator of the Women's Leadership Academy at the University of San Diego and an adjunct faculty member in the Department of Leadership Studies. Lorri is a founder and the principal consultant for Lotus Leadership Institute—a leadership development and training company. Lorri has written several articles and chapters on leadership issues, specifically women's issues, as well as presenting and speaking on a variety of leadership topics. Her expertise includes girls' and women's leadership, as well as group and team dynamics. Her research focus is on women's leadership, specifically on voice, power, and authority. Lorri is the cofounder of Blossom, a program dedicated to helping girls and women improve their leadership and develop their overall sense of self. She was a college basketball coach from 1998 to 2010. Lorri earned her PhD in leadership from the University of San Diego, her MA in sports psychology from San Diego State University, and her BA in English from Cal Poly San Luis Obispo.

**Leah Witcher Jackson Teague**, associate dean of Baylor Law School, has worked closely with Dean Brad Toben as Baylor Law School's executive leadership team for 22 years—an exceptional, if not unparalleled, leadership tenure in legal education. In addition, she teaches taxation and leadership classes. Leah developed and directs its leadership development program; she also serves on the national executive council for the American Council on Education's Women's Network and chairs its New Initiative Committee. She is founding chair of Texas Women in Higher Education, Inc., and is on the board of directors for the Texas Woman

Lawyers Association. Leah has participated in or organized numerous women's leadership development programs in the last three decades, including two Oxford Round Tables. Appointed by the Texas Supreme Court, she serves on the State Bar of Texas Ethics Advisory Committee. She writes and speaks on tax, business, nonprofit, and leadership topics.

**Judith S. White** has been president and executive director of Higher Education Resource Services (HERS) since June 2005. During her tenure, the original HERS Institutes program was redesigned so that three institutes now offer an enhanced curriculum to serve 200 women participants annually. She currently directs HERS leadership and partnership initiatives, including a biannual summit for women presidents and a research collaboration with the Center for Creative Leadership. Before coming to HERS, Judith was an administrator and faculty member at Duke University, Dartmouth College, and the University of North Carolina-Greensboro. She has been a senior fellow at the Association of American Colleges & Universities and serves on the board of Re:Gender (formerly the National Council for Research on Women). Her degrees include an AB from Princeton University, an MA from Columbia University, and a PhD from the University of Virginia. Judith is a HERS Bryn Mawr alumna 1996.

CPSIA information can be obtained at www.ICGtesting.com
Printed in the USA
BVOW08s1135150415

396223BV00004B/49/P

9 781623 968199